THANK GOD AHEAD OF TIME

The Life and Spirituality
of Solanus Casey

Michael H. Crosby, O.F.M. Cap.

THANK GOD AHEAD OF TIME

The Life
and
Spirituality
of

Solanus Casey

ST. ANTHONY MESSENGER PRESS
Cincinnati, Ohio

This book includes quoted material from the archives of the following sources: Office of the Cause/Guild of Venerable Solanus Casey: *Collected Writings of Father Solanus Casey, O.F.M. CAP.*, and *Written Reports Concerning Father Solanus Casey, O.F.M. CAP.*; and a publication of the Solanus Casey Center: *Journey to Holiness*. Excerpts from *Spiritual Passages: The Psychology of Spiritual Development*, by Benedict J. Groeschel, ©1983, are used with permission.

Scripture passages have been taken from *New Revised Standard Version Bible*, copyright ©1989 by the Division of Christian Education of the National Council of the Churches of Christ in the U.S.A., and used by permission. All rights reserved.

Cover design by Mark Sullivan
Cover portrait by Timothy Bodendistel
Book design by Jennifer Tibbits

LIBRARY OF CONGRESS CATALOGING-IN-PUBLICATION DATA

Crosby, Michael, 1940-
  Thank God ahead of time : the life and spirituality of Solanus Casey / Michael H. Crosby.
    p. cm.
  Includes bibliographical references (p.   ).
  ISBN 978-0-86716-919-5 (pbk. : alk. paper) 1. Casey, Solanus, 1870-1957. 2. Capuchins—United States—Biography. I. Title.
  BX4705.C33573C76 2009
  271'.3602—dc22

                          2009001481

ISBN 978-0-86716-919-5

Published by St. Anthony Messenger Press
28 W. Liberty St.
Cincinnati, OH 45202
www.SAMPBooks.org

Printed in the United States of America.
Printed on acid-free paper.

09 10 11 12 13   5 4 3 2 1

"Why not foster confidence in God's divine Providence by humbly and in all childlike humility venturing to remind him in the person of our divine brother Jesus that we are his children. We should remind him that we are, and at least want to be reckoned, as among his 'little ones.' Therefore we should thank him frequently for, not only the blessings of the past and present, but THANK HIM AHEAD OF TIME for whatever he foresees is pleasing to him that we suffer. We should do this not only in general but in each particular case. We should leave everything absolutely in his divine disposal, including with all its circumstances, when, where, and how he may be pleased to dispose the events of our death."

Words of Father Solanus Casey

CONTENTS

INTRODUCTION

On August 31, 1956, I met someone deeply gifted by God; so blessed by God that he would become the first man born in the United States to be declared "Venerable" by the Vatican (this represents the first major step in being declared a saint). I was at Saint Bonaventure's Friary in Detroit. My brother Dan had entered the Capuchin Franciscan Order. After his investiture with its habit he said: "Come and meet Solanus Casey; someday he's going to be a saint." Less than forty years later, on July 11, 1995, in the presence of Pope John Paul II, a decree about the sanctity of Casey's life was promulgated: He could be called "Venerable." It stated:

> There is proven evidence that the theological virtues of faith, hope, and charity toward God and neighbor and also the cardinal virtues of prudence, justice, temperance and fortitude as well as other virtues have been exercised to a heroic degree by the Servant of God, Francis Solanus Casey, a professed priest of the Order of Friars Minor Capuchin.[1]

Earlier, on June 20, 1995, the Congregation for the Causes of Saints unanimously determined that the Wisconsin-born farm boy baptized "Bernard," nicknamed "Barney," who later entered the Capuchin

Franciscans and received the name "Francis Solanus," had cultivated "the theological virtues [and] other virtues to a heroic degree."[2] The Congregation deemed his life proved worthy of imitation.

The events in Rome proved newsworthy enough that *The New York Times* featured them in a story about Solanus Casey entitled: "One Man's Life of Virtue Earns the Papal Spotlight."[3]

Little did I know when I shook Solanus Casey's frail hand in 1956 that I would become a significant contributor to the volumes accepted by the Congregation of Saints as the basis for its decision. How did this happen?

In 1982 my superiors asked me to write the "official" biography of Solanus Casey. I began by reading all his writings and testimonies of people who knew him. Next I interviewed those who lived with him, ministered with him or came to him for help and inspiration. The more I listened to their stories, the more convinced I felt that Solanus Casey had a message for our increasingly secular age that still yearns for meaning. His is a story of one person's unswerving faith in God's abiding presence continually calling us to cooperate with God in bringing about the unity of all.

Given the success of the first edition of this book, which appeared in 1986, I was appointed "External Collaborator to the Relator" for the Vatican (1987). This involved reading a volume of collected testimonies of people who answered the Congregation's questions about Solanus and then, building on this, writing the other two volumes of the *Positio*. These three volumes would become the official materials offered to determine his holiness.

The Congregation appointed as "Relator" for the Cause of Solanus Casey Father Peter Gumpel, S.J. Never have I met a Vatican official with so much insight and integrity. My visits to him in Rome lead me to echo the fine things said about him by Kenneth L. Woodward, religion editor of *Newsweek*.

Woodward had gone to Rome admittedly to write an exposé about the process used by the Vatican to determine who will be declared a saint. However, because of Peter Gumpel's full cooperation, Woodward became a believer. His respectful interpretation of the process became his *Making Saints: How the Catholic Church Determines Who Becomes a Saint, Who Doesn't, and Why.*[4]

By the time I finished my part in the trilogy that constituted the *Positio,* the biography of Solanus was 327 pages. The third part, while the smallest of the three at 145 pages, discussed "The Virtues." It showed how Solanus practiced fifteen key virtues. These include the theological and cardinal virtues, the spiritual and corporal works of mercy, the three evangelical counsels and humility. This volume contains over thirteen hundred footnotes, many with multiple sources.

After being approved by Father Gumpel, the three volumes were reviewed by a "Designated Committee of Theological Consultants." Each of these nine theologians prepared a report. On April 7, 1995 the Committee unanimously decided "that the *Positio* contains reasons and elements sufficient to reach the necessary moral certitude" that Solanus lived a life of heroic virtue. They stated, "the Servant of God, Francis Solanus Casey, was an authentic master through his words and example. His entire pastoral activity took place within the context of his apostolic zeal, the integrity of his Christian life, and his exquisite fatherly love toward all who came to him."[5]

When the decision of the Designated Committee reached Pope John Paul II, he accepted their judgment and ordered that a decree be written about the heroic virtues of Solanus. This was prepared by the Congregation for the Causes of Saints and brought public in that audience with the pope on July 11, 1995.

Less than fifty years before, while in "semi-retirement" in Huntington, Indiana, Solanus had pondered the role of saints in our spiritual journey. In his mind saints were exemplars to help us attain "familiarity with God." His words about them echoed in the decree about himself:

> Self-understood there can be no thought of our know-
> ing God in our present state directly and as he is known
> in heaven. Our privilege here is to start such knowledge
> as can be perfected only in the great, blessed Beyond.
> Nevertheless, if we stop to think as we ought to do,
> there must be ways and means close at hand whereby,
> according to the lives of the saints, we may if we try, to
> ascend to great sanctity and to an astonishing familiar-
> ity with God even here as pilgrims to the Beatific
> Vision.[6]

In researching his life and writing his biography, I have been challenged to find my own "ways and means close at hand," whereby, as I
reflect on his life and spirituality, I might move toward my own kind
of "astonishing familiarity" with God. For this I always will be most
grateful. In fact it no longer seems critical to me whether or not
Solanus Casey moves to the next steps of being declared "Blessed" and
then "Saint Solanus Casey." Whatever happens officially will not
change my deep gratitude for being touched by his life and message.
He has become, for me, a "saint."

This gratitude has kept me part of the effort to share his story
with more and more people. This involved my work with others in the
creation of the Solanus Casey Center and subsequent terms on its
Ministry Council, which makes recommendations about its operations, programs and materials.

Before writing this book I interviewed many people in Wisconsin,
New York and Detroit, Michigan. While I thanked these, and others, in
that earlier edition, I continue to be indebted to the tireless dedication
to the cause of two key Capuchin Franciscans in my Province of Saint
Joseph: Richard Merling and Leo Wollenweber. I also thank my
brother, Capuchin Dan Crosby, for his help in this revised version. To

these, the members of the Father Solanus Guild who work so diligently to share his message with the world, as well as past and present
members of the Solanus Center Ministry Council I dedicate this third
revision of *Thank God Ahead of Time.*

Ellen Murphy Casey and Bernard James Casey.

Earliest picture of Casey family, Superior, Wisconsin, 1892. Bernard Casey, Jr. (Solanus), is in the top row, third from the left.

1

THE EARLY YEARS

NOVEMBER 25, 1870–
DECEMBER 24, 1896

In 1930, the then-sixty-year-old Solanus Casey reminisced about his parents and how they came from Ireland to Wisconsin:

> Surely we were fortunate children that the good God gave us such sturdy, honest, virtuous parents. How can we ever be grateful enough? Thanks be to God! May their dear souls rest in the peace of the beloved! I often think of the wonderful designs of Divine Providence as revealed in the plans and strivings of these and similar "children of Saint Patrick." They were often pioneers indeed. Our own dear parents were directed from city life in Boston and Philadelphia away to "The River Bank" [to] Prescott. It must have been little more than a village.[1]

In 1852, in the aftermath of the Irish Potato Famine, eight-year-old Ellen Murphy accompanied her widowed mother, Brigid, an older sister, Mary Ann, and three brothers from Camlough in County Armagh to Boston.[2] Five years later, seventeen-year-old Bernard Casey

1857

emigrated from Ireland's County Monaghan for Boston as well. There he learned shoemaking.

For her part, Brigid felt that Ellen had become mature enough that Brigid could leave her in Boston while she moved to Hastings, Minnesota, to be near other relatives. In 1860, Barney met the now-sixteen-year-old Ellen at a Fourth of July picnic. When their courtship continued to the point that Ellen wrote her mother that Barney Casey had proposed, Brigid told Ellen to leave Boston immediately for Minnesota.

The official excuse for Ellen's move was that her sister, Mary Ann (who had married at sixteen a few years before with no apparent objections), had just given birth to twins. The true reason is clear from Brigid's words to Ellen upon her arrival: "You're still a girl. You should enjoy the years of your girlhood; then you can take on family responsibilities."

Brigid arranged that Ellen would live with the Donnelly family. Here Ellen found herself thrust into an entirely new world. Ignatius Donnelly was a well-known writer and lecturer. Later he became the youngest member of the United States House of Representatives and then a senator from Minnesota.

After three years with the Donnellys, Brigid permitted Ellen to marry Barney. Ellen accompanied the Donnellys to Boston and, on October 6, 1863, Ellen Elizabeth Murphy and Bernard James Casey were married.

The newlyweds could have only a half-day honeymoon. The Civil War had begun in 1861 and Barney was swamped with orders for shoes for Union soldiers. At the war's end, in April 1865, the couple moved to Germantown, Pennsylvania, and soon after that to New Castle, Pennsylvania. In both places they opened shoe stores with the help of Bernard's brother Terrence.

While the Pennsylvania business faced failure, in Minnesota, Ellen's now-grown brothers, Owen and Patrick, experienced increasing success as farmers. They urged their sister and brother-in-law to file a claim on some land just below the town of Prescott, on the Wisconsin side of the Mississippi. After many discussions the decisions were made: Terrence would go to Boston (where he subsequently became a lawyer); Bernard and Ellen would take their children on the train to western Wisconsin.

Upon their arrival in fall 1865, Ellen's brothers helped Barney clear some of the eighty-acre claim overlooking the Mississippi. They also built a three-room log house. Here Bernard Casey was born on November 25, 1870, the sixth of sixteen children. On December 18 he was baptized at Saint Joseph Mission Church in Prescott and given the name Bernard Francis Casey.

Here "Barney" Casey, Jr., spent his first years. Later, as Solanus Casey, he recalled the beauties as well as the difficulties of those first years of his life:

> Here it was, smiling down on the "Father of Waters," that five of us were privileged to breathe our first morning air and "sing our first baby music." No doubt little Bernard must have been proficient in that music; because it was during his term of babyhood that Papa went blind with ague. For two weeks he had to be led by the hand, and his little namesake got a rupture from which he never completely recovered. Like in all other trials, however, the good God had his designs herein also, and we can say with fullest conviction and in all gratitude today: "The Lord knows best." May he be in all his plans eternally blessed!
>
> How we must have thrived there in real unworldliness and innocence! Dangers of course were not wanting, to keep dear Father and Mother "on edge" and often, no doubt, in anxiety. Wild beasts and rattlesnakes seem to have been the most common cause of such anxiety, though two of our little cousins were

drowned together just below our little retreat near that River. Otherwise it was so generous, so noble, so majestic.³

In their home Barney and Ellen Casey introduced young Barney to an Irish Catholic environment. This nurtured in Barney the deeply held religious conviction that would be evidenced in his later life. Part of the family's daily practice would be meal prayers and regular night prayers during which everyone would pray "for a happy death and a favorable judgment."⁴

By 1873, Barney Casey, Sr., had become successful enough to move a few miles away to Big River, Wisconsin. The new farm was part of an area called "The Trimbelle" after the nearby river. As Solanus described it:

> The public road, such as it was, ran just past our little log cabin—a one-story mansion about 12 × 30 feet. You may smile at this title to honor it with, especially when you learn that it had a single partition only below. This was for "the bedroom" with Father and Mother on the one side and the little girls, Ellie and Mary Ann and little Mattie on the other. In the loft above, the little boys slept. In the morning, they sometimes played till they quarreled as little boys are wont to do....
>
> Winters were often severe and snowbanks sometimes mounted as high as the top of the gable roof. But poor, dear Father took care before the cold weather set in to bank well wherever he might. As a result, we were fairly comfortable no matter how the wind howled or the mercury sank.⁵

Farming at "The Trimbelle" brought Barney Casey more success. He not only had enough grain to feed his milk cows during the long Wisconsin winter; he had enough to sell to neighbors. The pasture provided good feed for the cattle (as well as deer and other animals).

His vegetable and fruit garden produced a year-round diet of wholesome foods.

Solanus believed "he had never seen a picture—in Bible history or elsewhere—so nearly like an earthly paradise as he remembered that scenery to be—with deer in twos, threes and more, stopping on the hillside or valleys to gaze at what he might be doing." The land produced "an abundance of wild flowers and fruits and nuts and berries."[6]

In his mind, Solanus believed that "what heightened the appreciation of those days was our innocence (from sin)."[7] His own "innocence" was cultivated through the regular religious practices that defined the patterns of nineteenth-century Catholic pioneers. Besides prayers in the morning, at meals and at bedtime, whenever possible the family traveled six miles for Sunday Mass. Fasting since midnight, those going to the 10 AM Mass would leave at eight. With only one horse and wagon, the ever-growing members of the family had to take turns going to church. One Sunday half of the children would go with one parent and the next Sunday, the other half would go with the other parent. Those at home would have their own service. There, precisely at 10 AM, the home-staying parent would gather the remaining children and read the prayers of the Mass for the day.

Barney loved those Sunday morning services at home. In his mind they made the little log house a real "mansion." It could be called "a mansion," he believed, because, "every decent mansion has a chapel of some dimensions."

> Ours was at times all chapel, and at times something of a church. As long as we lived in that little abode—a "hovel" possibly outside, but clean and neat as a palace within—we were wont to say morning and night prayers together; and on Sundays at 10:00 A.M., Father would read Mass Prayers.
>
> Of course when the weather permitted and the roads were any way decent, he would trudge away to

church about six miles taking short cuts. Then Ellie or James or one of the others would lead the prayers (at home).

If a child's attention span can be measured a minute for every year, even for young Barney, "sometimes they seemed pretty long."[8]

It was during "such a Sunday," Solanus recalled:

> that Papa and Jim had gone to church when we saw the black cloud of smoke rising from the far side of some of the hills off to the South. The wind was pretty strong too and poor dear Mother seemed quite anxious. She was giving instructions what to do and getting ready for what must have looked like a probable burnout.
>
> Ellie scratched a little "hoe-mark" out in front of the house and sprinkled holy water in it about half way down to the barn. By this time the fire was crackling through the grass and brush this side of Lamb's Road and the smoke rolled over our heads in thick, dark clouds. Then the barn took fire, some ten rods east of the house, and we all went down, carrying some bed-clothes, to the lone tree that for a long time stood in the middle of the original, four-acre field.... As we huddled together under said lone tree (my own little face hidden in mother's dress from the smoke) I heard mother saying in accents of relief: "Thanks be to God! Some of the neighbors have come and let the pig out." It was a big white one and had broken out of the pen itself where it had been a contented prisoner right near the barn. We saw it running for safety.
>
> Papa and James got home shortly after noon and some of the neighbors came to sympathize with us. It seemed a fresh, clear day, but our barn was in ruins and the hills were black in every direction, except our fields

and up to the northwest where the fire did not cross the highway…except to burn our barn.[9]

On the Trimbelle farm, the older brothers helped their father in the fields and barn; the younger Barney helped his mother in the kitchen.

The chance to go into the fields often provided wonderful childhood memories. As he recalled it:

> Those hills formed a great part of our pasture lands where we boys, especially Maurice and I (till he left for Stillwater to study) used to watch the cattle and study our catechism. Sometimes we'd roll rocks down the hillside…or pick berries, or fish and swim till the cattle would stray away and get into mischief. Then we would have our own anxieties finding them. Sometimes we got our medicine for carelessness.[10]

Being rambunctious, at times young Barney "got his medicine" for other kinds of mischief besides carelessness. In such cases this medicine would be prescribed and administered by the stern and exacting Barney, Sr. Thus, when Solanus was six and threw a fork at one of his sisters his father warned: "This is the first time you have ever done anything like this. So your punishment will only be three lashes. But if you do any such thing again, you'll receive six lashes. And if it should happen a third time, you'll get nine lashes."

When he was about seven, Solanus recalled how his "dear parents," Irish Catholics that they were, had mutually dreamed of the privilege of being parents to a priest in their family. In their mind it would be Maurice:

> This ideal seemed to have buoyed their hopes from the earliest years wherein they recognized holy matrimony as a state of life in which to serve God and help him to save souls. Furthermore, when the writer was in his seventh year and there were three brothers among

their five dear ones ahead of him, it just seemed self-understood as though planned before birth that Maurice was to be the Priest. Not only was this the case in our immediate family and relatives, but our neighboring children often spoke of it and seemed to revere him as so fortunately destined and chosen. So much was this true that someone even at that time and perhaps earlier, began to wonder if possibly there couldn't be two priests in a family—hardly hesitating that he would be the other himself.[11]

Maurice entered the seminary around 1883. But "health failure of the senior brother in his early classics had sent him home from the seminary, heavy-hearted—a family disappointment."[12] His departure from the seminary three years after entering was precipitated by a nervous condition that would plague him for the rest of his life.

Other health problems troubled the Casey family as well. Black diphtheria had struck in 1878 when Solanus was eight. It slowly took the life of his twelve-year-old sister. "Who will take the place of Mary Ann?," Ellen Casey wondered aloud as she held three-year-old Martha. Climbing down from her mother's arms, Martha walked to the corner and picked up the broom so often used by Mary Ann. "I will, Mama. I will sweep the floor for you like Mary Ann." Three days later, though, the disease claimed little Martha's life as well. Although several of the boys, including Barney, also contracted the disease, all of them recovered. In Barney's case, however, it had residual side effects. It made his voice weak and raspy. This may have been the cause of the peculiarly high pitch that defined his voice for the rest of his life.

While such tragedies and illnesses sometimes brought worry and grief into the Casey household, the pioneering Caseys brought even greater joy to their children through the folk songs and stories they brought with them from Ireland. Evenings found many of these being shared around the table in the log cabin. Other times Barney, Sr., and

Ellen gathered everyone around the dining room table for an evening of literature. There Barney, Sr., would read the poems of Tom Moore, Henry Wadsworth Longfellow and John Greenleaf Whittier. Stories like James Fenimore Cooper's *The Deerslayer* held the children fascinated for long periods of time.[13]

In his later life Solanus continued the tradition of sharing songs and stories with his nieces and nephews. In this, Solanus was a true *seanchaidhe* (shan-a-kee), the Irish word for storyteller. In the process, like every good seanchaidhe, he probably embellished the story further than it had been embellished for him. A nephew recalls one such tale:

> A certain overgrown John Joseph M., a contemporary of your Great Grandfather, a namesake and probably a relative, skipped school at thirteen because he was ashamed to go to class with little boys. He joined the British navy and went to the Far East. Later he failed in an enterprise in London. He first joined the Hudson Bay Company and then joined an Indian tribe and became the famous "Chief Black Eagle of the North." He was very charitable to the poor Indians whom, from the beginning, he had learned to love. But he was called to something greater.
>
> Deep in the wilderness he came across a sort of little clearing. There in the crotch of a big tree he met a weather-beaten statue of our Immaculate Mother. Calling his braves together shortly thereafter, he resigned. He disposed of his vast estates, went to Rome and after five years was ordained a priest. He returned to Ireland and after several years of mission in London, became the famous Fr. John of Cork.
>
> Who does not get a taste of the Cross one way or another and, if only with resignation: "The bigger the cross, the greater the crown."[14]

At a time when movies, television and video games could not be imagined, such stories provided the Casey family with their own home entertainment center. Especially when snows isolated the family, such amusement buoyed their spirits.

Another family practice, which remained with him throughout his later Capuchin life, involved the way Solanus would kneel upright at prayer, without support. This he learned from his mother and his sister Ellen. Solanus also learned from his parents a kind of "ecumenism" (before the word was used) that would influence him greatly in his later years. His family mixed well, not only across ethnic lines within Catholicism; but with neighboring Protestants as well. Possibly because many of these Irish, German and French-Canadian neighbors had experienced bigotry and left their countries because of discrimination, the Caseys realized the futility of arguing over religion and how it often led to alienation.

The town of Alihue was four miles away and home to many Methodists and Lutherans. While some Catholics belittled their ways, Solanus remembered the people of Alihue simply as "mostly honest, good Christians."[15]

Five miles beyond Alihue was Burkhardt. Needing a bigger house and convinced he could capitalize on his farming success at Trimbelle, Bernard Casey moved the family to a 345-acre farm there in 1882. The clapboard house had six rooms, two barns, a large ice house and a deep root house. The Willow River flowed nearby and Dry Dam Lake (which proved excellent for fishing and swimming) bordered the property.

An interesting feature of the land was the railroad line that ran through it. This made Saint Paul, Minnesota (thirty miles to the west), less than an hour's ride away. Not satisfied with meeting the basic needs of his family (there were now twelve members), Barney took advantage of the train to become a distributor for religious goods. After buying books at the religious goods store in Saint Paul, he'd bring them on the train. As it neared the farm, he lugged the heavy canvas bag to the train's rear platform. Then he'd heave the bag into a snowbank where the boys waited. When the train stopped at Burkhardt, he would walk back to the farm. He encouraged the children to read the books (keeping them unsoiled) before he sold them so that they might be aware of the latest in religious thought. Another way of supplementing the family income came by selling subscriptions to the *Irish Standard* and *Extension* magazine.

Nine miles from the farm, in Hudson, was St. Patrick parish. Two weeks before his First Communion, Barney, Jr., went there to review Catholic doctrine. It was 1883, and he was thirteen—a year older than the typical age for First Communion. Sickness and family chores had delayed Barney's First Communion a year.

Although the Casey children began studying their catechism when they were seven, the two-week course provided Barney a concentrated miniseries in his faith. Staying in the houses of city parishioners, communicants like Barney would attend morning and afternoon instructions. Pastor Thomas A. Kelly wanted to be certain his young parishioners could defend clearly the church's teachings. Only when he was satisfied they had sufficient knowledge could they receive Communion. Following the tradition in many Irish parishes at that time, Barney, Jr., used the occasion of his First Communion to "take the Pledge"—a promise not to drink alcoholic beverages until his twenty-first birthday.

When he was fifteen, Barney had nearly completed his elementary grades at the District School. However, because the last two crops had failed and the winter of 1886 proffered more bleakness, he left school to help out. The crisis found the Caseys adding another petition to the usual fifteen minutes of family evening prayer: that the harvest not fail totally.

After evening prayers with the family, Barney had decided he would recite the rosary nightly at his bedside. Once, after a hard day of chores, he decided to skip it to get more sleep. However he felt he should pray at least one decade. So he knelt down and began. To his surprise, he was able to stay awake until the whole rosary was completed.

That night he dreamed he was suspended over a huge pit of flames and nearly falling into it. Looking for something to save him, he saw a huge rosary hanging just above. Clinging to it saved him from falling into the pit. Later he said that it was this dream that began his special relationship with the Blessed Virgin.

When the financial situation of the Caseys did not improve, it was decided that Barney, Jr., should leave the farm to find work in Stillwater, Minnesota, twenty miles away. He got a job at the log booms, unjamming the felled trees that filled the Saint Croix River (a tributary of the Mississippi). Barney's job was to feed logs into the Stillwater mills. When he finished work he stayed with his mother's brother, Father Maurice Murphy, the pastor at a Catholic church in Stillwater.

When the waters froze in winter, Barney returned home to finish school and help on the farm. Although the summer wheat had failed, other crops had produced good results. This harvest, combined with Barney's income from work, made it possible to not only cancel the family debts, but to produce the first surplus in a long time.

Now seventeen and in his final year of grade school, Barney had become interested in rhetoric and debate. At that time, debates were not only an academic exercise; they were a public affair. Attending debates was a form of entertainment.

Debate provided a natural outlet for Barney's rebel side. It was a good forum for his natural tendency to argue about the facts and his desire to compete. He was open to challenge from all comers. It provided him a nonviolent way he could engage in combat (given his aversion to violence itself). He actually went out of his way to provoke a debate.[16]

One formal debate in Burkhardt addressed a controversial subject in those days preceding Prohibition: "Resolved: that the intemperate consumption of alcohol has been a greater evil than war." Barney's older brother John and his father joined him on the team. Although the debate began with decorum and dignity, it quickly became heated with hard feelings the result.

One person who seems to have attended the debate was fifteen-year-old Rebecca Tobin. Although Barney was older, the two began to spend time together at school as well as afterward, even after he graduated from elementary school in 1887.

After graduation, Barney returned to Stillwater to work in a brick kiln. One day when the workers stopped for lunch, they saw that Barney hadn't brought one. Some of the German-speaking workers offered him some of theirs: Limburger cheese sandwiches. After he had eaten, they asked if he had ever eaten this kind of cheese. "No, I never ate it before," the young Irishman responded, "but I often stepped in it."[17] Such humor, then and later, endeared him to all.

Ellen Casey had given Barney a Brown Scapular of our Lady of Mt. Carmel. As Solanus later recalled, it proved to be most providential while he worked at the kiln:

> Outside next to the building there was a large deep pit filled with water. I saw a man fall in, and I dove into the water, with all my clothes on and grabbed hold of him. He struggled with me and was pulling me down among the weeds so that I couldn't free myself.
>
> Suddenly I grabbed at the scapular I was wearing and with it I was somehow pulled up. Then another man who saw us, dove into the water and pulled the man away from me. However, the drowning man struggled so hard that the would-be-rescuer had to let him go, and so he drowned. I think I could have saved him. I know the Scapular of our Lady saved me.[18]

After his work at the kiln in Stillwater Barney worked at the local penitentiary as a part-time guard. There he became friendly with many prisoners. People person that he was, befriending the prisoners was easy for Barney. However, because he found it difficult to say no to their many requests, he had to be on guard (literally and figuratively) so that the prisoners did not take advantage of him.

Two of the most notorious prisoners were the Younger brothers, Jim and Cole. Formerly part of Jesse James's gang, Cole Younger was befriended by Barney, who spent lots of time talking with him. Cole gave Barney a clothes trunk that he kept for many years.

Although he liked his job at the prison, he discovered he could make more money working on the newly opened electric streetcar in Stillwater. He got a job as a motorman. Soon he was driving the new trolley cars.

During this time Barney and Rebecca found ways to communicate through correspondence and periodic visits. Around the time she was seventeen and finishing school, the relationship got more serious. It was not long before Barney decided to ask for Rebecca's hand in marriage. Even though she respected young Barney Casey, Jr., Rebecca's mother would hear none of it. She sent Rebecca to a boarding school in St. Paul. Barney would never see her again.

Nothing has been recorded as to how this decision affected young Barney. However, it seems it did not stop him from developing other relationships. One to whom he felt especially attracted was Nellie O'Brien (who later became his brother John's wife).

As a youth Barney had learned to play the violin; this talent helped him as a young man because he knew how to play popular tunes at dances. Although he played the violin only passably (and never improved), he did so with great energy. This was another good reason why Barney Casey, Jr., was a welcome guest at any party.

With his skills as a motorman, Barney went to Appleton, Wisconsin. There he worked for a couple of years for a new streetcar company. Then, in the spring of 1890 he moved to Superior to work on streetcars there—his fifth job in three years. While these many moves might indicate instability or, at least, a basic restlessness, they finally brought him closer to his family. They also proved valuable for the Casey family finances.

Drought and chinch bugs on the farm caused successive crop failures in 1887 and 1888. Another failure in 1889 dealt a devastating blow to the once prosperous Bernard Casey, Sr. Not quite forty-nine and with many mouths to feed, he felt in no condition to continue relying on the uncertainties of the local weather to provide for his family.

At that time Superior was one of the largest cities in Wisconsin. Barney, Jr., wrote home about its boom. With jobs readily available, he urged the family to move. At first the three oldest brothers arrived, including Maurice. By now he had been home from the seminary for several years. The four rented a house. Then came a sister, Nell. She left her teaching job to keep house for them.

In 1891 Barney Sr., sold the Burkhardt farm. He loaded the furniture, farm implements, fodder, cows and horses into two boxcars at the railroad siding. These were shipped to Superior where the brothers had rented a farm of forty acres. Another one hundred and sixty acres were soon added. These provided good supplies of oats and hay for the livestock, plus vegetables and fruit for the family.

While the move brought the family enough security to build a ten-room house in Superior, Barney, Jr., felt little security or peace. While interesting, being a motorman did not give him a sense of purpose. Increasingly he found himself wondering if he might not have a vocation to the priesthood. While this idea had come and gone for years, he seems never to have taken it seriously. With the family secure again, any excuse about needing to help out financially no longer applied.

Then, on a late afternoon in the fall of 1891, as he worked at his conductor's job, something jarred him into action. It was a cold, dreary evening. As his trolley rounded a corner in Superior's "rough section," the car stopped with a jolt. A crowd was gathered, watching something terrible take place on the tracks.

As Barney and two crewmen ran to the scene they saw a very inebriated sailor looming over a young woman. She lay bleeding on the tracks. Knife in hand, the sailor was cursing at her. In a few moments two policemen arrived and disarmed him at gunpoint. Then they took the sailor to jail. Upon returning to the trolley, Barney began to think about his future—probably more deeply than he ever had done. As he did he felt he could not interpret this brutal stabbing and the sailor's cursing as an isolated incident; rather he saw it as a kind of microcosm of the all the violence and anger in the world. While he prayed for the woman and her assailant, Barney realized he had to do more than just pray for them. He had to do something about the violence that seemed so prevalent in his world. Something told him that what he had to do would not be linked with trolley cars.

Still shaken two days later, Solanus decided to visit his pastor at Sacred Heart rectory. He told Father Sturm that he wanted to change his life. Furthermore he felt called to try to make the world better by serving God in the priesthood.

Father Sturm recommended Saint Francis de Sales Seminary, just outside Milwaukee. This was the "German Seminary" for the Archdiocese. Maurice had attended it and failed in his effort. For some reason, neither Maurice's failure, nor the German language used there, deterred Barney. He would go. This meant he must go through four years of high school with candidates many years younger than his own twenty-one years.

For his first year, Barney excelled academically; he also received high marks for application and conduct. However, after this his grades began to decline. In his 1894–1895 semesters he raised his marks enough to enter fifth class, the equivalent of the first year of college, in fall 1895.

For the second semester he got low- to mid-70s in Latin, algebra, geometry and history, high 70s to low 80s in German, and the equivalent of today's "B" in vocal music, U.S. history and natural philosophy. He was now twelfth of fifteen and steadily dropping a notch in his class each semester.[19] Although he was technically not failing, the seminary officials did not believe Barney could maintain the level of academic excellence they demanded of their seminarians.

How did this happen? Understanding the dynamics involved shows how the future "success" of Solanus Casey was linked to this increasing "failure" of young Barney Casey, Jr.

Barney was not limited in knowledge. However, while he could process information quickly, he also had a tendency to skim the surface. Information most easily available was processed; he did not probe much further. This natural tendency, coupled with his lack of proficiency in German—to say nothing of the Latin—created increasing academic problems for the young Irishman.

Although the seminary leaders decided he could not be ordained a priest, they sensed he might have another kind of vocation. They knew from observation that his interest and concern for things religious were very strong. They sensed that God (if not theology) was paramount in his life. Within the Catholic orthodoxy of that time, he was firm in his beliefs. At the same time they found a young man who was not rigid; he seemed open to sound ideas. This enabled him not to be closed in a way that would prevent him from learning from others and broadening his horizons.

The faculty also valued the positive influence he had on the younger seminarians. They respected Barney in a way that enabled him to exercise positive leadership among them. They also admired Barney's ingenuity in the way he helped pay for some of his education by cutting hair.[20] While they did not approve of his refusal to wear a catcher's mask for baseball games—a sign of the rebellious spirit that never left him (and also a sign of the imprudence that sometimes followed him in the future)—they told him they believed he had the makings of a religious vocation.

At their suggestion, Barney visited another Saint Francis Seminary nearby. This one was named after Saint Francis of Assisi because it was conducted by the Capuchins, a group of bearded and sandaled men who followed the Rule of Saint Francis. Traveling the five miles from the lake shore campus of the diocesan seminary to the heart of Milwaukee, he was not impressed with what he found at the other Saint Francis Seminary. Possibly it was the Capuchins' austere appearance and strict observance of the Rule that repelled him, or perhaps it was the setting of the place—in a busy section of Milwaukee, not far from downtown. Or, even more likely, it could have been that, if he joined them he would have to speak German, since these Capuchins were also German-speaking (at least in their studies).

Whatever the reason, Barney reacted negatively to the Capuchins. He returned to Superior for his summer vacation of 1896 uncertain and confused. He had come to Milwaukee quite sure of his calling; now he did not know what God wanted for him. Added to these mental and spiritual troubles, his quinsy (sore throat) had gotten worse during his seminary days. Now chronic, it could easily have been aggravated psychosomatically by the deep anxiety he felt.

Barney confided in his former spiritual director, Father Eustace Vollmer, the assistant at Sacred Heart. Unlike Father Sturm, Eustace was a Franciscan. He belonged to the Observant branch of the "First Order" of Saint Francis (which also included the Capuchins and Conventuals). As Father Eustace listened to Barney he heard words coming from a young man who appeared to be very generous and open to do the right thing. Despite his independent streak, he loved people, especially those in need—a good sign for a vocation. His background showed him to be responsible, if somewhat unstable—but that could be because of his lack of meaning with a "regular job."

He recognized a tendency, however, that Barney could become quite set in his ways once his mind was made up.

However, this time, when Barney came to Father Eustace this tendency was a problem of another kind: His mind was not made up! Barney was very confused, frustrated and concerned about his future. While he had negative feelings about joining the Capuchins, something about their commitment attracted him. Furthermore, if he joined them, he wondered whether he would be able to succeed. After all, hadn't he shifted in many jobs and then failed when he tried to settle into one by entering the diocesan seminary? How did he know if entering religious life would go well?

While honoring Barney's questions, Eustace tried to relieve his anxiety a bit by making a joke about the Capuchins: "You above all, Barney, should value the Capuchin beard," he said. "Those beards protect the throat and chest. With that troublesome quinsy of yours, a heavy beard is precisely what you need!" Barney was not impressed with such humor.

Whatever else transpired in that meeting, Barney decided to send a letter of application to the provincial of the Capuchins, Father Bonaventure Frey. He resided at the Province of Saint Joseph's headquarters in Detroit. At the same time, he also decided to hedge his bets: He sent a letter to the Franciscans of Eustace's Sacred Heart Province asking how he could be admitted to their formation program as well.

Barney's letter to the Capuchins brought a positive response. However, in subsequent correspondence Barney had said he still owed $525 at Saint Francis for school. He asked, "What should I do about that before I go to join you—supposing I could not pay cash?" Bonaventure replied with a practical solution: "In the Seminary of Milwaukee you will easily settle your accounts. If your father and brothers will offer the Rev. Procurator half of the amount of your debt, I have no doubt it will be accepted. I know neither the Most Reverend Archbishop nor the Reverend Rector will object to it."

Earlier in the letter, Bonaventure had given his support for entrance to the Capuchins, based on the positive recommendation he received from Saint Francis de Sales Seminary: "I will make no objection now to your application of joining our novitiate, as the Rev. Rector of the Salesianum thinks you have a vocation for monastic life. You may therefore come to Detroit, as soon as circumstances will allow you, or the sooner the better for yourself."[21]

Ordinarily one would think that Barney Casey would be excited at getting such a positive response. Given his initial negative feelings about the Capuchins, he thus read the letter without enthusiasm. By his own later admission, Barney was prejudiced against the Capuchins; being part of them was one of the farthest things from his desires that this Irishman could imagine.[22] Still wondering whether it would be better to join the other branch of Franciscans, to which Father Eustace belonged, he decided to make a special novena to the Blessed Virgin. She had helped him so many times in the past; possibly her approaching feast of the Immaculate Conception would give him some insight.

During the novena, Barney Casey concluded that, even if he might never become a priest or religious, he felt called to live celibately. Thus on December 8, 1896, the Feast of the Immaculate Conception, he decided to take a private vow of chastity, dedicating his whole life, including his sexuality, only to God. However, when it came time to make his vow, something powerful came over him. "At once"[23] he became intensely aware of the presence of the Blessed Virgin. At the same time, he heard the words: "Go to Detroit."

Later friars said that Solanus told them this experience (as well as an earlier experience of the Blessed Virgin at the time of his First Communion) was an actual vision.[24] Whether visions or not, their impact remained forever in his memory and helped influence the certitude by which he approached his understanding of faith itself.

Since he had shown interest in both the Observant and Capuchin branches of the Franciscans, and because the Capuchin's novitiate was in Detroit, Barney concluded that the message saying "Go to Detroit" meant he should join the Capuchins.

While he might not have been excited about what he heard, at least he was relieved. Somehow the same God who had inspired two German-speaking Swiss diocesan priests to found the Order in the United States could help this former diocesan seminarian. They had founded the Order at Mt. Calvary, Wisconsin, the same year Barney Casey, Sr., had arrived in this country. Perhaps something good might happen with the Capuchins and a Casey coming together in the Saint Joseph Province.[25] With clearance from his local bishop ("no doubt you will become a good religious"), Barney began to prepare for Detroit.

Knowing that once he entered the Order he might never be home for Christmas again, his family urged him to stay until after the holiday. But Barney's mind was made up. He was determined to respond as soon as he could to what he considered his call. He must "go to Detroit" as soon as possible.

On December 20, 1896, he left Superior for Saint Paul on the 11 PM train. In many places, drifting snow slowed the train to a crawl. Inside, when the crowded cars were not stifling and hot, they were bitterly cold. The air was dry and stale. Finally the train reached Milwaukee for a layover. Barney traveled the two miles from the depot to the Capuchin seminary of Saint Francis. Receiving a warm welcome, he spent part of the evening in "friendly recreation."

The next day he boarded the train for Chicago. There he transferred to a Detroit-bound train. Because of the increasing snow two locomotives pulled that train, yet it averaged only twelve miles an hour. It arrived at dusk on Christmas Eve. From the station in Detroit he made his way to Saint Bonaventure's to enter what he would later call "the privileged novitiate."[26]

The Casey Family, July 8, 1900. Bernard Casey, Jr., is now Solanus Casey and is not pictured. He is stationed at St. Francis Seminary in Milwaukee.

St. Bonaventure Chapel and Monastery as it was in 1896 when Barney Casey came to the Novitiate. The Novitiate wing is in the back of the building, not pictured here. (*Detroit News*)

Sacred Heart Church and Monastery and the adjoining field at Yonkers as it was when Solanus Casey came in 1904 for his first assignment.

Solanus with his priest brothers at Maurice's ordination to the priesthood, June 1911, in St. Paul, Minnesota: Maurice is on the right. Edward, on the left, was ordained in 1912.

2

NOVITIATE & EARLY FORMATION

DECEMBER 25, 1896–
AUGUST 3, 1904

Lugging his belongings—probably in the trunk given him by Cole Younger, the gangster he befriended at the Stillwater prison—Barney took various streetcars to get to the Capuchin "monastery" of St. Bonaventure. The porter, the superior and his future novice-master, Gabriel Messmer, warmly greeted him. They offered him a meal, but Barney was too exhausted. He just wanted to sleep.

Walking through the first floor cloister and up the winding stairs, Barney noticed the simplicity and starkness of the building. Its architecture reflected the Capuchins' poverty and austerity. The wood latch to his "cell" opened to a nine-by-twelve room; it had a single curtainless window. The window overlooked the large grounds behind the friary. While he would discover the beauty of those grounds in summer, the snow and his exhaustion made them look desolate. Opposite the narrow iron bed was a one-drawer wooden desk with a straight-backed chair. The two clothes hooks on the wall would hold all the clothes he needed once he began wearing the Capuchin habit.

Once by himself in the room, Barney began to wonder: What had he gotten himself into? Yet, recalling his earlier, December 8 experience, he asked himself: "Why did our Blessed Lady send me here?" He was revisited by the old, negative feelings and prejudices against the Capuchins that he thought he had forgotten. These thoughts, combined with his fatigue, overwhelmed him with fear and depression. Taking off his coat, he lay on the bed, throwing a blanket around him. The deep sleep that came almost immediately overtook his fears.

The next sounds Barney heard came from the corridor, down the hall. As they grew closer, he figured out that someone was ringing hand chimes as voices sang *Stille Nacht*. As the sounds got closer to his room, he also could smell incense.

Barney Casey's first night at Saint Bonaventure's gave him the experience of one of the most tender and touching rituals of the Capuchins: the awakening of the brothers for Christmas Midnight Mass with songs, bells and incense. Opening his door, he saw a group of smiling, singing friars. As they moved from door to door, more friars joined them. Putting on his shoes, Barney became another voice in their procession. Somehow the gloom that had descended on him shortly before was forgotten. Maybe, he thought, the Capuchins were not so austere and inhuman after all.

Midnight Mass, and the Christmas Day Mass, plus the friars' feasting and recreating would help erase anyone's doubts, fears and anxieties—at least for a while. It was no less with Barney. Indeed, the whole Christmas season offered him so many new and memorable experiences that Barney's Christmas Eve concerns seemed to recede into the past.

However, with Epiphany they were resurrected again.

In those days, Epiphany began one of the several fasting periods of the Capuchins. This was "the Fast of Benediction." It lasted forty days, often merging into the regular lenten fast. Rather than offering Barney an occasion for growth, the thought of the fast evoked his prior doubts and fears. As January 14, 1897, drew closer—the day of his impending investiture into the Capuchin habit and its novitiate—his negative feelings and foreboding only compounded. Just one day before receiving the habit, Barney's depression reached a peak. In the small book of the Rule of Francis and the Constitutions of the Capuchins he had been given, he noted that it was a "day of anxiety" and "dark indeed."[1] Something in him told him, however, to move ahead.

Barney's fears seem to have remained with him until the very point of taking off his suit coat to be invested with the chestnut brown habit of Saint Francis. At that point a deep peace settled into him. He received the name of Frater[2] Francis Solanus, after Saint Francis Solanus, the violin-playing seventeenth-century Spanish Franciscan missionary who worked in South America.

Solanus's novitiate was unique in timing. It straddled two other groups of novices. For the first six months he was classmate of Fraters Leo Steinberg and Salesius Schneweis. In July seven new novices were received.[3]

By now Solanus had fallen into the regular pattern of the day that began with the sound of the "clappers" at 4:45 AM. These were two pieces of wood, each eight by four by two inches. They were clapped together to the tune of *"Sur-gi-te, Fra-tres"* ("Get up, Brothers"). With few exceptions, the early morning pattern followed the same schedule:

5:15	Lauds (Morning Praise) followed by Litany of the Saints
5:40	Meditation in common in choir
6:00	Angelus followed by Mass
6:25	Thanksgiving meditation after Mass
6:40	Personal time in silence
7:00	Breakfast

Such a patterned routine fit the new novice well, given his natural conscientiousness, which bordered on the scrupulous.

At breakfast the Capuchins drank their coffee from bowls. If such a ritual caused negative feelings in Solanus, they were certainly short-lived. He not only put coffee in his bowl, but his juice, cornflakes and whatever else seemed to fit, making a kind of porridge which he ate with gusto.

Novices such as Solanus who were on the track to become priests in the Order (cleric novices) had three classes a day. They learned how to pray the Divine Office and how to chant. Once or twice a week they would rise to chant Matins at midnight. Outside of class and study times, the novices helped with household chores.

The more Frater Solanus got into the routine of classes and "clericalia" (household chores), the further away and more meaningless his former work in Stillwater, Appleton and Superior seemed to be. The first entry in his little book of reflections notes: "I labor for eternity; not $100 per day or $1,000 a month."[4]

During his novitiate, Solanus came to realize that his motives were not always the highest. While he definitely did want to serve God's glory, the human tendency to get some reflected glory and the respect of others was not far behind. He jotted a quote to remind him of the need to purify his intentions:

> As for desiring to do things which may deserve glory, though it is what magnanimity desires, yet the magnanimous man desires it not for the glory that arises therefrom but only that he may deserve the glory without possessing it. On the contrary he has raised himself so high above the opinion of the world, that finding nothing estimable but virtue and looking with the same eye on the praise and scorn of man, he does nothing for love of the one or through fear of the others; his flight is higher. It is for love of God and virtue that he is moved to perform great actions; all other motives have no influence on him. Virtue is so excellent a thing that men cannot either reward or recompense it sufficiently. God alone can do this.[5]

If God alone was what Solanus should desire; his heart must become purified. Yet, to reach this goal of the spiritual life, he had to make changes in his life. In this he was helped by what he had heard from Saint Bonaventure: that perfection consists principally in love and its perfection and that this perfection must exclude those inordinate attractions (like avarice, pride and lust) which are the enemy of charity. Such tendencies, he was discovering, also represented opposite characteristics to principle of perfection which Francis called "most high poverty."[6] He also came to realize the inability of attaining the ultimate goal of loving God wholeheartedly—the aim of "most high poverty"—without certain practices. These "means" Solanus wrote down in his notebook to serve as a continual reminder:

Means for Acquiring the Love of God[7]
1. Detachment of oneself from earthly affections; singleness of purpose!
2. Meditation on the Passion of Jesus Christ
3. Uniformity of will within the Divine Will
4. Mental prayer, meditation and contemplation
5. Prayer: "Ask and it shall be given to you" (Matthew 7:7)

In many ways, what the young novice listed as the first means to acquire the love of God, represents the most essential requirement if one is to achieve union with God. If he was going to experience and remain in God's love, Solanus realized, he had to develop a pure heart, free of any obstacles which might interfere. In this way he could balance the negative element of detachment with the positive step of single-mindedness.

Single-mindedness was not just a spiritual goal for Solanus; it was part of his personality. In the past, when he set his mind to do something, it would get done. However now he discovered that this natural tenacity was tinged with a strain of perfectionism which he inherited from his strict upbringing as well as a scrupulous conscience. In the novitiate he was learning that, by trusting in God more than himself, he could become freer from both excessive rigidity and anxious scrupulosity.[8]

While detachment and singleness of purpose were the first of Solanus's five "Means for Acquiring the Love of God," it is significant that the last "means" he noted for becoming closer to God was found in his unique embrace of one of the four forms of prayer (besides thanks, adoration and praise): the prayer of petition. Thus he noted the Gospel passage: "Ask and it shall be given to you." This promise of Jesus to his followers, combined with Solanus's single-minded trust in God's Word would serve as the foundation of a powerful healing ministry that would come to characterize much of his future interaction with people.

As he interacted with his fellow novices, Solanus noticed that, at times, he was judging some of them harshly. In the process, he realized he should be judging himself instead and, furthermore, should be more empathetic about what may have led the novice to act the way he did. He was challenged to do this by a passage which he added to his notebook:

> If a fault of anyone disturbs you, know that it is more a weakness for him than for you, and that he suffers more from it. Perhaps, however, it is but "a mote in thy brother's eye" which, on account of "the beam in thy own" appears so great. At all events, have the charity to pray the Lord to deliver your brother and if the latter be the case, it will prove a double blessing.[9]

In his formation, Solanus learned to pray more intentionally. He was given tools which would serve him well not only for prayer in common, but for his personal prayer. Aided by the silence of the monastery, Solanus discovered the value of recollection. It provided him the means he could use to maintain a sense of God's abiding presence. Two aids to prayer he found particularly helpful. These mantra-type disciplines were added to his notebook: "I. Raise your heart to Him by frequent ejaculations and II. Make a good intention at the beginning of each work and frequently during its execution."[10]

Another prayer form he found helpful was meditation on the Passion of Jesus, especially in the form of the Stations of the Cross. Meditating on Jesus' self-sacrificing love enabled Solanus to move further toward his aim of acquiring the love of God because he began to understand how much God first loved him.

At a certain point in his novitiate, the professed friars (who were not allowed to talk to the novices but who observed them every day) had to vote as to whether he and his companions should proceed toward vows. Solanus passed the first two "scrutinies" with nine votes in favor. On the last scrutiny, November 17, he and Frater Maurus received eight positive votes and one negative vote. At that time there was no necessity for a dissenting friar to register the reason for his vote. However, it could have been that the negative vote came not because of Solanus's failings as a Capuchin but because his problems with Latin and German might have been thought to hinder him from being an effective Capuchin priest. From the less formal classes (in German) with Father Gabriel, the novice master, it was clear the fears registered at Saint Francis Seminary in Milwaukee had foundation.

The Capuchin superiors approached Solanus with their concerns about his academic prospects. They feared he did not have the necessary grasp of his subjects. With first vows coming soon, they also wanted to be sure that Solanus had the right motives. Did he enter the Order to be a Capuchin or a priest? To make sure, they asked Solanus to state his intentions clearly on this point. To allay any fear he might not be qualified to become a priest, Solanus signed an "Attestation" on July 20, 1898, the day before he would make his first vows:

> I, Fr. Solanus Casey declare that I joined the Order of the Capuchins in the Province of St. Joseph with the sure intention to follow thus my religious vocation.

> Although I would wish and should be thankful, being admitted to the ordination of a priest, considering the lack of my talents, I leave it to my superiors to judge on my faculties and to dispose of me as they think best.
>
> I therefore will lay no claim whatsoever if they should think me not worthy or not able for the priesthood and I always will humbly submit to their appointments.[11]

Whether it took much struggle and purification of motives to write this "Attestation" will never be known; however no one recalls Solanus showing any negativity about doing so. In the freedom with which he signed the statement, Solanus seems to have evidenced that he had been purged of any serious obstacles to moving to a higher stage in the spiritual life. This is called the "illuminative way," or the way of positive growth that builds on a life of detachment.

Having already committed himself to celibacy and to be totally given to the Lord on December 8, 1896, and with the previous "Attestation," on July 21, 1898, Frater Solanus knelt before Father Bonaventure, the provincial who had accepted him into the novitiate twenty months before, to declare his commitment to live the gospel as a Capuchin Franciscan "in obedience, without property, and in chastity."[12]

After making his vows, Solanus and his classmates traveled to Milwaukee by train to continue their studies at the Capuchin Saint Francis Seminary. The friary seminary extended like a *U* from the left of the large Romanesque church and friary chapel which was behind the sanctuary. Inside the U was a cloister garden that created an ideal place for relaxing, as long as you did not talk or laugh in a way that might disturb those on the second floor. On the second floor, in the upper left corner was the classroom. Due to the low number of students at that time, the classes were rotated on a four-year basis.

The student director was Father Anthony Rottensteiner. While some might have found his surname strange, nobody made fun of his approach to education, especially the young Capuchin clerics. All seriousness, he demanded the same of the seminarians. He established the educational program for the province. He also was the province minister from 1888–1891, the first provincial who was not one of its two founders, Francis Haas and Bonaventure Frey.

Anthony was elected only once, for a term of three years. To be elected for only one three-year term was rare in the province then as well as now. It indicates some kind of displeasure about the exercise of leadership. At the chapter of 1891, the general minister of the Order, Bernard of Andermatt, stressed the need for leaders to be more sensitive and humane in their approach. The fact that Anthony was known to be a severe taskmaster may have contributed to the fact that he was not reelected.[13] Now, returned to teaching at Saint Francis, Anthony oversaw other assignments for the students besides studies. Solanus's charge involved oversight of the friary chapel and the altar boys for the parish church of Saint Francis.

In this task, it seems, Solanus's conscientiousness became quite evident. According to a classmate, Father Boniface Goldhausen:

> He was very exact and painstaking. At times I would go down to the choir when he was busy there. I would observe him. I was highly edified. On feast days he would put perhaps three candles and three bouquets out. Then he would put candles on each side and he would go way back and look at it. If it wasn't exactly perfect he would go back and move one candle until they were just where he wanted them. It was the same thing with the bouquets. If everyone would take so much care for the Lord it would be wonderful. It took him at least a half hour to trim that simple choir altar. But at the same time he seemed so recollected. When he was finished, he made his adoration. One would

notice that he was deeply absorbed spiritually. That's one thing I cannot forget.[14]

Besides this detail of Solanus's days in the seminary, little is known about how he dealt with the other seminarians, except that he fit in as well as anyone else and had an affinity for checkers. For himself, he was quite aware of failings others didn't see. In his notebook, he wrote about one, challenging himself: "Patience, therefore, *with* your faults."[15] In another place he cautioned himself about his ongoing tendency to be judgmental: "Beware of silent criticism."[16]

His notebooks of the time show that Solanus's concerns went beyond the confines of the cloister. For him, the "Traits of Saintly Characters" consisted of three things: "(1) Eagerness for the glory of God; (2) Touchiness about the interests of Jesus; and (3) Anxiety for the salvation of souls."[17] Since a key group which "interested" Jesus were the poor, Solanus believed concern for the poor was at the heart of his vocation. "As Capuchins," he would later write: "our lot has been cast among the simple lives of the poor."[18] One of the first quotations in his notebook came from Pope Clement XIV while still a cardinal:

> Be not contented with giving, but also lend to him that is in need, according to the precept of the Scriptures. I do not know a more contemptible object than money if it be not employed to assist our neighbor. Can the insipid pleasure of heaping up crowns be compared with the satisfaction of conferring happiness and the felicity of attaining heaven?[19]

In his letters to his family he also urged them to do what they could for the poor. He reminded his sister Ellen to "admonish" their brother Owen "not to neglect the most salutary (deed)—almsgiving for the poor and orphans."[20]

Given Anthony Rottensteiner's stress on excellence, Solanus began finding difficulty in his final semesters of philosophy. He was just below average in his class of six. Textbooks were in Latin and discussions were in German. When he began his first semester of formal theology, in the fall of 1899, the superiors wondered aloud whether Solanus could survive their academic regimen. Instead of acknowledging part of his problem might be connected to a system which demanded German and Latin rather than the English language which nurtured Barney Casey, Jr., they identified any problems Solanus might be having with his own deficiencies; in their minds he simply was not smart enough.

Despite their concerns about his academic problems, Anthony Rottensteiner witnessed much good about Frater Solanus. He did whatever he could to coax answers out of him and the others having difficulties, especially when he believed their hesitation and stumbling were not for want of understanding, but because of the nuances of the languages. Nevertheless, a report card[21] of his first year of theology shows that Solanus did not do well. His grades were below average.

With solemn vows approaching for Solanus in July 1901, the superiors were very concerned. If he would take solemn vows, they again wanted to be sure that Solanus should not think that this meant he would be ordained, or, that if he was ordained, he would be able to fully function as a priest.

While Solanus was apprised of his situation and accepted it, the superiors wanted the matter written and signed. Thus, on July 5, 1901, Solanus signed a statement declaring his intentions. Typical of the Province, it had been written in German:

> I, Fr. Solanus Casey, having entered the Order with a pure intention and of my own free choice, wish to remain in the Order, and I therefore humbly ask for admission to solemn profession. However, since I do not know whether as a result of my meager talents and defective studies I am fit to assume the many-sided duties and serious responsibilities of the priesthood, I

hereby declare (1) that I do not want to become a priest if my legitimate superiors consider me unqualified; (2) that I still wish to be able to receive one or other of the orders, but will be satisfied if they exclude me entirely from the higher orders. I have offered myself to God without reservation; for that reason I leave it without anxiety to the superiors to decide about me as they may judge best before God.[22]

Having heard for almost ten years that he was academically challenged, Solanus seems to have accepted as truth what he had been told: He was not very smart. In this sense of "humility" as truth, Solanus would be considered very humble in signing the statement. This sentiment of humility, along with its sister of self-deprecation, would accompany him throughout his life.

Periodically in his notebooks we find items mentioned which indicate Solanus's world was not limited to the monastery's walls. We read of the rise of Count Leo Tolstoy and his strong influence over people of that time. Other entries note periodic visits from family members and the news that Maurice had decided to return to the seminary. Closer to home it mentions the need to split the northern section of Saint Francis Parish into a new parish to be named after Elizabeth of Hungary, the Franciscan queen, noted for her concern for the poor. Solanus and the other seminarians were recruited to help in its construction.

Around this time, an eye problem created some anxiety, in fact, more anxiety than Solanus thought was good. The more he thought of his pain and the way he was reacting in such fear, the more ashamed he felt. Not able to find peace by worrying, he decided to be more positive and thankful. If energy follows thought, his changed thinking had a positive effect. In his notebook he briefly penned: "Thanksgiving for same June 12; consolation on 13th, 1902."[23]

Another consolation of an academic nature came with the fact that, with the 1901–1902 school year, Solanus's grades began to improve. This contributed to the superiors' decision to have him move forward toward priesthood by receiving the Minor Order of Tonsure. In his second year of theology, Solanus's efforts also showed a slight improvement.The first semester of his third year gave Solanus his best marks thus far in theology, although they were still not that good in comparison to his peers.

As a result the superiors again raised questions as to whether he possessed the necessary ability to function fully as a priest in the German-speaking province, with its only German-speaking ministries. For his part, Solanus realized he had to let go of any self-determination and do real penance. Thus he wrote: "Penance is the primary end of the Friar Minor. Therefore a vocation to the same implies *penance* first of all, and whatever is of pain or death must be received at least with res-ignation and, better yet, with gratitude…. If the *Creator* desires or requires penance, what better can the creature do?"[24]

For the first time in his notebook, this entry marks the first time a key phrase in Solanus's spirituality would appear: *"Deo Gratias!"* This way of resignation would not only reflect a willingness to accept what might seem desired by God but actual gratitude in embracing it. As a sign of this gratitude, in the face of his own fading dreams, Solanus added and underlined the words that would be on his lips for the rest of his life: "Deo Gratias!"[25] Somehow, if his will was united to God's and God's will was somehow communicated through his superiors' decisions, he had to give thanks, even though it might be terribly hard.

Solanus celebrated the seventh anniversary of his call to "Go to Detroit," by receiving the subdiaconate. While this signaled his inau-guration into major orders, it still did not mean he would be ordained a priest.

The final decision about his impending ordination seems to have been deeply affected by something which occurred two months after his subdiaconate. In February 1904, Solanus's report card shows no marks at all for sacred Scripture and liturgy. This opened the door again to new questions as to whether he would be considered qualified for further orders. He wrote his sister that he would "probably be ordained deacon and priest before August," but immediately indicated the uncertainty by adding: "May the Holy Ghost direct my superiors in their decisions in this regard and may his Holy Will in all things be done."[26] This time, under his signature, Solanus wrote "Resignation+"; this was one of the few times he added this word to his name.

In the next few months, his grades in dogma, morals and canon law improved significantly, giving him the best average he had ever achieved. However, as before, he failed to get grades in sacred Scripture and liturgy. In relationship to his classmates, Solanus found himself in the middle of his class. Three had mostly all "good and very good" and "average" marks; three others almost all "average" and "passing" marks. Solanus came just behind Frater John O'Donovan and quite a bit ahead of Frater Damasus Wickland. None had ever received a "good and very good" or even a combination of these with "average." Furthermore, none seem to have completed their Scripture and liturgy courses to satisfaction.

Despite his academic difficulty, Anthony Rottensteiner came forward with prescient advice regarding his impending diaconate and priesthood: "We shall ordain Frater Solanus," the director of studies had said, "and as a priest, he will be to the people something like the Curé of Ars"[27] (referring to John Vianney, whose faculties for hearing confessions and preaching dogmatic sermons had originally been withheld, although they were later instated).

The superiors decided to ordain Fraters Solanus and Damasus, but to withhold from them any "faculties" to hear confessions or preach dogmatic sermons. It is unclear what they proposed for Frater John O'Donovan but he was ordained and later is known to have functioned with full "faculties."

Frater Solanus and his five classmates, Damasus, John, Fabian, Pius and Maurus were ordained at Saint Francis Church on Sunday, July 24, 1904. Archbishop Sebastian Messmer, the brother of Solanus's former novice master, ordained them. Two days later, in Rome, the head of the Capuchin Franciscan Order, Bernard of Andermatt, followed the traditional form of signing a letter giving Solanus "Preacher's Patents" for the Order. Though he received the papers from the Capuchins' headquarters in Rome, the provincial superiors decided otherwise. They would not allow him to use it, nor to hear confessions. Solanus would remain a "Simplex Priest" for the rest of his life. Simply put, the superiors did not believe Solanus had a grasp of German sufficient to be an effective minister in the confessional.

Their decision cannot be linked to any anti-Irish bias, because his fellow Irishman, John O'Donovan, who also received poor grades, fortunately "knew German better than the Germans." Furthermore, an objective investigation into his intellectual acumen, evidenced by his handwriting shows he had an IQ around 135.[28] Why, then, did he not make the grade? He also had evidenced fine abilities in rhetoric and debate as early as later grade school years.

Certainly part of the problem was the system that demanded solid Latin and German; Solanus was proficient in neither. However, it seems an added problem was Solanus's own personality. While he was logical and loved facts, he did not probe complex issues deeply. He tended to skim the surface. If he did not grasp something immediately he tended to give up. To himself and others this indicated a lack of sufficient intelligence; to observers today he might be considered more intuitive or intellectually lazy or not sufficiently tutored in ways that might balance this way of functioning with more concentration on developing greater skills at probing.

The superiors did not challenge Solanus's mind by giving him methods to go beyond the surface facts to logical insight and understanding. Instead they accepted the conclusion reached by the diocesan seminary professors at Saint Francis de Sales (who also were German-speaking). In the process the seeds of a self-fulfilling prophecy about Solanus Casey were planted: He was not smart enough.

If blame is to be placed as to why this happened, it would have to include his seminary instructors, his superiors and Solanus as well. However, as his life would play out, one can say of the decision that it too was a "happy fault."

At that time province legislation stated that "First Masses" be celebrated in the Capuchin parish closest to the newly-ordained's home. Since Appleton was the closest to Superior (two hundred miles away), Solanus celebrated his "First Mass" at Saint Joseph's Parish there. It was also one of the cities where he had worked as a motorman. This took place on the Sunday after his ordination. Included as part of the ceremony was a procession that featured a "bride" for Solanus—four-year-old Irma Roemer—and his brother Maurice as one of the servers.

It was a grand day, Solanus would later recall: "On that occasion I met dear Mother for the first time since joining the Order eight years before. She and Father came down from Superior and Maurice, who was with the Railroad Mail Service, came from Chicago." He recalled also: "Papa wept all during the Services at the thought that God had finally blessed his family with a priest."

After the Mass he and Maurice went for a walk. There he learned some good news: "Maurice, who was destined to follow to the same sublime privilege, brought a tear to my own eye that day, when the two of us were strolling in the Monastery garden. He half-soliloquized, as though revisioning his twenty-year vocation: 'By George, Barney, I think I'll have to try it over again. I'm getting tired of this blamed railroading!'"[29]

By now Solanus had received word that his first assignment as a priest would be Sacred Heart Parish in Yonkers, just north of New York City. His "Obedience," the official letter of his appointment, said he should arrive there by August 4, 1904, four days after his "First Mass" in Appleton.

Solanus Casey (top row, center) with high school seminarians, Sacred Heart, Yonkers, 1912.

Solanus Casey with other Capuchin friars at Our Lady of Sorrows, Manhattan, 1918.

Queen of Angels Church, Harlem, as it was when Solanus Casey was stationed there, 1921–1924.

3

YONKERS, NEW YORK

Solanus Casey had never been so far east in his life. Situated on the top of one of its many hills, Sacred Heart Parish and especially the monastery in Yonkers were known for the ministry of the "Capuchins on Shonnard Place." Solanus considered it to be a "city of fine schools, villas, and terraces."[1] Like Trimbelle, it too was "picturesque and beautiful."[2]

A main reason for Yonkers' beauty lay at the foot of its many hills, the Hudson River. Solanus's room offered him a view of it. The view elicited thoughts about God, along with a parallel desire to thank God from whom he had received so many benefits in his life thus far. He wrote as much soon upon his arrival there:

> Surely the natural scene now before me when I turn my head to look at it is as picturesque as any scene of long ago. The mouth of the Hudson shines like a silver lake away in the horizon in the clouds. I was going to say, "with hills and valleys and human achievement between." But what is nature in light of the supernatural? Ah, a substratum!

And what are natural blessings compared with the hope of immortality? I believe that I'd go crazy, yearning for something higher if I had nothing to enjoy or to hope for but the natural, even had I all the natural gifts and blessings enjoyed by man. But thanks be to God for the True Faith! Thanks be to God for the simple, honest, faithful parents that God gave us! Thanks be to God for vocation and for strength to follow the call, at least imperfectly! Thanks be to God for the blessed hope that he gives us here in our exile of once being eternally united with his chosen ones in the peace of our true home, in the love of his Sacred Heart![3]

"The ideal monastery of the Sacred Heart in picturesque Yonkers"[4] had for its superior and pastor the man who had built it thirty years before and, as provincial, had accepted Barney Casey, Jr., into the Order: Bonaventure Frey. Since Solanus was a priest, but not allowed to preach formal sermons nor hear confessions, finding him enough work to do proved quite a challenge. He assigned Solanus care of the sacristy and the teaching and oversight of the altar boys. These jobs were hardly full time.

For a priest to be assigned such work in the province—which had clear distinctions between priests and brothers at that time—it might also be considered something of a put-down. But Solanus had accepted the fact that he would always be limited to such work. Not only had he accepted such; he embraced his assignment with deep gratitude and a sense of being privileged. This attitude is found in a letter he wrote:

> ...something came to mind of our ineffable privilege in doing the little things we are able to do for the general welfare—most especially in a religious community. Each one is in his own place without thought or distinction as to what the work may be. To whatever

office or service one may turn, it is not easy to say just
which is more privileged, possibly excepting that of a
sacristan.[5]

While Solanus might consider being sacristan a distinct privilege, others did not see it that way. They felt that a priest taking care of the sacristy and sanctuary was a real humiliation. One who did try to understand was Solanus's brother, Edward. Not understanding why the
Capuchin superiors not only limited his brother's priesthood, but now
gave him work usually assigned a lay brother, Edward, who would later
become a priest as well, wrote him a poem. He titled it "The Brother
Sacristan," and tried to put a positive spin on the situation by linking
the notion of fidelity to duty with the concern about details which he
knew earmarked Solanus's approach. Reading the poem brought
Solanus much joy.

In his capacity as sacristan, Solanus worked with the women's
Altar Society. He also oversaw the altar boys who served the many
public and private Masses of the friars. James Lawless was one of these.
He recalled: "Father Solanus was the personification of patience when
it came to teaching us our Latin for serving Mass. He was a patient,
dedicated, and devoted servant of God."[6]

Despite such a positive memory, Solanus became impatient when
he saw some altar boys behaving poorly or without sufficient conscientiousness at Mass. When he observed this, he would let them know,
in no uncertain terms, of his frustration at their pranks or their lack
of devotion.

Once, when such corrections did little to change the situation, he
decided to make the Novena of the Immaculate Conception. By the
time he finished it, he noted, "immediately good boys asked to be
servers!"[7] The day was December 8, the anniversary of his decision to
join the Capuchins—which came during another such novena.

Some altar boys did not like to serve Solanus's Mass. It took too
long, given his sense of reverence, his scrupulous concern for exact

wording and his poor Latin. However, they did love it when Solanus took them on outings. James Lawless recalled:

> I have fond memories of the good times we had under his supervision, such as the yearly outings for the altar boys. I remember on these occasions that we had to attend Mass and pray for a safe journey to and from our destination. These visits were to Rockaway Beach, to Saint Patrick's Cathedral, and other places.
>
> Before heading home, Father always treated us to an ice cream soda. After that we would stop at the nearest church and say a few prayers for a safe return home.[8]

The boys liked it that Solanus played baseball in his habit. But what really impressed them was that he would never wear a catcher's mask—a continuation of his practice with the Casey brothers' team in Superior and at Saint Francis in Milwaukee.

Despite such good experiences with the servers, it would not be long before Solanus would find himself having to address their insensitivity and lethargy at the altar. Another time their poor performance reached such a point—despite his frequent corrections—that Solanus decided to make another novena, this one in honor of Our Lady of Perpetual Help. As in the case before, "every one showed new zeal."[9]

This entry represents one of four notations Solanus made between 1901–1910 under the heading: "Favors of Our Lady and Blessings." Another entry calls himself to task for being too easy on the boys and for being a bad example by passing "so many churches without making a visit to Jesus, before, during, or after the first outing."[10]

In 1906, Father Aloysius Blonigen succeeded Bonaventure as pastor and superior at Sacred Heart. One of the first things he did was to give Solanus a ministry that would have a powerful and lasting impact on himself and others: He was to serve as doorkeeper, or porter, of the friary.

Once at his new assignment, when people came to "talk to a priest," Solanus told them that, while he was a priest, if they wanted to go to confession he could not give them absolution. This confused them. They had observed him celebrating Mass at the side altars, why couldn't he hear confessions? "I'm not able to," is all Solanus would usually reply. As word spread about Solanus's compassion for the many people who now were coming to see him, the parishioners developed their own rationale for his inability to hear confessions. One of these was: "Father Solanus loved God so much that he could not hear confessions because he might not be able to take it if he discovered how many people were hurting God!"

What impressed people when they came to see him, little Loretta Brogan (later Sister Dolora, c.s.a.) remembers, "He never acted as though he was what he wasn't. He accepted people wherever they were. If you were sick, he hurt with you. He was very compassionate. He could say a few words to you and you would be perfectly at ease."[11] Others recall that, of all the fine priests at Sacred Heart, something about Solanus made him the easiest to approach. He put people at ease and tried to do as much for them as he could.

Those who attended the high school preparatory seminary at Sacred Heart also recalled Solanus's humanness: "One time we were called to Midnight Mass by Solanus. Here he was," Walter O'Brien (later a Capuchin) recalls, creating a one-man ritual for the annual Capuchin Christmas Eve wake-up: "the censer on one finger, the bell on another, and he was playing *Stille Nacht* on his violin!"[12]

Because of his approachability, people were unafraid to come to Solanus with their problems and concerns, asking for prayers or guidance. Generally he'd listen to the situation, then close his eyes a few moments or look off in space in a reflective mood. Then he would respond. His answers invariably brought them new insights as to how they might deal with the problems. At the same time they began to sense that Father Solanus was in special touch with God; this gave him the grace to help them the way he did.

When people with troubles could not come to the front office, they often asked Solanus to visit their homes. These included not only the Germans and Irish—who felt a natural kinship with Solanus because of language and background; the newly immigrated Italians who also came believed he would show them equal concern for their needs.

As an eight- or nine-year-old girl, Carmella Petrosino acted as Solanus's interpreter for the Italian community. "If anything went wrong in the neighborhood, the people would say, 'Go, get the Holy Priest,'" she recalled. She expanded on what happened then, as she often accompanied Solanus going from house to house:

> My first experience happened with Mrs. Maria De Santo in our neighborhood. She had come from Italy with her three or four children, and was about to deliver another. In those days instead of doctors, they had midwives, so my mother went over to help. In the process of delivering the baby, the woman got very, very sick. As the days went on infection set in. The doctor came, very concerned about her failing health. My mother said, "I don't think Maria is going to get over this; she's going to die."
>
> So right away I suggested that I go and get "the Holy Priest." To the Italians, they wouldn't say, "Father Solanus;" they would just say, "the Holy Priest." So I went to Father Solanus and told him that one of the ladies who just had a baby was going to die. So we started down the hill into the valley where we lived.
>
> As soon as Father came in, he asked for holy water. But they had no holy water. Father Solanus said, "Oh, poor, poor, poor." I ran over to our house and got some. When I came back he prayed over her, blessed

her and from then on the woman got over her infection and lived a long time afterwards.[13]

In another incident where she acted as interpreter, Sister Agrippina (Carmella) recalled:

> I don't know where this woman came from, but she came to our house. The woman had been having headaches for many years and felt she couldn't take it any more. She said to my mother: "Mrs. Petrosino, I heard that they have a holy priest up at Sacred Heart. And that if he prays over you, you get over your illnesses." (We didn't say "miracles" in those days, just that "you'll get better.") Then she said, "Could your daughter go up and get him?"
>
> So I ran up the hill and Father came right away. He had a little book with him. The woman said, "Father, would you put your hand on my head?" So he did that, as he read from the book.
>
> I just imagine the woman got better because she never came back.[14]

During their walks to the neighbors' houses, up and down the hills of Yonkers, Solanus and Carmella would have good talks. One day he asked: "Carmella, what are you going to do when you grow up?"

"I'd like to be a Sister of Saint Agnes," she replied, thinking of the Sisters from Wisconsin who staffed the school.

"You will be a Sister of Saint Agnes," is all that he said. A decade later Carmella became Sister Agrippina Petrosino, C.S.A.

This incident indicates another dimension of Solanus's unique giftedness: his keen insight into people's needs and how they fit into God's plans. These days at Yonkers found the seeds being sown which would flourish in his future ministry of healing and prophecy.

In some of the accounts told by Sister Agrippina about Solanus's house visits, he used holy water as well as other prayers. Invariably,

Solanus always used some "instrument" in the form of a sacramental of the church or invited his petitioners to get involved in some corporal or spiritual work of mercy. Thus, when any favorable response came to those who came to him in need, while they saw the source as Solanus, he attributed the positive results to the efficacy of the church's rituals or the works of mercy practiced by the petitioners.

One such work of mercy promoted by Solanus involved participation in the Capuchin's Seraphic Mass Association (SMA). The SMA had been the brainchild of a Swiss laywoman who wanted some way to help the foreign missions. She convinced the Capuchin superiors that, if she could get people to make contributions to the missions, the Capuchins should remember them in their Masses and other prayers. To formalize this mutual promise she suggested that an association be established. Benefits would go both to the Capuchin missionaries, in the form of donations, and to the people donating, in the form of Capuchin Masses and prayers. The superiors accepted the idea and the SMA was launched.

The front office of every Capuchin friary had SMA memberships available. Thus, when people visited Solanus at Sacred Heart asking for favors, he would often talk with them a while, pray for their healing or intention and then ask them to support the missions by joining the SMA as their way of thanking God for the favor they requested— even if it would not be forthcoming in the way they desired. The action requested did not always involve participating in the SMA; other times, Solanus asked them to perform some other action.

Solanus didn't limit his ministry to Catholics alone. Indeed he actually sought out Protestants to be with them. Sometimes they would come to the door in their need. Other times he went to their homes simply to be friends with them. Still other times, because some were quite wealthy, he tapped them to give jobs to people looking for work. "Non-Catholic neighbors over on Hudson Terrace especially where the more wealthy and the millionaires lived were wont to employ Catholic girls and young men," he recalled. Thus, on "such visitations I found that many of these dear good people would feel slighted if we failed to see them too. It just seemed sufficient to ensure employment if a Capuchin father sent anyone over where there was work to do."[15]

When it came to praying, besides mental prayer, Solanus daily prayed the Divine Office as well as the Little Office of the Blessed Virgin. When he missed it, he would correct himself as being ungrateful and insensitive. After all hadn't the Blessed Virgin Mary been solicitous of him throughout his life? Hadn't she been at the heart of some of the many unique religious encounters he had experienced?

His intimacy with Mary developed in a remarkable way shortly after being ordained. He wrote:

> I heard of a "Life of the Blessed Virgin." I was skeptical. "Who could think of presuming to write the life of the Blessed Virgin these days?" So I figured, erroneously taking it for generally understood that it had never been written. However, I was determined to see if it possibly might be more than a compilation of favors, etc., like the "Glories of Mary" which my Father used to peddle in the wintertime and give away.
>
> We found an abridged copy of *The Mystical City of God*. WHAT A REVELATION! What a treasure!
>
> From that first perusal of the simple but masterly introduction by the humble secretary, the actual writer...[Mary of Agreda, the Spanish mystic], my conviction has grown that the same *Mystical City of God*...is not only a genuine "Life" of the same Blessed Mother Mary, but, having studied it for more than forty years and on my knees having prayed the whole four volumes, I am convinced that the work has been rightly referred to as the most opportune and authentic autobiography of the Blessed Virgin herself, the

> Queen of all Creation and chosen by the Divine
> Creator himself to be his own Spouse and our Mother.
> Glory be to God![16]

Solanus knew *The Mystical City of God* inside and out. He noted the key passages: those which helped Mary's role in salvation, how these might apply to the church and their relevance for issues he was concerned about.

Another devotion which Solanus began to cultivate at Sacred Heart involved Thérèse Martin, the "Little Flower" of Lisieux, France. He read her autobiography, *The Story of a Soul*, at least fifteen times during his own life. He wrote of his admiration for her in a letter to his sister, Margaret. He suggested the Carmelite nun might help Margaret with her daughter, also named Therese, as well as other family members:

> Dear Margaret, if ever there was a good for a family like
> yours, her autobiography is one. She died only fifteen
> years ago. Her cause for beatification is now in Rome
> and I am asking her for entire reconciliation between
> J.T. and T.L., as well as other favors.... You ought not
> fail in procuring this book. She makes sanctity so really
> attractive and so beautifully simple. I think the book
> costs $2.00 at P. J. Kenedy and Son's, Barclay, N.Y. Do
> not fail to bless your family with its presence.[17]

While Solanus's spirituality was influenced by devotion to Mary and saints like "The Little Flower," he also found ways to translate his faith concretely in the way he related to others, especially those in need.

The parishioners noted that, when he portered, Solanus would feed the "tramps," as many in need were often called in those days. When strangers arrived who were hungry, he'd get them a big bowl of coffee, as well as whatever else might be available in the friary. The lore at the parish was that Solanus even gave them his own food.

Solanus had a special love for the children who often came to see him. Cletus McCarthy, later a Capuchin, remembered him joining them in playing fungo and how he would bat fly balls to the boys or hit ground balls "to see if they were good shortstops."[18] For her part, Loretta Brogan reminisced:

> It was 1912 and I was seven years old. We were having a Field Day in school. We were free from classes and celebrated with outdoor activities. I had gone to the eight o'clock Mass. I lived in a valley below another hill and valley.
>
> Father Solanus saw me going by the monastery and said to me, "Loretta, where are you going?"
>
> "I'm going home to get my breakfast."
>
> He put his arm around me and said, "No, you're not going to walk down all those hills. You come with me."
>
> He took me inside to an inner office. He brought me a plate with the biggest piece of bread on it I had ever seen in my life and a bowl of cornflakes and a great big cup of coffee. I had never seen such a cup of coffee in my life either.
>
> I was a very picky eater and never sat still long enough to eat much of anything. And I was so embarrassed to be in the priests' house. I was afraid what my father would say if he knew I was eating the priests' bread. I don't remember how much I ate, but when I was done, he took me over to school and saw to it that I was in good hands.
>
> That's the way he was; he just had to help you. Everybody respected him.[19]

After a while working as sacristan, altar boy supervisor and porter, Solanus received another task: liaison to different parish groups. One was "The Children of Mary," a sodality for young ladies. At the end of its meetings Solanus always made sure a big tray of cookies would be available for the young girls. Another group was the Sacred Heart League. Although he had not been allowed to give extended, formal sermons, Solanus used the occasion of League meetings or devotions in church, to give what the Capuchins called *"ferverinos."*

In the early days in Yonkers, these ferverinos did not come spontaneously to Solanus. He wrote them out with great difficulty. Yet, given his flair for the English language, he rather enjoyed the tedious process of perfecting his thoughts on paper. One of his notebooks covers fifteen pages of such reflections. These make it clear that his approach was quite a departure from the typical fire-and-brimstone style used by many preachers in those days. Instead of hell and damnation, Solanus stressed the love of God, the roles of the Sacred Heart and the Blessed Virgin, the nature of the church and the need to cooperate with God's graces. Drawing from his theological background, his preaching also reflected his own life's struggles and experiences.

He wrote one such sermon on marriage. Using the text from the Wedding Feast at Cana, Solanus's reflections for his era need not be altered greatly to apply equally well to our time:

> The Holy Gospel of today brings us at once to the really beautiful and sublime subject of "Christian Marriage." It is a subject that the Church has always proclaimed holy. It is a type of the love of Christ for his Church. It is fundamentally necessary for every kind of true progress and human prosperity.
>
> Not that everyone must marry who wishes to have peace in this world and gain heaven in the next. That would be contrary to the counsels of Jesus Christ and his Church. But marriage should be held as it ought to be, and is, as something sacred, to be prepared for with purity and holiness of heart and embraced in a Christian manner. Those who embrace it should do so determined to bear the burdens of the holy state they enter. They should remember that their duties and

privileges are one and the same and must be taken as such if peace is to reign in the individual soul, in the family, and in human society.[20]

Moving from this theological grounding for happy marriages, Solanus then addressed the pastoral problem of the growing alienation and divorces among married people:

How is it that there are so many unhappy unions in the holy state of matrimony? How is it that, where peace should abide and conjugal love reign (to the edification of the earth and the delight of heaven) that there is so much discontent, so much suspicion, so much hatred and quarreling? How is it that the divorces in our country alone are running away into the hundreds of thousands? One single divorce is a lot of scandal in a community. Why is it?

Is it not because of the levity with which so many of our young people prepare for and enter marriage? They worship at the shrine of amusement and pleasure while preparing, dreaming of nothing else. They cast away the thought of duty and obligation which indeed is so grave and so manifold. They trust to material advantages and to natural attractions in creatures, forgetting the Creator of all beauty and joy and holy pleasure. How can they but be disappointed? But alas, the worst of it is not for themselves but for poor children who grow up practically without father or mother and in cases of mixed marriages without definite religion.

But the marriages are not all so discouraging. Thank God there are still many who do prepare for this holy state and embrace it as God-fearing people ought to do. Many marriages in the Church, where the parties begin their new state at the steps of God's altar, receive the blessing of the Church and of God upon them and receive Jesus in their hearts. Such marriages are an edification to the parties themselves, a delight to friends, a joy to angels and surely at such weddings the Mother of Jesus is undoubtedly there also. For when Jesus is in our hearts, Mary will not be far away.[21]

While Solanus was very conscious of the problems facing married people and others, he knew that powerful societal forces influenced many. Their alienation and problems became compounded by the ever-more materialistic world around them.

While at Sacred Heart, tensions between nations in Europe brought about World War I. As he read the thirteenth chapter of Matthew's Gospel (wherein Jesus talked about the weeds sown among the wheat), Solanus found the weeds in the "sources of scandal" that Pope Benedict XV had said were causing wars among nations. Reflecting on the "sins" of his days, Solanus enumerated them:

The general craze among all classes for pleasure and amusement—very often sinful in itself—craze for the dance hall, the moving picture, the gambling hall, the ballroom. The Gospel's cockle can also be found in the sources of scandal which our Holy Father Pope Benedict XV complains of in his Encyclical to the Warring Nations: 1) Lack of mutual love among nations; 2) Disregard for authority; 3) Unjust quarrels among different classes; and 4) Material prosperity becoming the absorbing object of human endeavor as though there were nothing higher and better to be gained.[22]

Again, in making the link about societal influence on the behavior of the people who would be hearing his preaching, Solanus added:

As Leo XIII commented, "Our lot has been cast in an age that is bitterly opposed to justice and truth." And besides all these external dangers, there is a war going on within our own hearts as determined and as uncompromising as the world conflict now raging in the fields of Europe—a war between right and wrong—between the virtues of the soul and passions of our corrupted nature. As Saint Paul expresses it, the spirit wars against the flesh and the flesh wars against the spirit. What are we to do? "And the servants said to him, 'Do you want us to go and gather it up?' And he said, 'No, lest you might root up the wheat as you are gathering up the cockle....' " But what are we to do?[23]

At this point in the sermon Solanus offered some ideas that might help the people live peacefully in the midst of both their own wars and those of society: patience, awareness of obstacles to God's grace, as well as prayer and avoidance of those situations that undermine fidelity. He concluded by urging the people: "Let us not sleep, therefore, in God's service, but be grateful and vigilant that when the time of harvest comes on the day of judgment, we may be gathered into the heaven of eternal glory. Amen."[24]

Because of his awareness of social influences that impacted individual lives, Solanus felt he and other priests had an obligation to make sure the people were aware of their responsibility to get involved in public issues as their way of promoting the gospel and the social teachings of the church. Quoting Pope Leo XIII, he made such an entry in a notebook:

Let those of the clergy who are occupied with the instruction of the multitudes, treat planning of this topic of the duties of citizens; so that all may understand and feel the necessity of conscientiousness in political life, and of self-restraint and integrity. For that cannot be lawful in public, which is unlawful in private affairs.[25]

A social issue that deeply troubled Solanus which he felt he must address at this time involved a problem of injustice being experienced upriver at Graymoor, New York.

Solanus had become friends with the well-known Anglican convert Paul Francis Wattson. Wattson had founded the Franciscan Friars of the Atonement as an Episcopal group in 1899. His was the parallel group to one of Franciscan women founded by Sister Lurana White. In their common effort to promote Christian unity the two found their effort led them to Rome. This led them to bring their respective communities into the Roman Catholic church in 1909. Solanus went to Paul Francis' subsequent ordination and preached for his first Mass on July 3, 1910.

Upon their conversion to Catholicism, a benefactor who had deeded their convent to them now wanted it returned, alleging it had been given to them as Anglicans. The matter had created a legal scandal. Solanus was edified at the "Franciscan" way they represented themselves in their justified effort to keep the land. He wrote Sister Lurana:

> I take this occasion also, Dear Sister, to assure you that I thanked Almighty God—and do thank him—for having inspired someone with such truly Franciscan sentiments as were manifest in your gentle protest to the plaintiff attorneys of that Graymoor Church property case.
>
> I am fully confident that there are too many upright lovers of justice, even among our separated brothers and sisters, who read *The Lamp* [the Graymoor magazine] and paused at that letter ever to hold their peace while an act of such injustice were perpetrated as would be perpetrated should your community be ejected from Graymoor. In my opinion there is no sane man who has a spark of Christianity who will hesitate (when he knows the facts and the present circumstances at and around Graymoor) to second these

sentiments, and acknowledge your sentiments as really
Christian. Continue, Dear Sister, in your determination
never to quarrel, as our Holy Rule enjoins us and be
sure you will have more powerful patrons on your side
than intrigue with irreligion and silver and gold can
ever procure.[26]

After a lengthy legal battle, the sisters lost their appeal in 1917. They
were evicted from the property. True to his personality, which could be
adamant on matters of justice, Solanus tenaciously believed the sisters
had morality and justice on their side. He felt that their eviction represented "the killing letter of the law." He believed that "the majority
of our separated brethren will condemn it as done in their name and
will regret it."[27]

Despite the sisters' "persecution for justice's sake," Solanus did not
urge retaliation. While writing Sister Lurana: "Needless to say, we all
hoped that things would never come to such a farce against common
justice and charity," he tried to put the situation into a larger perspective of faith. He wrote:

However, the victories of the world are short-lived:
"Man proposes but God disposes." We may be sure that
Almighty God has not permitted things to take such a
course without some good design of his own—to turn
evil into good.

At all events the words of our Divine Master,
"Blessed are you when they revile you and persecute
you...," should be a consolation to you and an encouragement. The sisters will hardly be able to do anything
better than pray earnestly for their persecutors, according to the same divine authority: "Do good to those
who hate you, and pray for those who persecute and
calumniate you."[28]

In concluding his supportive letter, Solanus enclosed a "little dona-tion…to help you in your present need." It came from the superior of Sacred Heart, a very human response to some friends and coworkers facing a very difficult situation.

Life for Solanus wasn't all front office work, visiting the sick and helping the poor or those in trouble. There were plenty of times for celebration as well. These celebrations brought out the human side of Solanus, which delighted people.

One of Solanus's favorite celebrations at Sacred Heart was its Labor Day parish reunion. After a High Mass, parishioners and non-parishioners alike would mill around the playground, mixing with each other, playing games of chance and drinking good German beer. Solanus liked playing the wheels of fortune, eating hot dogs with onions, renewing acquaintances and enjoying the other parts of the festivities.[29]

Solanus's outgoing personality was at its best in such celebrations. His natural desire to be around people, to befriend them, and to share his enthusiasm and optimism for life and God was especially evident. It was clear to the people that Solanus simply loved them. Not only was he their "holy" priest, he was one who loved a good joke—as long as no person or group would be hurt in the process. The parishioners' admiration only increased Solanus's enthusiasm and zeal to be their friend and helper.

A highlight of Solanus's years at Sacred Heart came with the cel-ebration of his parents' fiftieth wedding anniversary. In the autumn of 1913 all the remaining family—four daughters and ten sons, including three priests—gathered to celebrate their dear parents' fifty years of married life. Father Edward, now ordained for two years, was cele-brant. Maurice, ordained for three years, was the deacon. Solanus, ordained for nine, served as subdeacon and preached.

Recalling the impact made by Barney and Ellen Casey on their sixteen children, Solanus could only be thankful. Consequently he developed the theme of appreciation for the past years shared between husband and wife and their children, gratitude for their present health and prayerful thanks for their holy and happy future.

During the week of celebration, the family spent much of the time reminiscing. Some of this was recounted years later, in a letter Solanus sent his brother James:

> Probably you remember when, at the Golden Wedding in 1913, we were all musing over scenes and events on the River Bank and in Old Trimbelle. Someone remarked, "Wouldn't it be nice if we could go back there again!" Dear mother, gently sighing as if revisioning the trials of those days which outweighed their beauties and pleasures, half-whispered an exclamation: "Thanks be to God, I'm glad it's over."
>
> Many a time since I've thought, how beautiful was that little exclamation. It was really Christian![30]

Two years after the golden anniversary, Barney Casey, Sr., died. Three years later, Ellen Casey joined her beloved Barney in a "beautiful death at the second ringing of the Angelus."[31]

Solanus was in his mid-forties and, as is the case of so many at this stage of life, he now experienced the loss of those closest to him. Far from embittering him, his parents' deaths led Solanus to deepen his desire to draw closer to God. He sought to deepen this relationship in prayer; at the same time, he seemed to grow even more concerned about God's people—a sign that his mystical approach to prayer had an active component as well. This concern for others led them to find in his words strength and peace.

Solanus tended to take people at their word. When they came with their problems and needs, he did not spend much time probing nor did he show curiosity about their phobias. He seemed unconcerned about details; indeed he even seemed to skim over them to get to what he considered their core issue regarding their relationship with God and others. To some this way of dealing reflected superficial thinking; others thought it implied that he might be too easy with them; still others said it reflected a practical way he could deal with the many who came to the office.

Seemingly unaware of the many things happening to people through his ministry, Solanus confidently offered responses to their needs. At times, it appeared to some that his approach bordered on bravado. Actually, what seemed like audacity reflected what the Scriptures call "courage" or "boldness." Encouraged by the positive results people had, Solanus grew to more deeply trust that God would respond to people who asked; they would receive.

Probably at no previous time in his life was Solanus more grounded. The time at Sacred Heart found him gaining more control over his strong emotions. His earlier tendency toward argument and debate was waning. He no longer had time for temper flare-ups. He was becoming more sensitive and empathetic.

Solanus also was discovering that the scriptural promises about Jesus' healing sickness and diseases of every kind were as relevant for the people of Yonkers as for those in Galilee. The confidence people sensed in Solanus was really the fruit of his own growing confidence, not in himself but in God's promises revealed by Jesus. In fact, it was becoming clear that precisely because he had balanced self-confidence with humility, Solanus was able to have more confidence in what God wanted to do in him and through him for others.

In July 1918, the Capuchins had their triennial chapter, at which new assignments were given. Deciding that Solanus had been at Sacred Heart long enough, they transferred him to Our Lady of Sorrows in Manhattan on the Lower East Side.

In his "first assignment, first love," the years at Yonkers had built a solid foundation for Solanus's future ministry. In his ministerial niche in the province, he had come alive; he found himself. His desire for responsibility found its expression in a unique ministry that helped others physically, relationally and spiritually. Whatever earlier doubts and confusion he may have had about the religious life and priesthood seemed resolved; there was little or no confusion as how he could minister as a Capuchin Franciscan. He had developed a rhythm and timing that spoke of solid integration and openness to the future.

Also, true to the notion of "first assignment, first love," Solanus found his transfer bittersweet. He would be leaving many friends; yet he also felt God's work in him would continue in this new assignment. He shared these thoughts in a note to his sister Margaret:

> I am just about to leave Yonkers for a new field, down in the very heart of the metropolis. In a way I almost feel sad to leave the Sacred Heart Monastery and Parish where I've been laboring (if laboring is the right word) for close to fourteen years. We had a provincial Chapter in Detroit last week (July 11–14) and we just learned today (July 16) of the changes made.... Well now, "Good-bye" for the present from Yonkers. My new address will be 213 Stanton Street, New York City, New York.[32]

Solanus left Yonkers immediately. He began his new assignment on Manhattan's Lower East Side the same day.

Solanus next to soup kettle at the Soup Kitchen.

Solanus handing out bread at the Soup Kitchen.

Solanus serving a meal at the Soup Kitchen with other friars, circa 1940.

4

MANHATTAN

JULY 15, 1918–
JULY 31, 1924

When Solanus arrived at Our Lady of Sorrows, most parishioners still constituted the same ethnic group of German immigrants who helped create the parish in 1867. With Solanus's arrival, he was given the tasks of being director of the altar boys and the Young Ladies' Sodality. It does not seem that he was given the job of porter.

He used the extra time to deepen his understanding of the Scriptures. He wrote many of his favorite passages in a new notebook. Covering some thirty-five pages (with some blanks) entries in his little book covered biblical themes of resignation, patience, gratitude, injustice, the Eucharist and the Blessed Virgin.

Solanus also entered into the book comments related to himself, including his perceived failings. "Affected to be little conscious of the beauty or success of sermon yesterday,"[1] was one such entry. Another time he chided himself for being insensitive to the needs of the poor who approached him for help: "Refused 5¢ [one time and] 2¢ to unfortunate."[2] In two entries from this notation, he jotted a reminder of what Deuteronomy said about the way the poor should be treated: "I command thee to open thy hand to the needy and poor that live with thee in the land (Deut. 15:2)."[3]

Besides these items, not much is remembered about Solanus's years at Our Lady of Sorrows. The only available recollection of anyone who knew him at that time was from Sister Rose Cecilia Ascherl, an Amityville Dominican. She was in grade school while Solanus was at Sorrows. Though still a child she recalled, "Father Solanus made a deep impression on me. His gentleness with the children, his way of speaking and friendliness I always cherished."[4]

From his notes and writing, it seems that Solanus was moving from more practical goals to visionary goals. In his retreat notes for 1919, of all the references noted, the most refer to "Zeal for Souls." He copied Luke's words of Jesus and underlined the first words: "*I am come* to cast fire on the earth and what will I do, but that it be kindled" (Luke 12:49). He then noted the link between the union with God that is achieved in ecstatic prayer and the desire to bring others into a similar union with God. He quoted approvingly Saint Catherine of Siena's words after she woke from an ecstasy: "Oh wonder! Oh wonder! How can I begin to describe the ineffable and the indescribable?" This led Catherine, Solanus commented approvingly, to be "ready to give her life a thousand times to save even one sinner for such glory."[5]

An entry like this gives a glimpse into the possibility that Solanus himself was moving well on the spiritual path as outlined by one of his favorite writers, Saint Bernard. Bernard described the spiritual journey as going through three levels of truth. The first of these, the truth of self, ends with the self having ecstatic knowledge of God.[6]

For Solanus, this first level of truth involved the recognition and admission of himself as a sinner. His sensitivity to his sinful tendencies at this time was very keen. Often he would ask people to "pray for my conversion." In his eyes (unlike those who could find no fault in him), he was not a holy man but a sinner in need of growth and conversion. The second pathway and level of truth was Solanus's knowledge and truth about others. His self-knowledge led him to greater acceptance and love of others.

The first two stages of truth—that about one's self and that about others—led automatically to the third level. Not afraid to face the truth about himself and others, Solanus was open to experience the truth of God "with unveiled face" (see 2 Corinthians 3:18). The more time he took to be still and know the Lord, the more the peace, joy and consolation of God seemed to invade his being. This experience invited Solanus to further union, including ecstatic union.

While Solanus never wrote explicitly about his experience of this union, his writings about Catherine of Siena and the fruits of the Spirit gradually becoming more manifest in his charity toward others bespeak the mystical reality already beginning to flower in his life. Paradoxically, an experience he had under the influence of drugs might just reveal what was happening internally in Solanus at this time.

Solanus came close to Sister Death as a result of a gangrenous infection. He recalled, "I had been in agony for at least forty hours, though no one else seemed to know it, and while I tried to thank God for it all, my principal prayer—at least a thousand times repeated—was 'God help us.'"[7]

In his recovery at Saint Francis Hospital on East 142nd Street, Solanus wrote about his experience. It had brought him in touch with the possibility of death. His reaction to it is described in a detailed letter to his sister:

> You will probably wonder what the cause for my being in the hospital. Well, I did not come here for pleasure, of course. Yet I thank God for the whole experience here since my arrival. No doubt a few details will be interesting, and I hope, profitable. I will give you some of them now and tell you their purpose afterward.
>
> When I was examined by Dr. Edgerton (an excellent physician) Saturday night, my case was pronounced gangrenous. Because of its urgency, it would be a Sunday case. "Tell Dr. Kirchen to be here at 10:00

tomorrow," he said, and then said to the nurse (our cousin Joseph Parker), "We'll give him a whiff of gas and slit that open."

I had counted the hours all night. I wondered at times if I'd be possibly able to say Holy Mass at 6:00 as prearranged. I considered how I might hold out until 10:00. Thank God I said Holy Mass, but with great difficulty.

At about 11:00 "Parker" came in to tell me that an urgent case of appendicitis had come in just as they were about ready for me. He said, "Have a little patience." I had started a couple of cards to our Reverend Brothers (Maurice and Edward) by this time and I think my pain had become less acute. My most frequently repeated prayer was "God help us!" Sometimes I said, "Deo Gratias!..."

After some joking with the doctors...they took off their "long faces" although they kept on their white caps and gauze-covered mouths. Dr. Edgerton concluded: "Well, roll him in here now, head first." With my sixth breath of gas, and with effort, I called out: "All right!" (after the first couple of breaths, I almost doubted if the stuff was any good).

Life and light were going by fast when beautiful bells began to ring (from Saint Joseph's Hospital for Consumptives across the street). A voice gently and piously reminded: "There's the Angelus." Oh, how sweet was that music to my soul and the announcement, how confidence-inspiring!

Then I realized that consciousness had come to the very end. The description of Mother's beautiful death three years ago at the second ringing of the Angelus flashed on my memory and my heart was only able to respond: "Behold, be it done to me according to your holy will."

I can realize now as never before how beautiful in the sight of heaven Mother's death must have been. With the above act of resignation, I came to "perfect darkness and death." A shorter instant, however, than that death lasted could not be imagined. With electric quickness the bubble broke. What peace! What solemnity!!! The very breath of my experience seemed to be principles of wisdom and truth, such as "To the pure, everything is pure." "Charity knows no evil...is not suspicious," etc.

At about 12:15 p.m., I heard Dr. Kirchen urge Dr. Edgerton: "Hurry up! Hurry up!" I seemed to see the latter cutting away the last fleshrags as I actually felt him do it without the slightest pain. I could only weep out with joyous wonder: "Deo Gratias! Deo Gratias! Thanks be to God!...[8]

In Solanus's experience of "perfect darkness and death" it seems he experienced deep unity with himself, others and God. While Solanus's reflections were induced by the anesthetic, since it called up scriptural archetypes to his consciousness ("to the pure, everything is pure" and Paul's Canticle of Love), one can surmise that Solanus's unconscious had been at the point of purity of heart; the peace and solemnity which he experienced at this level were surface emotions of mystical reality present before and present later.

After Solanus left the hospital that specific infection never returned, although he would begin in a short while to be bothered with what would become chronic poor health.

On October 25, 1921, a trade was made between Our Lady of Sorrows and Our Lady Queen of Angels in Harlem. The *Chronicle* for Queen of Angels starkly notes: "Father Cajetan transferred from here to Pitt Street at 'Mater Dolorosa.' His place was taken by Father

Solanus from Pitt Street."[9] No rationale for the transfer is noted; but in those days only one rationale was given: the vow of obedience.

The most significant thing about Solanus's new assignment at Third Avenue and 113th Street was that, for the first time, he was not appointed to the sacristy nor given the task of caring for the Young Ladies' Sodality. Aware of the good that had been done through his door-ministry, the superiors gave Solanus the main assignment of being porter.

When people came with their problems, one of the practices Solanus continued was his invitation to them to participate in the Seraphic Mass Association. In his eyes, the SMA was a most powerful way people could have their prayers answered as they helped the Capuchin missions. He explained its purposes and benefits to someone whose child Jenny was "very low with polio and asks for prayers, that, if it be God's holy will, she recover:"

> The members of this Association are asked to pray for our foreign missions and their work and for one another—those members, of course, who can pray. Also those who can afford to do so are asked to help with an offering of some kind (for the missions) besides by prayer and Masses. I am confident that this will help your Jenny. This (will help) especially if you and yours do your part.[10]

Although Solanus wrote this letter later in his life, what he outlined describes the way he himself dealt with those who came to him. After the people shared their problems, Solanus usually made comments about their physical, relational and spiritual condition, addressing their pain or concern with deep sensitivity and care. Many times he spoke to an area that might not have been shared as a concern by the person. After commenting on the problem, Solanus usually talked about God's goodness, and the need to "thank God ahead of time" for whatever was being requested. Then he would invite his petitioner to manifest their thanks, ahead of any possible outcome (that might or might not accord to the petitioner's original desire). He also asked them to manifest their thanks by doing something concrete, such as enrolling in the SMA or performing some spiritual or corporal work of mercy. He stressed the need for some kind of action as a sign of "expectant faith"; thus his previous quote to the mother of "Jenny": "I am confident that this will help…especially if you and yours do your part." The "part," which more and more people did, was to enroll the object of their concerns, or "the poor souls," in the SMA.

When people understood that they were helping the Capuchin foreign missions as well as receiving spiritual benefits for the people, they eagerly joined the SMA, not thinking that the requested fifty cents for an annual enrollment was too extravagant. When people could not afford it, Solanus simply enrolled them without cost. By being named an official "Promoter" of the SMA for the Capuchin Order by the superior in Rome, Solanus was free to give such memberships gratis to those he determined were in need.

As he promoted the SMA to the people coming to him, or urging them "to do their part," more and more people found their needs and prayers being answered. Soon the word began to spread about the phenomena taking place at Queen of Angels. Personal problems were being resolved; troubled marriages were experiencing peace; people with sicknesses were saying they were healed. As the word spread, Solanus became busy all day counseling people, praying with them and for them about their problems, getting them involved in doing some charitable work, and, as always, inviting them to bless God for "all his designs."

The news that so many people were reporting positive responses to their requests not only traveled around New York; it reached the ears of the provincial minister in Detroit. Thus, when Father Benno Aichinger made his annual visit to the parish and friary in 1923 he talked with Solanus about his portering and what was happening to people in the front office. As he spoke about the various favors being granted and how many came upon their enrollment in the SMA, Father Benno told him to start keeping a record. That very day the recording began.

Solanus got a twelve-by-ten-inch letter-type book with heavy covers and lined pages. The first notation under "NOTES ABOUT SPECIAL CASES—November 1923" referred to Benno's request: "Nov. 8th, 1923. Today Visitation closed. Father Provincial wishes notes to be made of special favors reported as through the Seraphic Mass Association."[11]

The choice of words Solanus used for his notebook—favors reported as through the Seraphic Mass Association—is significant. Solanus Casey had an almost unshakable faith in the efficacy of the Mass, sacramentals and membership in the SMA. He was convinced that any favor people might receive came, not because of himself, but because of their membership in the SMA or whatever other good deed each was asked to perform, be it "going to confession" or helping the poor and needy. So convinced was he of this vis-à-vis the SMA that he believed anyone who enrolled in the SMA, at any Capuchin office, could be hopeful of having their requests answered. Other Capuchins, he said, "can enroll you in the Seraphic Mass Association as well as I can, and that is a big feature in the 'secret' of the many notable favors reported…. Thanks be to God."[12]

His first entry regarding a specific petition in the "NOTES ABOUT SPECIAL CASES" book opened with the phrase Solanus used to begin and end so many verbal and written utterances: "Deo Gratias!" Then it continued in Solanus's unique method of abbreviations:

> This p.m. Marg. Quinn—who enrolled her neighbor Mr. Maughan against drink and consequent anger [on] October 26, as also her sister, E. Remy of Philadelphia against severe inflammatory rheumatism, reports wonderful improvement in former and [reception of] letter

this a.m. from [her] sister [writing]: "Thank God and the good prayer society, I'm feeling fine."[13]

The first page has notes about people in many stages of life and death. Someone asks for "the grace of a religious calling and strength and grace to accept it." It mentions hitchhikers who had been "terribly beaten-up." A woman (whose husband drinks) had "two partial strokes." A woman's "16-year-old had vanished a week before" and was "found next day in Jamaica."

Another woman had "a nervous breakdown." Someone else whose brother had "been drinking for five years" and was "very careless about Church" had lost sight in one eye. The period for these entries is November 8 to December 9.

At about every third or fourth entry, another notation is written in such a way as to indicate that a positive resolution of the problem had taken place. Page after page sketched what Solanus called "pathetic stories."

- An eighteen-year-old boy was staying out Sunday mornings until 4:00. Although he was a practicing Catholic, he remained in bad company. That and his drinking were upsetting the family's peace. Nineteen days after this entry, another entry is made noting that he "went to the sacraments Christmas," escaped the "terrible and notorious misfortune of [the] former comrade" and was doing "ideally." His sister noted it was "Nothing less than miraculous."
- A mother with two fine babies suffered pneumonia; her doctor gave her three days and then three hours to live. She "recovered completely."
- A woman with an address on Lexington Avenue improved after serious heart failure. The doctors were surprised that she lived.
- A man working on the subway enrolled his wife. Eight years before she fell and lost "her memory completely" so that he had to leave "a note on table for Sunday morning [saying] 'This is Sunday' to

remind her to go to Holy Mass." He came back to report, "My wife's memory is evidently improving. Thanks be to God!"

- A woman enrolled herself and her husband who was "an inmate of asylum on Ward's Island." She came back to report that her husband was home and mentally well.

About half of the cases reported in the first pages give full names and addresses. Peoples' places of residence range from a few blocks from the church to Danbury, Connecticut, and locations in New Jersey. Solanus's reputation was growing. This became clearly evident when he celebrated the silver jubilee of his first vows January 14, 1922; the house *Chronicle* notes that it attracted "a great multitude of the population of New York."[14]

The first extended entry came on Valentine's Day, February 14, 1924. Solanus detailed the account of a seventy-three-year-old woman living on East 88th Street:

> Extremely anxious lest operation for double cataract be necessary. Promises to do all in her power for missions if use of glasses be restored without operation. This was November 1. She returned on January 20th, wearing her glasses but not yet satisfied. She renewed her promise that day. Today she returned jubilant and perfectly cured. In fulfillment of her promise, she joined herself [to the SMA] perpetually, and re-enrolled her parents and brother besides paying for a heathen child ($5.00).[15]

Incidents similar to the above filled seven such notebooks by the time of Solanus's death. From Solanus's perspective, his notes were made simply because he was told to make them. From the superiors' position, it was a matter of verification. They needed Solanus's comments about what actually was happening in face of the inevitable stories going around about Solanus being a "miracle worker."

While some people at Queen of Angels sought out Solanus for his blessing, to share their problems with him, or that they "might be cured," still others were led to a deeper sense of God's presence by observing their religious faith. The Italian children in the school spontaneously referred to Solanus as "the Saint." "We just observed him," one former third-grader recalls, "especially when he was in the back of the church where the Calvary scene was located. We all looked in awe at him and were compelled not to talk or cause any disturbance as though [to do so would be] a sin."[16]

Others, like Justin Joos, remember how Solanus not only brought consolation to his family at the time of the death of his brother, but a prediction that he (Justin) would become a Capuchin. He recalls:

> He was a great friend of my mother and father. My Mother was Prefect of the German Third Order and my Father was head of the Ushers in Harlem. This was in 1924. I was only eleven at the time, kind of a roustabout who never took things too seriously.
>
> My brother was a Capuchin seminarian, Frater Romuald. He had been in a hospital in Appleton, Wisconsin. He was at Marathon, Wisconsin, in theology and was about to be ordained subdeacon. He got sick and they thought he had a thyroid, although he never had a goiter problem. They gave him medicine and then he developed tuberculosis. For awhile he had to recuperate at Calvary; then he went to Detroit for treatment and finally to Appleton.
>
> My father went out to Appleton where Frater Romuald was in the hospital. They assured him that everything was going to be all right. Two weeks later, on February 24, my father got a phone call that he was dead.
>
> My father wanted his body brought back here but it was not permitted, so my father was the only one able to go out to the funeral. After he came back, he was

quite distressed about the sudden death and that he alone was at the funeral. He went to Father Solanus to share his concerns. He explained that he wanted to have a priest in the family. Father Solanus told him, "Don't worry, you will have a priest in the family."[17]

At that time the eleven-year-old John Joos had no intention of going to the seminary. Years later when John had become Frater Justin, Mr. Joos told his son the story as well as how it brought comfort to him and his wife in their bereavement. He had kept from telling the incident to his son because he didn't want Solanus's statement to influence John's decision to go to the seminary.

Others remember Solanus as not tolerating the antics of servers who misbehaved during Mass (as occurred earlier in Yonkers). When he discovered their "shenanigans," he would get frustrated and correct them "quite consistently."[18] Despite his frustration, his impatience never got expressed in actual anger.

Another situation that actually generated the emotion of anger in Solanus clearly related to situations wherein he perceived that the rights of other people were abused or violated. Often such occasions involved situations of social injustice.

Probably his harshest extant writing is found in a stinging letter to the editor of *The Catholic News* of New York. His specific concern arose from an editorial in the archdiocesan paper about relations between Ireland and England. He scorned the editorial writer for "a regrettable one-sidedness of information." Solanus believed this bias resulted from what he considered was the undue influence of the "atheistic" news agencies. The paper's treatment of the anti-Irish tensions, Solanus wrote, "might be expected rather in a London Daily, or in any of our Metropolitan Yellow Jackets—everyone of them heart and soul in sympathy, not with a crucified nation [Ireland] or with Catholic principles, but with the Brazenly Brutal British."[19]

Solanus wrote his letter to "aggressively" challenge the Catholic press to publish the kind of information which Popes Leo XIII and Pius X said was a necessary alternative to the secular press. These popes believed the latter was often "bitterly hostile to justice and truth."[20] Solanus's passionate letter (which extends five full pages of single-spaced small type) recalled "centuries of Britain-broken treaties" and other incidents.

Solanus perceived himself as a "correspondent not doing this [writing] in any spirit of vindictiveness or out of malice to anyone." Rather he used many principles of debate which he had learned as a teenager. His energy, enthusiasm and determination to right wrongs were at their peak when he used his pen to hammer away at his point, marshaling example after example to support his position. He peppered the editor with one argument after another to show why the paper was not being even-handed toward Ireland. "Aye, Ireland unarmed except by her Faith in God! Unoffensive except for her surpassing determination to stand by the principles of righteous Freedom—principles for which from 1914 to 1919 humanity has bled white! Great God! Is it to be all for nothing?"[21]

Garnering all the arguments he could muster, Solanus even attacked the allied nations for allowing Britain to continue its control over Ireland. In almost a jeremiad, he wrote:

> Let no nation, much less individuals deceive themselves: God will not be mocked forever! And the allied nations, and their civilization have been mocking the honest peoples of the earth, and surely not less the Eternal God of honest people. Who is to blame? Where is our ideal Catholic Press? Offensive and defensive? God help us! Aye, God help us, and forgive us!
>
> That individual leaders have been and are guilty of that criminal silence and that mockery, is as positively clear as the fact that nations are made up of individuals.

They seem now, however, to be going further into crime. Instead of blushing for shame, personal as well as national, that no one has arisen like Daniel of old to convict the hypocrites, some of them are beginning to come out on the side of shame itself, on the side of the bulldog and the lion [England], the side of the archravager of nations. They speculate with the coolness of gamecock gamblers on hair-splitting points of morality. Thus they wittingly or unwittingly divert attention from the real source of [the] troubles in Ireland—the presence of British soldiers and of British corruption. Is not this clearly a case of the Scriptural, "Straining at a gnat, and swallowing the camel?" Shame on the "blind guides!" Pardon me if your correspondent [Solanus] seems acrimonious, and may the Lord help us to see clearly! For bitterness like falsity and exaggeration are to no purpose in an honest cause.

But history, it seems here as well as elsewhere, must repeat itself. It was a bishop that condemned St. Joan of Arc for witchery and who, a little later (duressed as he was by the British who were supposed to be Catholic) exposed her to unmentionable cruelties and finally burned her at the stake as a heretic. If reports be true, there are one or two priests in America who would do the like for a number of Irish "Joans," even without British duress.[22]

Probably because of his allusions to the bishops of Baltimore and Boston (who had made negative comments about Eamon DeValera, the leader of the IRA who later headed the Irish Republic), as well as the passion and rhetoric of the letter itself (to say nothing of its length), *The Catholic News* rejected Solanus's letter. Undaunted, Solanus sent it to *The Irish World*. It ran the letter *en toto*.

Someone reading the entire letter cannot help but question the anti-British sentiments of Solanus Casey. What happened in Solanus's past that could trigger such passionate and negative feelings? How can such an incident square with the fact that people think Solanus Casey should be a candidate for sanctity?

As a descendant of Irish immigrants, Solanus Casey could never be separated from his roots. One is not raised in a family with parents who were forced to leave a country because of famine (which they knew was caused not only by weather but by economic policies of the occupying British government) without passionate feelings which would be communicated to their children. And if that one had an uncle killed by the British in defending the Blessed Sacrament, such feelings would be supported by claims of martyrdom.

Solanus fully believed in the innocence of the Irish vis-à-vis England. Consequently, he would have been the first to believe that he wasn't prejudiced. But he was. Prejudice is a social sin that is nurtured in one's culture and its background. It is not necessarily willed, but it is part of one's emotional response received from society. Because it is so deep-seated, it is not eliminated overnight. If it took Jesus until the Resurrection to extend his and his disciples' ministry beyond "the lost sheep of the tribe of Israel" (Matthew 10:6; 15:24) and to people he and his coreligionists could call "dogs" (Matthew 15:26), certainly Solanus Casey should be allowed time to mellow (which he did). His struggle to overcome his received cultural biases is evidenced in the way he never limited the gospel to any person coming to him, no matter what nation or racial group they may have represented.

While Solanus believed his anger was justified in the case of the Irish "troubles," he could be equally strong, though more gentle, in dealing with justice and injustice among the Capuchins themselves. During his days at Queen of Angels, a brother was being pressured to leave the Order under some degree of duress. He confided in Solanus. The brother seems to have had few friends in the Order; in fact, the

friars seemed to have shunned him. The clear impression was that he
was neither welcome nor wanted.

Solanus was aware of how the community had dealt with this
brother. While he himself did not approve of many things the
brother had done, he tried to find some saving features. Believing the
possibility of conversion existed, Solanus wrote to the provincial,
Benno Aichinger. He noted the faults he had pointed out to the
brother, but also his belief that the local superior may not have given
him a "fair deal":

> I told him as much as that I had not been personally
> edified at what seemed to me was his want of fervor or
> devotion to Holy Communion while he was with us in
> Our Lady of the Angels. I thought he ought to turn
> earnestly to Headquarters—meaning the Tabernacle—
> and make some promise to do better in this, or some
> other regard, if things adjusted themselves favorably
> to his peace.
>
> Then he said something about making a retreat
> with the Jesuits. I told him that would, in my opinion,
> be the best thing he could do. I told him I would write
> you about him and he said he wished I would. I wanted
> to tell Father Guardian of my visit to him (which was
> made without the Guardian's knowledge) and of my
> proposition to write you all about the case, but I
> decided it as prudent to say nothing to him about it.
> Before I had a chance to do so, before deciding, he for-
> bade me to correspond with "Br. P." and at culpa before
> dinner gave quite a little admonition, in a general way,
> bearing on this case, while we all knelt as [though we
> were] novices.
>
> Now Dear Father Provincial, I do not wish to
> blame anyone or to excuse anyone else. "Brother
> _____" seems to me willing to be directed. He seems

quite conscious that he did not receive entirely "a fair deal" with the superior above. Well, may our dear Lord direct him and us all![23]

What happened with the particular brother and the "bad blood" between him and the local superior is not known. Who was right? And was Solanus right in taking up his cause? Sometimes Solanus's insights were strikingly accurate; however it could have been another case in which he was taken in by another's hard luck.

Even though Solanus's unbounded trust in the goodness of every human being could be exploited, nevertheless he could be counted on to speak his mind whenever he believed people were treated unjustly. As for the times he himself was misunderstood, however, he never was known to justify himself or to try to make his detractors look negative or foolish.

At the July chapter which preceded this letter, Father Benno was reelected provincial. At that time it was also decided that Solanus should come to the headquarters of the province, St. Bonaventure in Detroit. Stickler for detail that he was, Solanus noted that he received word of his transfer at 1:15 PM, July 30, to be in Detroit by August 1. A follow-up note finds him saying he arrived by his deadline.

In Detroit, Solanus often recalled his days in Yonkers and Manhattan with deep joy and gratitude, although, once told to transfer he did so without question, seeing it as God's will for him. He noted, "While I never long to go back to any old place from which Divine Providence has seen good to remove me, yet I must acknowledge that I have a natural inclination that way—like the Israelites in the desert naturally yearned (many of them) to go back to Egypt. No doubt, we are all naturally inclined that way."[24]

Solanus with his priest-brothers when Maurice entered
the novitiate, 1929.

5

DETROIT

AUGUST 1, 1924–
JULY 22, 1945

When he arrived in Detroit, Solanus found St. Bonaventure basically the same as when he entered the Order in 1896: a friary, the novitiate and the provincialate.

Solanus's "official" day started at 4:45 AM with the sound of the clappers calling the friars to rise. Lauds or morning praise began at 5:15 followed by the Litany of the Saints and meditation in common. At 6:00 Prime and Terce were chanted, followed by the "Conventual" or community Mass at 6:15. If he had not celebrated Mass privately beforehand, Solanus would do so after Conventual Mass. Then he would eat breakfast in his unique way. At noon two more "hours" of the Divine Office, Sext and None, were chanted for about fifteen minutes, followed by the main meal. Afterward, there would be a short time spent in relaxation. Vespers and Matins were recited at 5:15 or 5:30 until 6:00 when supper was served. Before retiring prayers, evening prayers were offered, including the Litany of the Blessed Virgin. In between these structured times for "regular observance," the friars would perform their various ministries.

Things were quiet at the friary, novitiate and provincialate at St. Bonaventure because not many people came. Consequently the front

89

office did not have much activity. As a result, the porter, Brother Francis Spruck, had the added job of being habit-maker and tailor. At the right side of the entrance was the tailor shop; the porter's office was on the left. This arrangement made it easy for him to answer the doorbell no matter where he was. Francis was very affable—a kind of Friar Tuck. His wit and humor made him very popular not only with the friars but with the occasional visitors to St. Bonaventure.

At St. Bonaventure Solanus was assigned to be assistant porter. Although he had been the main porter at Sacred Heart and Our Lady Queen of Angels, this meant he, a priest, would be under the direction or supervision of a lay brother. The fact never seemed to have registered with Solanus; it was just a matter of obedience.

Within a few weeks of Solanus's arrival the number of people coming to the front door increased dramatically. They were coming not to see Francis Spruck, but Solanus Casey. This jarred the pattern Francis had established.

For his part, Solanus seemed oblivious to Francis' increasing consternation. As in the past, he continued filling his notebook with reference after reference about "people of every illness and disease" coming to him (see Matthew 4:23; 9:35). An early account is that of a woman who came during his first month:

> (August 30) Mrs. Clara Kowalski (23, of 3392 Palmer Ave.) on August 18, extremely anxious lest x-ray examination demands [an] operation for dead bone in [her] ear. Joins Mass Association. Today [says] nothing was found yet in photo x-ray.
>
> (Sept. 1) Danger disappearing, good color returning.
>
> (Nov. 1, 1925) Perfectly cured. Deo Gratias.[1]

As one month flowed into another, Solanus's notebook shows more and more problems, with many being positively resolved:

(Sept. 7) Protestant woman enrolled for the sake of peace by a Catholic neighbor. Mrs. H. Johnson and Emma Smith run the Scientific Beauty and Corset Shop. They are very much at variance. Each is having a lawyer, to the scandal of [their] surroundings. Papers [have] already been served in Court.

(Sept. 12) Amicable settlement effected. Deo Gratias.

(Sept. 12) Lost Mental Faculties Restored. Wilfrid J. Vincent Noonan, 27. He [has been] in Saint Joseph's Retreat, Dearborn, since June 15. Once a very successful student, seemingly called to be a priest or religious, but to help poor parents decided on course of medicine. Broke down completely. Is enrolled today for two years by [his] broken-hearted mother.

(Oct. 24) Saw him today. Naturally not much hope; [his] poor Mother weeps bitterly....

(Aug. 2, Portiuncula, 1925). Now back home since March and [spent] first night [as] intern doctor in hospital. Deo Gratias. Loss of mental faculties restored indeed. Now thanks be to God!

N.B. Said that W.J.N. got his "degree M.D." in October 1927 [and] in June, 1928 was made superintendent of (a) big hospital in Detroit, Delray Hospital.

(Oct. 6) Sugar Diabetes Cured. Joseph Kajeski, 3320 Montgomery (35 years old) had been an invalid for two years with diabetes. He is a hopeless case. He was enrolled on Sept. 3. He went to work Oct. 6. Deo Gratias.[2]

(Nov. 18) Gall-Kidney Stones Cured. Mrs. Margaret S. Homan (45) of 1063 E. Grand Boulevard. Enrolled Sept. 6 against terrible kidney stones. She was to have

operation which took place on Sept. 9. Operation sur-
prisingly successful as also the rapid recovery. Today
returns to report as perfectly cured after seven years
suffering.

(Oct. 20) Suicide Positively Averted. James John Kulick,
37, of 4933 Vinwood, makes all preparations for death
by suicide (final will in all details, even to the choice of
coffin). Ready to go on boat to Cleveland. His two sisters received a leaflet and word of explanation about
the SMA, at their father's funeral. They enroll their desperate brother that day, October 16. Today, sister Grace
returns in tears of joy that every vestige of danger dis-
appeared that night. Her brother is now in hope and is
praying. Will go to work November 24. Today enrolls
brother, Ed, against tuberculosis.

(April 18) Same Edward reported in perfect health. Deo
Gratias!

(Dec. 5) Father away from Church two years enrolled
by anxious son. Theophilis Rohr, 65 years old [has
been] away from practice of religion for two years. The
children of his second wife [have been] taken out of
Catholic School. Estranged and bitter against older
children and against religion. Is enrolled for year by
oldest son, who reports a week later: "Father is completely changed."

Because so many people had begun coming to see the new porter at
St. Bonaventure, the room was enlarged. Solanus's desk was placed at
the right of the entrance, a few feet in front of Francis'. More chairs
were added along the wall. Their addition came not only because of
the growing numbers, but because Solanus gave full attention to all,
for as long as they wanted.

When asked why they were willing to wait so long without complaining, invariably the same answer was heard: They also would have Solanus's fullest attention when their turn came. Thus nobody would become impatient—except Francis. His frustration often came in outbursts directed at Solanus. According to Father Marion Roessler (a novice the year Solanus came):

> Brother Francis was a very efficient person and couldn't stand Father Solanus's slow easy manner, letting people talk on, letting people wait for hours to see him. He felt he had to keep people moving. He would scold Father Solanus before an office full of people, calling him "Casey" when he was piqued. Brother Francis would tell people that they could bring their enrollments to his desk and he could take care of them. Father Solanus would acquiesce and say that Brother Francis could enroll them also. Of course people would want to wait for Father Solanus and did so no matter how long it took. But it was a humiliation before all these people.[3]

As word spread about what was happening at St. Bonaventure, the numbers coming there increased. "There were so many callers that I had to give personal attention to," he once recalled, "that I worked for 18 hours a day. Sometimes I could not attend to one quarter of my personal letters."[4]

"I have plenty to keep myself busy for at least eighteen hours a day," he wrote his sister:

> I console myself occasionally with the thought that sooner or later the day will come when they will say of poor Father Solanus: "He's gone." Please God the struggle for existence will then be over. I just hope that by that time I'll be able to exclaim with St. Paul, when shortly before he died a martyr he said, "I have long

desired to be dissolved and to be with Christ!" O well, it will not be long. What are fifty years of pain to the endless joys awaiting us above?[5]

Outside those eighteen hours Solanus practiced the regular rituals of community life like the other friars, only more so. While they arose at 4:45, Solanus often was already praying in chapel. And when the friars retired just as Solanus could be saying good-bye and "God bless you" to the last person in the office, he would then take out a pail and mop to clean the office. After this he would go to chapel to pray some more. Finally he'd go to bed.

The January after his arrival, Solanus struck up a relationship with Earl Eagen. Eagen lived in Smiths Creek, about forty miles from Detroit. Years later Solanus recalled their first encounter in a letter to Eagen's daughter Dorothy:

> It was Saturday morning, January 10, 1925, that a neighbor-friend of theirs from Port Huron, brought your dear parents to St. Bonaventure Monastery in Detroit. Your poor father was hardly able to talk. He tried, however, to tell briefly how he felt and that the doctors said he had "ulcers of the stomach." Later on I learned that they had sent him home as a hopeless case of cancer. I told him quite a little about the Seraphic Mass Association and suggested that he do something for the missions.
>
> "Now I have your name. Mr. Eagen," I said. "And you can enroll perpetually if you wish. If you are any-way short, however, I would advise that you enroll for just a year now and promise perpetual enrollment as soon as convenient, if things go favorably."
>
> I took him to be seventy-five years old or upwards. Your poor mother looked old too. Sunday morning, eight days later, your father drove his own car down to keep his promise. From their appearance alone I would

hardly have known them; but the moment he spoke I thought, "This is the fellow from Port Huron!" He looked thirty years younger. He was only thirty-nine at the time.

"But, Father," he said, "The doctors in Port Huron want to take an x-ray. What do you think?"

I asked him, "How much is it going to cost you?"

"Twenty-five dollars."

"What do you think?" I asked your smiling Mother. They were both smiling all over.

"Father, he doesn't need it. Look at him," she exclaimed.

"Listen," I said. "You make a promise to the poor souls in purgatory that, if you are able to forget that appointment tomorrow, you'll enroll them for a part of it."

"Gee," he said. "I'll give them half of it. I'll go fifty-fifty!"

After that he drove down every week for several months. On February 29 I believe he had the whole family down. After enrolling some other member, as he nearly always did, he concluded about as follows: "Now, Father, I want to enroll the Poor Souls as I promised them I would do. Put them down for a good half of that twenty-five dollars. Enroll them for fourteen dollars."[6]

Solanus wrote this letter twenty-two years after the event took place, in response to Sister Cecilia Eagen's request for an SMA enrollment. In it, she never mentioned her baptismal name Dorothy; yet Solanus knew it was her and vividly recalled what happened on that first visit.

Solanus had asked to be introduced to the family. Eleven-year-old Dorothy was embarrassed to come downstairs; she didn't have any shoes. Sensing someone missing, Solanus asked if he had met all the children. At her mother's urging, Dorothy was coaxed downstairs. In the way Solanus greeted her, Dorothy forgot her bare feet and immediately relaxed. Solanus also reminded Sister Cecilia Eagen in his letter: "And just incidentally, it was on that occasion that I remember seeing little Dorothy as a possible candidate for a convent or a missionary."[7]

On March 12, 1925, shortly after the Eagen event, Solanus entitled an entry in his notebook: *"Big Company Enrolled."* Later he explained what happened when a company got enrolled in the SMA:

> I hardly think I ever told you about our enrolling companies and projects in the Seraphic Mass Association. The following, first of several similar to it since, I am sure will please you.
>
> The slump of the 1925–26 winter was a tough one on Detroiters. Every auto factory in the city shut down for at least a week at Christmas, without a word when they would start up again. Only a day or two before New Years' it was announced that Ford would start up again, on such and such a day after New Year's Day and would continue at three days a week till further notice. That was quite a "beam of hope" for perhaps millions. The other auto companies followed lingeringly, but most of them just worked one and two days each week. One of the slowest seemingly was Chevrolet. As we learned only a year or two later, it had already started negotiations toward bankruptcy.
>
> On the 12th of February, Thursday after 9:00 p.m. John McKenna, who had become enthusiastic about the SMA the first months after my arrival back from New York, August 1, 1924, came to the Office. He was evidently discouraged, notwithstanding his otherwise wonderful Faith.

"Father," he began, "I don't know what to do. I can't support a wife and family with the hours I've been working. I haven't had a full day now in two weeks. Today I had only two hours. They're always finding an alibi to send the men home." All at once, as though by inspiration, he said, "Father! Enroll the Company! (Chevrolet)."

"That's new," thought I. Twenty times quicker than I could tell it, however, so that it seemed absurd to hesitate, (something) flashed on my mind: "If a single Holy Mass must help any legitimate cause, why should not five hundred Masses daily in connection with the holy foreign Missions help?"

"All right, John," I answered.

"Yes, Father; I'll give them fifty cents" (for an annual membership in the SMA).

That same night the company received an astounding order. Two nights later McKenna waved triumphantly: "Father! We had overtime yesterday and today and we heard this afternoon that the company has an order for 45,000 machines, wanted in thirty days."

It was believed that order saved Detroit itself from bankruptcy.[8]

Moralists might raise all sorts of rationales to say why such a corporation (despite its legal constitution as such) is not a person. However, by now, Solanus was influenced not only from the laws and canonically correct procedures he had learned in the seminary but another law flowing from the gifts and fruits of the Holy Spirit—gifts everyone has, but not everyone uses.

Traditionally mystics have gotten in trouble with people who consider the law from the traditional categories of knowledge and understanding. Mystic-in-action that he was, Solanus revealed another kind of wisdom in his response to McKenna's idea: "That's new, thought I.

Twenty times quicker than I could tell it, however, *so that it seemed absurd to hesitate…"*

Many things Solanus did—instinctively, prophetically or from the gift of wisdom—were highly unorthodox in his time. Yet now they seem quite acceptable. His approach to non-Catholics and Jews, wherein he did not pressure them to become Catholic, serves as an example. The way he counseled couples having marital problems or those who were divorced is another.

Another example is the way Solanus "heard confessions without giving absolution." It was as exceptional as it was humane—from the perspective of the penitent, if not the casuist. Solanus (who had not received the canonical permission to give sacramental absolution) had developed a unique arrangement with Father Herman Buss. According to Father Herman (who began working with Solanus in 1926):

> A person would come in (to Solanus) and talk and talk.
> Father Solanus got the story. Then he would say to the
> man or woman, "Now go over to the church and I'll call
> Father Herman and he'll go over to hear your confes-
> sion." Father Solanus could not give absolution, but
> many, many persons told him of their lives. Father
> Solanus would say, "Now you told the whole story. Just
> give a resume to Father Herman. He will understand
> that you talked to me and he'll give you absolution."
> Then Father Herman heard their confessions.[9]

Like Jesus, Solanus's approach to people arose from "a heart moved with compassion." Realizing many were in very embarrassing situa-tions, especially when it came to matters of sin, they way he listened with total attention to them became a burden-lifter. He related the same way to everyone whether that person was Mayor Frank Murphy of Detroit or Brother André of Saint Joseph's Oratory in Montreal (in front of whom he knelt for a blessing after André had asked Solanus for a blessing).[10] Unemployed people, women, Jews, blacks, as well as his fellow Capuchins found him unaloof and open. Even crying babies seemed to relax when Solanus would leave his desk, take them from their perplexed mothers' arms and hold them.

When people approached Solanus for a favor, his method followed a pattern. Hearing their request, he never allowed people to remain passive. He always invited them to some way to grow in their relationship with God and others. After talking with people, he would build on some positive thing they said; then he would embellish that point with references to God's goodness and love for them. Then he would invite them to deepen their relationship with God or do some good work for others. Once he got people to "do something" as their way of commitment, Solanus would bless them with the Sign of the Cross, holy water, a relic of the true cross or some other sacramental. If something positive happened as a result, he attributed it to the power of these sacramentals.

Other times he used different means. To an avowed atheist whose son had drowned, Solanus invoked the example of the man's wife, Kathleen. Solanus invited him to remember her "example of never failing Christian virtues." But then, "just six weeks after the son's death," it seems that "his wife Kathleen also was taken, leaving him three children to mother for himself as best he might."[11] Despite this, Solanus was not afraid to invoke her faith to encourage her grieving husband.

He might ask non-Catholics to discover for themselves the differences between their own religion and Catholicism or why Catholics "try so much to imitate Jesus in his love and reverence for Mary, his own dearest Virgin Mother." While inviting non-Catholics to "investigate the claims of the Mother Church," if they showed no interest or were happy in their own faith, he did not pressure them. Instead, he told them, they should be faithful to their own beliefs about religion and act on them:

If religion is the greatest science of all ages—"The science of our happy dependence on God and our neighbor," which no one seems to question—then there can be but one religion. In like manner if—"We are Christians only inasmuch as we believe in Jesus Christ and keep his words"—his doctrine—so there can be but one Christianity. Therefore, it is up to each one of us individually to examine into our own conscience whether we be Christians in reality or only in name. Too, it ought to be our happy privilege to perfect ourselves in the faith more and more, and to find out its infallible Guide on earth.[12]

To nonpracticing Catholics he might be a bit more challenging than he was to Protestants and Jews. Often he asked them about the frequency with which they celebrated the sacraments. Invariably he'd invite them to be more faithful. Solanus used this approach not only with individuals; he also challenged groups of people to greater faith and fuller participation in the sacraments. Here too, he sometimes did this in unorthodox ways. William Tremblay recalled:

I drove Father Solanus to St. Joachim's Church, which is the old French Church of Detroit. As they were short of priests, the Capuchin Fathers used to go and say one Mass there sometimes. It happened one Sunday that I drove Father Solanus there for 10:30 High Mass. When it came to Communion time, he turned around and held the Host waiting. But there was nobody that came to the holy table for Communion. There weren't many people in the Church. Maybe one hundred people, but it used to happen that nobody went to Communion. He was so surprised and seemed to be hurt about it. He said to the people as he held up the Host, "Please come, the Lord wants to go to you, please." And everybody was so surprised that they all just looked at him. Then

he turned around and put the Hosts back in the tabernacle. It was just another incident to show you his love
for the Holy Eucharist and how he wanted the people
to be helped. He knew that God could help them
through Holy Communion. He was just surprised and
hurt that nobody went to Communion and he just had
to tell them.[13]

At times, if he sensed people might be uneasy meeting him, Solanus
would use his Irish wit to full advantage by beginning to look very
serious only to end up telling a funny joke or story about the Irish.
He took advantage of his last name, Casey, saying he had the shortest
surname: only two letters—K.C. And when people came to him in a
very agitated state, he found ways to calm them and give them
encouragement.

His calm approach to people who were upset was recalled in a
now-humorous incident by William Tremblay:

One morning a man came to the Monastery at 4:00 and
as you know, Fr. Solanus was always the first one to go
to the door. He always thought that the poor Brothers
would be too tired, so he would always get up himself.
Well, that morning he answered the door and a man
was waiting there.

He asked, "Where's that guy, Solanus?"

Father Solanus said, "Well, he's here, what do you
want with him?"

He said, "I came here to kill him."

"Well, that's something that should be discussed,"
said Fr. Solanus.

The man had a few drinks, so Fr. Solanus invited
him to the office and helped the man talk. The man
told him that he was secretary of the East Side
Communist Party. His mother belonged to the
Monastery and she was a great friend of Fr. Solanus.

His mother cried all the time because he had those meetings in his home and the things they discussed broke her heart, because he didn't go to church and he kept meeting those Communist men and having them in his home.

So, Fr. Solanus let him talk until he sobered up a little bit and then after awhile, he began to talk to him. Before the man left, he wanted to go to confession. He got on his knees and begged Fr. Solanus for mercy and asked him to bless him and he wanted to go to confession. Fr. Solanus said, "No, I want to see if you'll make a man of yourself. I want you to come to confession during the day and some other priest will confess you."

And as far as I know the man went back to church with his Mother and he left the Communist Party.

In case anyone might doubt his tale, Tremblay added: "Father Solanus told me this story himself."[14]

While Solanus might be scoring points with outsiders, he remained a source of frustration for Brother Francis. Francis would call Solanus "that old fraud."[15] Other times he'd chide Solanus about taking so much time with people that he would be late for meals. At those times Francis often would enter the refectory saying Solanus was "still talking, still talking." Francis was not alone in recognizing Solanus's tardiness. Father Bernard Burke bet Solanus a rosary for every time Solanus would be *on time* for meals. Bernard never had to say one![16]

Sometimes, when they were allowed to talk, the friars would tease Solanus about his high-pitched, low-volume voice. "Nobody understands you," they would say. "Open your mouth." On such occasions he would merely respond, "Well, God understands me."[17] Although, at this time in his life such incidents hurt, he never retaliated in kind.

Within such occurrences, Solanus lived like the other friars. He never acted in any way but normal; he fit in like any average friar. Father Cosmas Niedhammer, recalled:

> When I was with him in Detroit, I recall that he would come into the recreation room on Sunday nights. He would draw himself a glass of wine from the gallon jug by holding it over his shoulder and then he'd tell some humorous incidents. Father Solanus was very gifted in that way. He could spin out a story just like that, and become personally involved in it. He was always very simple as though he had no context of uncharitableness. Sometimes he spoke of some incident that happened in their family of 10 brothers and 6 sisters. And Fr. Theodosius would poke fun at him about when he used to be a streetcar conductor. He would say that Fr. Solanus was now doing penance for all the nickels he had taken and didn't ring up. Fr. Solanus would laugh and have another anecdote ready. He was really quite human in that way.
>
> Other times he would come into the recreation room after the noon meal like the others. He liked to play pool or billiards. Often as not though, he would pick a cue and start to shoot and his call bell would sound. Then he would have to put it right back into the rack, but never with any expression of impatience. It was remarkable. And it meant that when he was called, he would be in the office until supper time. And sometimes he was so tired that we knew he would have to go into the last room of the office and lie down on the floor for a few minutes to take a catnap. He would just take off especially if he had an interruption....
>
> Sometimes I would drop in the choir at midnight or one o'clock in the morning and sure enough Fr. Solanus...was there with his fiddle in front of the

Blessed Sacrament. At other times when I thought I
was alone in choir, a figure would rise up from behind
the stall and Fr. Solanus would be there with a grin. He
was just taking a little nap after a fatiguing day.[18]

Solanus's understanding of and compassion for people in pain could
only have been helped by his personal involvement in the sufferings of
his brother Maurice. Toward the latter part of 1928, Maurice visited
Solanus. Some twenty years before, he had entered a seminary in
Berlin (now Kitchner), Ontario. From there he wrote Solanus, "I have
found the grace again I looked for so long."[19] He was ordained a diocesan priest in 1911. However, now disillusioned and depressed, he used
his 1928 visit to discuss with Solanus and the Capuchin superiors his
thoughts about joining the province.

Maurice returned to Detroit for Solanus's silver jubilee of ordination, July 28, 1929. While the day was joyful, it was clouded for both
brothers by the recent deaths of their two lawyer brothers, John and
Thomas, in a car accident. In September Maurice again returned to
enter the novitiate which had moved earlier to Huntington, Indiana.
He received the name Joachim.

"Thanks be to God, he seems well and hopeful of making profession in September,"[20] Solanus wrote his sister Margaret in April 1930.
However that was not to be the case. Something made the superiors
concerned about Maurice's profession, so they decided not to accept
the sixty-two-year-old's request for vows. Instead they offered him the
possibility of remaining part of the province, but as a Third Order
member. He would live the full Capuchin daily routine among the friars and accept regular assignments. While able to keep his own money,
he would be under the superior of whatever house he belonged to.
Father Maurice Joachim (as Solanus would call him) agreed to the
plan. Consequently, the superiors assigned him to Sacred Heart in
Yonkers. His time there began well but would not end that way.

With the novitiate moved to Huntington, it seemed appropriate to move the tailor shop there as well. However, Francis Spruck would remain at St. Bonaventure rather than make habits. And he would have to live with increasing numbers of Solanus's visitors.

By this time more chairs had been added to the front office. People sat in them as in a doctor's office, waiting to talk to Solanus. Previously locked, the front door was now always open under a simple invitation: "Walk in."

On Wednesdays the front office was particularly busy. This was the day of the "Saint Maurus Blessing of the Sick." It had been a weekly devotion at the monastery long before Solanus. However, with his arrival and periodic presiding at the service, the number of people increased rapidly. An instance noted in the house *Chronicle* of February 29, 1928, noted: "A very large crowd at the blessing at 3:00 P.M. Fr. Herman acted as traffic cop, while Fr. Solanus offered the relic to the people."[21]

Unlike other Capuchins, when Solanus presided, he included a reflection. Father Marion, who lived at St. Bonaventure at the time, remembered:

> His simple discourses in connection with this weekly
> devotion consisted in admonishing the people to strive
> to come closer to God through the frequent reception
> of the sacraments, prayer, and conformity to God's
> Holy Will in all the events of their lives. He insisted that
> penance was very necessary to make up for sin and for
> the salvation of their souls.[22]

Because Solanus spoke in such a weak voice, people came early to get closer to the front. Often many stood immediately in front of the pulpit that they might hear his words. Invariably, his theme was the same: Trust in God and use the gifts of faith and of charity to show gratitude.

He often mentioned examples from his notebook or other incidents in which people found solace with their problems. He attributed many of these to the Wednesday blessing.[23] After his talk, he would say the prescribed prayers, incense the relic of the true cross, take it from its reliquary at the altar, and give the general blessing of the sick with the relic. Then the people would process to the Communion rail to receive individual blessings.

Because of his style with people in the office, Solanus often came late for the Wednesday service. Consequently Francis Spruck developed a routine to try to get him to the chapel on time. Fifteen minutes before the service he would loudly call: "2:45." At five-minute intervals and with increasing insistence, he would give the time. Then, at the very moment the service should have begun, he'd sternly say: "Casey!" or sarcastically: "It's time." Only then, the case usually showed, would Solanus sheepishly leave his desk and go for the service.

One of the people once left in the front office was Bernadette Nowak. She recalls:

> My sister, Geraldine Bieke, took me to Fr. Solanus. However, before I could talk to him, he rose and said it was time to go to the church for the blessing. I was disappointed, but went to church. As he passed before the people kneeling, he passed before me, gently touched my cheek and said softly, "Stop worrying now. You're going to be all right now," or words to that effect. I had not seen him stop to talk to anyone else and was surprised. That night I had the first sound good night sleep in over a month. From then on I was better.[24]

The chapel was generally filled with people of all faiths and races. However, it also occasionally had some skeptics. One was Casimera Scott. She recalled:

> I went thirteen weeks not believing that he could heal others. I was a doubting Thomas until one Wednesday, I saw a Rabbi with his cap, long beard and a heavy cane. He used to come every week too. Now he had Faith and

I was full of doubts. But when I saw him walk away
without the use of his cane, then I believed. I was in
excellent health then. Maybe I was blessed so because of
going to Fr. Solanus for his weekly blessing.[25]

On October 29, 1929, the stock market crashed. Industrial cities like
Detroit were especially hard-hit. This occasioned even more people
coming to St. Bonaventure. Solanus listened to story after story. His
heart could not help but be moved to pity at the sight of the crowds
now needing not only healing, but bread as well.

For as long as people like Father Herman Buss could remember,[26]
the Capuchins were always ready to share their own food with those
in need. For someone like Solanus, the rationale was simple: "The
poor have as much right to the food as we." If the food came from
their own table, it was not much: most often it consisted of coffee, a
bowl of soup, and bread. Before the Crash, about 100 to 150 people
came daily for such help. However, as the effects of the Depression
deepened, more people were coming to the front door. Only Solanus
and Francis were there to meet their needs.

With 200 and 300 coming daily, the superior concluded that it was
impossible for the friars to continue giving out bread in addition to
their other work. He asked Father Herman, the spiritual director of
the Third Order (known today as Secular Franciscans), if St.
Bonaventure's Fraternity might help. The hundreds of concerned
women and men who belonged to it only needed an appeal from
Herman to begin ministering.

On November 1, 1929, Herman shared the first cup of coffee with
a needy person. In time the Third Order hall, next to the chapel,
became a kind of restaurant. It became known as "The Soup Kitchen"
after its chief meal, a big bowl of thick meat stew.

The Soup Kitchen received special attention from Solanus. He
began asking people who came to him for favors to do some kind of
corporal work of mercy for the Soup Kitchen. He got the rich and

powerful to cooperate as well. Wealthy people from Grosse Point were tapped for cars to haul food. Well-known personages like Tom Bresnahan, the mayor of River Rouge, a Detroit suburb, and Frank Murphy, the mayor of Detroit (and later a justice of the Supreme Court) were enlisted in the effort. In his spare time Solanus himself would walk down the street and get involved, mingling with the people in the line as well as with the workers.

One of the volunteers with whom Solanus became well-acquainted was Arthur Rutledge, a fireman. One day he went to a hospital for observation for a tumor in the stomach. Solanus happened to be there and passed him in the hall as he was being wheeled into the operating room. Recognizing Art, Solanus stopped the cart and asked: "Where are you going, and what are they going to do?"

Art replied, "They say I have a tumor and are going to operate."

"Where is the tumor?" Solanus asked.

Art explained that it was in the abdominal area. Solanus placed his hand on his abdomen and said, "Have them give you another examination before they operate."

When the doctors made another check, they found no tumor. Art was discharged from the hospital the following day. He returned to the fire department and the Soup Kitchen to volunteer his talents. He never had a recurrence of the disease.[27]

Although Solanus "wasn't there all the time or directing the thing," Herman insisted: "through his holiness I believe he is the one who helped us to get help from Divine Providence. God was blessing the operation because we had a holy man right there."

By now more than three thousand people were being served on a daily basis. Herman recalled that, one day,

> I said, "Fr. Solanus, we have no more bread and two or three hundred men are waiting for something to eat."
> He went over to the hall and told the men who were waiting in line, "Just wait and God will provide." Fr.

Solanus said an "Our Father" after inviting the men to join him in the prayer. We just turned around and opened the front door to go out, and there was a bakery man coming with a big basket full of food. He had his whole truck full of stuff, and he proceeded to unload it. When the men saw this they started to cry and tears were running down their cheeks. Father Solanus, in his simple way, said, "See, God provides. Nobody will starve as long as you put your confidence in God, in Divine Providence."[28]

Occasionally, some people who are poor can appear as fussy as some who are rich, exhibiting an attitude of entitlement. On one such occasion, a guest insisted on jelly doughnuts rather than sugar doughnuts. The supervisor had had a rough day and didn't want to debate. Exasperated, he came complaining to Solanus at the front office. In a way that did not make the man feel misunderstood or offended, Solanus simply reasoned: "If we have jelly doughnuts, then why don't you give them to her?"

Although people came to Solanus asking for help, he went to God asking for the same. Often, when someone asked for a particular need, Solanus would sneak to chapel for a few moments of prayer. He would also pray there for extended periods late at night and, when he thought everyone was in bed, he would play his violin for the Lord in the Blessed Sacrament.

Like everyone at prayer, Solanus had his share of distractions. While he admitted there were times he prayed without distraction and said he did so from a power beyond himself, he didn't get upset when distractions came: "Do such distractions displease the Good God? For myself, I do not think that they do," he wrote: "Rather, I would answer, as I have occasionally done now and then to assure scrupulous souls: 'No, Jesus is no crank. He knows that we are not angels, but poor sinners.'[29]

At times the sheer repetition of people coming to him seemed endless. The pattern almost became routine, so much so that he confessed to his friend and fellow porter Brother Leo Wollenweber:

> Sometimes of course it becomes monotonous and extremely boring, till one is nearly collapsing, but in such cases it helps to remember that even when Jesus was about to fall the third time, he patiently consoled the women folk and children of his persecutors, making no exceptions. How can we ever be grateful as we ought to be for such a vocation, to such privileged positions, even in the Seraphic Order of the Poverello of Assisi? Thanks be to God that he has such divine patience with us.[30]

While Solanus worked long and tedious hours, he found time to leave the friary with friends. "I remember one instance when Father Solanus and I were driving out Gratiot Avenue and we passed a bar," William Tremblay recalled:

> This was not too long after they brought the liquor back. Fr. Solanus said to me, "Let's stop at that bar. There's a man there that is very good to the Monastery. It will please him to see me stop."
>
> So we went in, and when the man saw him, he was overwhelmed. He didn't know what to say when he saw Fr. Solanus. He was so glad he brought out a table and a chair. Father Solanus said. "Oh, no, we'll sit at the bar. Just give us a beer." Of course the guy was surprised.
>
> All the men in there kept looking at Fr. Solanus with his beard, taking a glass of beer and talking like any other man. When we left, the man handed Fr. Solanus something. I don't know what it was; it might have been a check. But Fr. Solanus said, "Oh, I didn't

come for that; I came for a beer. You have very good
beer and you have a nice place here."

Somehow going beyond the canon law which stated that priests
should not frequent bars, Solanus either did not recall the law or felt
that the value of fraternal charity went beyond it. The result was evident in the man's response:

> The man said, "Father, you don't know how proud I
> am. I get many customers but I never got one that I
> favor more than you. I hope you come back."
> I will never forget the reflection on that man's face.
> He was so glad to see Fr. Solanus come in and take a
> beer just like any other man. It just shows his humility
> and his good sense of understanding of good people,
> no matter where they are at or what job or what posi-
> tion. He was at home all over, you might say.[31]

Because Solanus mixed with people of all economic backgrounds and
all races, he was able to better understand their inherent goodness and
use that for their further conversion. Even when people showed their
impatience with God, Solanus gently but insistently reminded them of
his belief in God's power to turn all things for the good (see Romans
8:28). Mrs. Mary Therese McHugh narrated a case in point:

> It was in 1933 that my daughter Marianne (then two
> years of age) became very, very ill. The doctors said her
> temperature was 104 degrees and much, much too high
> for them to remove her to a hospital. She grew progres-
> sively worse and, after his house calls very late one
> night, the doctor stopped by again to see if it would be
> possible to remove her to the hospital. But she had
> slipped into a temperature of 105 degrees.
> After he left I called Bishop Murphy (then pastor
> of St. David's and a close friend of the family). He had
> seen Marianne that afternoon. He said to call Fr.

Solanus at once and do whatever he (Fr. Solanus) asked me to do. I called and Fr. Solanus told me to wrap the baby up in a blanket and bring her down to the monastery immediately—about a fifteen minute ride from our home. My mother and I were watching over her as my husband had fallen asleep. So I wrapped her up warmly, slipped out of the house and went to see Fr. Solanus.

When I got there he was waiting at the door for us. He took the baby from me and held her in his arms for some time, praying silently and smiling down at her. Then he carefully placed her back in my arms and took us to the car. He said, as he closed the car door after placing the baby on the seat beside me, "Therese, be sure to bring her back on Saturday" (three days later). I told him that the doctors did not expect her to live until Saturday. But he said, "Just do as I wish. Bring her to me; she'll be ready."

I drove home, feeling much at peace. I put her back in her bed and sat beside her, placing cool towels on her hot brow. About six o'clock in the morning she opened her eyes, smiled and said. "Mummy, I'm hungry." The sheets and pillow cases were soaking wet. The temperature had broken. I called the doctor and he came right over. When I told him what I had done, tears came to his eyes and he said, "I cannot help but think this was a miracle." Then Bishop Murphy came over an hour or so later and he could not grasp the change in the baby. But he repeated also that it was "another miracle by Fr. Solanus."[32]

Solanus often operated in tandem with the medical profession in dealing with sick people. As a result, many doctors considered him a true partner. Sometimes he would advise people to go to a doctor. Other times, he suggested they do so, but then added that the doctor would not find anything. Still other times he'd say: "You don't need to go to a doctor." This response sometimes generated resentment or questions. However, despite rumors to the contrary, at no time has it been shown that anyone was told not to consult a doctor and subsequently suffered as a consequence.

Solanus himself had doctors throughout his life. He respected their powers. Yet he respected the healing power of God even more. Speaking of an experience she had with a doctor and Solanus in 1935 or 1936, Elizabeth Ann Maher wrote:

> At the age of six, I became ill. Many leading specialists in the city of Detroit were consulted. My ailment was diagnosed as osteomylitis.
>
> For six months, every other day, my dear mother took me to the hospital where the doctors would chip away the decayed bone in my shoulder. My doctor then decided to consult with the leading specialist in the city.
>
> A bone would be removed from my shoulder which would result in either making my arm shorter than the other or I would have a pronounced hump on my back.
>
> Two days before the scheduled operation, my darling Mother took me across town on one of the coldest days of the year to seek the guidance and advice of her dear friend Fr. Solanus.
>
> Fr. Solanus placed his loving hands on my shoulder, looked at me with those saintly blue eyes and said, "She will not have the operation."
>
> At the next day's appointment with the doctor, our visit to Fr. Solanus was related to him. Dr. Andrews (being a man of great faith) said, "Let's take a final x-ray." After reading the x-ray he said, "It's like a miracle. The operation will not be necessary." He put the arm in a cast for one year and the bones knitted together.[33]

Another woman noted a unique way Solanus responded to doctors' diagnoses for surgery or other radical forms of treatment:

> About 1936 or 1937, I had terrible pains in my right wrist. I was seeing my doctor who worked at Harper Hospital. He called in a bone specialist, Dr. Campbell. X-rays showed a tumor in the bone. It was badly swollen and for three months the doctors treated it. It continued to grow worse. Doctors were using radium. My doctor was the head of the radium therapy department at Harper Hospital. Finally, the x-rays showed the tumor spreading like a web. Doctors felt that it was impossible to operate on the tumor. It would only spread through the bones…
>
> When the doctor said that they would have to amputate, we went then to see Fr. Solanus. He looked at my wrist and talked to me; he spoke very softly, so low I had to listen very carefully. I felt so awed, it was (like) talking to God, to Jesus himself.
>
> Fr. Solanus took my hand, held the wrist, and his eyes were closed. He was praying like he saw a vision or something. When he opened his eyes, he said, "No, we're not going to let them amputate." I could just feel that he was seeing something like a vision, that he could see that I would not have to have that operation. After that was when the change began.
>
> Fr. Solanus asked me to do something for the Dear Lord on my own. I promised then that I would say all three sets of the Mysteries of the Rosary, that is, fifteen decades every day as long as I was able. I also promised to offer one extra day a week (other than Friday) without meat. I prayed if only I could do my work, care for my children. I made a promise to bear the pain and offer it all for the Poor Souls.

> The change started after I saw Fr. Solanus. I con-
> tinued the treatments for the next three months, but
> they did not have to amputate; the tumor no longer
> spread. The doctors' minds were directed. They no
> longer spoke of operating. They were so amazed that
> my arm was saved.[34]

Around the time this letter was written (1936), Father Maurice
Joachim was becoming increasingly agitated and depressed. He had
written his other brother-priest, Edward, now a monsignor (who
had left teaching at Saint Thomas in Saint Paul to become a missionary in the Philippines), about his displeasure with certain Capuchin
superiors. Maurice's negativity grew to such an extent that he was
removed from regular parochial work and sent to the Capuchin
seminary at Marathon, Wisconsin (which had been built in 1917 as a
house of theology).

Even though he was depressed, Maurice was not so sick that he
could not show his care for Solanus. In June 1937, Saint Joseph's
Church in Prescott, Wisconsin, would celebrate its seventy-fifth
jubilee. Maurice persuaded Edward to come from the Philippines and
Solanus to come from Detroit. The delightful experiences Solanus had
at the celebration became the basis for his longest letter extant: seventeen pages of reminiscences to his brother, Jim.

For the most part, it describes people met and places visited in
and around Prescott, the Trimbelle and Superior. Speaking in the third
person, he notes that at the Solemn Jubilee Mass at Prescott:

> Fr. Solanus had been about the same as appointed sev-
> eral months before the sermon. If it was satisfactory or
> no, I could hardly say. For him it was far from what it
> should have been. Perhaps it was fortunate that he did
> not foresee what caused him quite a disappointment
> before the Mass was over—not a Holy Communion

received save that of the Celebrant. Of course, we
hoped they had received at earlier Masses....

The funeral the next day drew quite a crowd, having been announced the day before as to be solemnly
conducted by the three brothers. It went off quite satis-
factorily, save one feature, however. Fr. Solanus gave
them a sermon in which he told them of his lamenta-
ble disappointment at the celebration the day before—
not a single person to come up and receive Holy
Communion![35]

During his time in Detroit, Father Charles Coughlin, the "Radio
Priest," had influenced Solanus. Solanus considered the controversial
priest "a prophet."[36] Solanus also agreed with many of Coughlin's
political opinions (although he never was taken in by Coughlin's
anti-Semitism). One of these involved President Franklin Roosevelt.
Originally a great supporter of the champion of the "New Deal"
which put people back to work, by the time Roosevelt entered his
third term, Coughlin had "soured" on him, as did Solanus. This is evident in a note Solanus wrote after his return from Prescott:

As for being for Roosevelt: Well, I say God bless him,
too, though my enthusiasm for him is almost, or fast
becoming ancient history. If he were a practical friend
of the laborer or of the poor, considering the billions
he's been demanding and having spent, you and your
class would hardly need worry for a decent employment. It seems to me he is simply of the bankers.[37]

In Solanus's eyes, many rich people were not concerned about those
who were poor. Whether the president or anyone else, if he believed
this to be so, he would indicate his opinion.

As a way of urging others to join him in alleviating the needs of
the poor, Solanus accepted an opportunity in 1937 to give a radio
speech to the people "on both sides of the [Detroit] river" (that is,

Windsor, Ontario, and Detroit, Michigan). The talk coincided with these cities' "thank-you" for the Capuchins' work among the poor. He said:

> Good Afternoon, My Brethren:
>
> An opportunity was offered to me today to speak to you on the radio. The occasion is the benefit party which some of our friends have arranged for us this evening at the Naval Armory on East Jefferson Avenue. We have always known that many of you have been our friends, but since the preparations for this beautiful party have been in progress, we are convinced of it. From all parts of the city men and women came to us asking how they might help. We Fathers are told that the city of Detroit wishes to show itself grateful for the help we have given during the days of the Depression. We admit that we have tried to be of service to the poorest of the poor, but must add that it was simple duty.
>
> St. Francis, our Holy Founder, impressed it upon his brethren that they must labor for their daily bread. And he added, "should the wages of our work not be given us, then shall we have recourse to the table of the Lord asking alms from door to door...."
>
> Our lot has been cast among the simple lives of the poor and our object is to give them spiritual aid and, if possible, material help as well. When speaking of those days of depression, we cannot forget that our work in relieving the misery and poverty was made possible only by the willing cooperation of such men as the bakers, who supplied the bread, the farmers who gave us the vegetables, and our numerous friends who made donations from their fairly empty purses.
>
> It is to these generous souls that we want to pay tribute today. May the all-bountiful God, who leaves no

glass of water offered in His name to pass unrewarded, recompense the generosity of our friends with true happiness—the peace of the soul.

Our gratitude extends to them and to all those who are now helping make this benefit party a success. We are deeply appreciative of all they have done for us, and, in return, assure you that you are remembered in all the prayers and good works of our numerous brethren.

It is our sincere hope that this harmony of interest and action may never be broken. Our community is at the service of those who may require it. And as long as we are among you here at Detroit, we will have the needs of the poor at heart and will relieve their misery as best we can.

Once more, let me thank you, my brethren, one and all, in the name of our Capuchin community. May mutual appreciation be the soul of our relationship in the future as this party in the Armory tonight seems to prove it has been in the past.

God bless you all.[38]

In April 1938 Father Edward came to visit Solanus. They talked much about their concern for Maurice. By now he had become dissatisfied at Marathon, even more so with the Capuchin life, and said he wanted to return to the Saint Paul archdiocese. Solanus rejected strongly the direction Maurice was contemplating. In a December 15, 1938, letter Solanus promised him prayer but made his disagreement quite clear:

I offered my rosary this morning out in the crisp, moonlit air for your intentions and your guidance. I am confident that though, like the rest of us poor children of Eve, you have your difficulties, your temptations, your falls even, and your occasional little triumphs, our dear Lord will keep you from serious blunderings. In fact, not only this, but notwithstanding our very sad blunderings in the past—possibly worse than my own, possibly not so bad—I still hope and pray that in the few years left us, you may do something to make up for lost time; something to save your soul and gain the one victory, the one crown, the one triumph really worthy [of a] rational creature's effort.

"The few years" did I say??? Who can tell? We hope so, of course, if it be God's holy will. But, oh, how uncertain [it is]! It may be tomorrow they'll say of you or me or of each of us: "He is gone."

If either of us lives ten years longer it will be passing the old-age mark for our clan. And after all, what's the difference if we only be ready? Nay, if it be tomorrow or fifty years hence, if we only save our immortal souls? What's the difference?

But dear Fr. Maurice Joachim, I hardly know what to say or to think of your present proposition to write back to your old diocese, to a prelate you've probably never met and who has possibly never heard of Father Joachim. Naturally you would hope to be received with open arms, dreaming as you probably do, of some cozy little place just smiling across the Wisconsin hills at you. Ah, dear Fr. Maurice Joachim! You may be sure, such would be only dreaming. Our age and your experience should rather exclude such dreams as belonging to the long ago. This we might think especially, considering your years of dreaming when and how you might get away from the world to a monastery. Think of it, Fr. Joachim....[39]

While he asked Maurice to "think of it," it might be argued that in a close family case such as this, Solanus himself did not think objectively. As had happened before with Maurice, it might be questioned if Solanus was not being too hard on his brother, especially so if

Maurice was suffering from some kind of nervous disorder. The letter also shows another case where Solanus's "confidence" about a positive outcome did not apply—especially when he was dealing with his own family, whether the Caseys or the Capuchins.

Maurice disagreed with Solanus's letter. In late winter 1939, a very painful carbuncle on the back of his neck was aggravating his depression. After doctors in various places could not help, he appeared in Detroit, increasingly bitter toward his Capuchin superiors and Capuchins in general. This led him to stay with Father Charles Coughlin in Royal Oak rather than Solanus and the other Capuchins. Coughlin finally persuaded Maurice to call Solanus. Maurice had become so agitated that Solanus did not recognize his voice. A subsequent visit with the provincial resulted in Maurice's "letter of exit" from the Order. He left only to wander about the eastern states before finding some respite in a recuperation center in Baltimore. For his part, partly because of this, Solanus suffered a monthlong bout with colds and coughing.

Besides his frustration with Maurice, Solanus also showed impatience when people indicated lack of faith in the "good God." However only those close to him could detect an increased intensity to his already high-pitched voice. In such cases Solanus seemed more eager than ever to spend more time and effort with people if it might lead them to faith.

Solanus also found creative ways to deal with people who monopolized his time rather than becoming impatient. Many times, he used his wisdom—as well as his humor—in dealing with such situations. At that time, St. Bonaventure had but one telephone line; it came into the friary through the front office. As porter, Solanus answered all calls, even if in the midst of counseling people.

A particular person called Solanus regularly, often speaking at great lengths about her concerns of issues of life in general. Brother Leo Wollenweber, who took the place of Brother Francis Spruck in

1940, recalls one such call when the office was particularly busy. After listening to the woman for quite some time, Solanus quietly placed the receiver down and continued to talk with the person at the desk. Every now and then he picked up the telephone and made a few sounds of recognition. Once, as he picked up the telephone to make such an acknowledgment, he realized that many of those in the front office were watching this routine. He placed his hand over the mouthpiece and whispered to them with a wink in his eye, "She's still there!"[40]

While Solanus might be an instrument of healing for outsiders who came to the front office, any such healing stopped at the monastery wall, eluding the Capuchins themselves. Solanus simply believed that, in general, Capuchins, like all religious, were "called to endure suffering." Possibly because he had not professed vows as a Capuchin, an exception to this rule was made in the case of Brother Daniel Brady. He was in the brothers' novitiate in Detroit. He recalled:

> I had a front tooth that had root canal work done on it about 1930. It never gave me any trouble until I was in the Novitiate in 1941. When I went to the dentist he opened it and found it infected. It had even infected the jawbone and was filled with pus. He said I should come every week so that he could drain it; but his efforts were to no avail. After many x-rays, he saw that the infection was deep in the jawbone; the only remedy was to remove the affected part surgically.
>
> When I came back to the Novitiate, I met Fr. Solanus in the sacristy. He had just finished the usual Wednesday afternoon devotions. He said to me, "What ails you? You look so downcast."
>
> I told him my problem. Then he scolded me for my lack of trust in God. But I told him my concern was more with the operation. It was more-or-less major, and being only a novice, it meant I would have to leave the Order [as was sometimes the practice at that time].

He then said, "Kneel down, and I will give you my blessing. When you go back to the dentist, he will be surprised." As he did so, he touched my cheek and when he did, I knew I was healed. I could feel it tighten up.

The dentist was surprised. He thought I came to arrange for the operation. He had me come back four or five times before he would even put in a temporary filling.

The dentist worried that the filling would surely have to come out and told me that anytime I got pain to come in. Then he would take it out. It never did flare up again; it was healed for good.[41]

On the last day, after getting the final OK from the dentist, Brother Dan came back to the novitiate through the front office where he told the good news to Solanus. "That calls for a celebration," said Solanus. With that he opened one of his desk drawers and produced two ice cream cones. Somebody had brought them in about a half hour before and Solanus had put them in the drawer. When he pulled them out, they were as good as new.

The more that people heard about Solanus and saw him in action, the more they came to believe God was working in and through him in a special way. Even people who were once skeptics were more than won over; some, like Casimera Scott, considered him to be a friend:

...my nickname is Casey and his last name was Casey. Believe it or not, he had a most delightful sense of humor. He used to say, "To those who don't understand, no explanation is sufficient and to those who do understand, no explanation is necessary...."

He used to say to me, "Life is to live and life is to give and talents to use for good if you choose. Do not pray for easy lives, pray to be stronger. Do not pray for tasks equal to your powers, pray for powers equal to your tasks. Then the doing of your work shall be no miracle but you shall be a miracle. Every day you shall

wonder at yourself, at the richness of life which has
come to you by the grace of God. But, everyone needs
someone, knowing that somewhere someone is thinking of you."

I remember crying when he told me one time, "I
am a lantern along the feet and I shall shine the lantern
to guide you. You shall work in the house of the Lord
and you shall keep his house clean and my blessings
will fall upon you my child. Only goodness and mercy
shall follow you the days of your life."[42]

From the recollections of someone like Casimera Scott, it would be
safe to say that Solanus exercised various prophetic gifts before people
called them such in the Roman Catholic tradition. While some of the
prophecies took the form of encouragement, such as the prophecy to
Casimera Scott, some served other purposes as well. Sometimes they
would challenge, as the time he told a woman that she was practicing
birth control.[43] James Derum tells of one that offered another kind of
challenge related to the practice of the faith:

In the early forties a supposedly practicing Catholic
bachelor came to him at the suggestion and in company of a devout Catholic couple with whom he
boarded. The young man desired prayers for his father.

"My father is a very good Catholic," he informed
Father Solanus.

"Yes, he is—but you are not," came the friar's
blunt response.

The man flushed, and the couple who had brought
him objected.

"Why, Father!" the woman said in surprised
annoyance. "We know Michael goes to Mass faithfully
every Sunday."

The young bachelor began to perspire.

"He has not been going to Mass," Father Solanus said. "And he has not been to the Sacraments in the last five years."

At this, the young man admitted that Father Solanus's statements were facts. The bachelor promised that he would return to the sacraments at once.[44]

Other prophecies involved the promise that someone's health would improve. In the case of Sister Joyce Pranger his prophecies took the form of foretelling the future. She recalled in a book about a visit to Solanus while he was taking time off in Huntington, Indiana:

> Every now and then we come across a person who deeply influences our lives. I can recall many people in my life who have been such a powerful force in my own spiritual formation. There were the nuns, my grandmother, my pastor, spiritual directors I have had along my pilgrimage of life. But one of the most powerful ones was a dear old Franciscan Capuchin priest. His name was Fr. Solanus Casey!
>
> I was only thirteen years of age when a friend of mine, Frances Harrison, invited me to go with her to visit the Franciscan monastery in Huntington, Indiana, where he was then acting as porter or gate keeper. It was a different kind of experience for me to go to the monastery; but since I planned to be a nun, I accepted.
>
> I watched this brown-robed friar from the long line of people waiting to see him. He wasn't a striking figure, but there was something that was different. What was it?
>
> Soon it was my turn to go into the monastery parlor. At first, my heart was beating very fast at the prospect of being alone with this servant of the Lord. But it didn't take me long to be perfectly at ease.

His warmth and joy were contagious. He talked to me of the love of God and what a joy it had been for him to spend his entire life dedicated to him. Father's eyes were crystal blue like a mirror in which I could see the depths of eternity.

It was growing dark in the room and he spoke, on and on, of the love of God. It didn't seem to phase him that a long line of people was still waiting outside to see him. He remained unruffled. He counseled me lovingly, as a Father of the desert counseled his disciples. For him, man's greatness lies in being faithful to the present moment.

As we rose to leave, he took my hand gently, and whispered in my ear softly, "God has great designs for you in your life. Through you, many people will come to the Lord Jesus. You will enter religious life eventually. During that time you will have much to suffer. Then the Lord will bring you out, into a ministry entirely different from any known to Sisters at that time! Through you, the Lord will heal many people of various afflictions. But you must remain faithful every moment or you will frustrate the plan of God for your life!" He blessed me and the door closed behind me. Never again in this life would I see this servant of God.

The visit and the prophecy all seemed to fade away in my memory until one day about twenty years later, when I was browsing in the community library looking at new books.

Among the publications I came across a book entitled "The Porter of Saint Bonaventure's." I stood aghast. I couldn't believe my eyes. Here this man with whom I had prayed was considered a likely candidate for sainthood. His counsel to me, "a little act of fidelity may

open the door to great graces," was truly a lived reality
in his own life…

He became the humblest of God's servants! And as
a result, his very humbleness drew forth the glory of
God within him.[45]

What was the origin of Solanus's various forms of prophecy, such as
this in the case of Sister Joyce Pranger? His ability flowed from his
depths, from the "glory of God within him." This form of prophesy-
ing came not from any intuitive abilities (in themselves), but from a
power building on those abilities. It did not have a human origin. It
would have to be attributed to another source: God. Many of his fellow Capuchins experienced in Solanus this God-centeredness and
were spiritually edified by it. One of them said: "When he was speaking with you, you felt that he was constantly God-centered, on fire
with love for God, and constantly God-conscious, seeming always to
have his eyes on God. He seemed to see everything as flowing from
God and leading back to God."[46]

On September 13, 1942, the *Chronicle* of St. Bonaventure notes:
"Father Solanus was sick in bed last night; he was unable to go to his
help-out at St. Paul's. Fr. Solanus was taken to St. Mary's Hospital with
104.5 degree temperature."[47] Belying the *Chronicle*'s brief comment,
what actually happened to Solanus was quite serious.

Trying to get respite from the chronic eczema on his legs, which
sometimes looked like "raw meat," Solanus often tried other people's
remedies. This particular cure was connected to the use of an electric
light. The remedy backfired. From his hospital bed he explained what
happened: "I had been fighting the grippe for about five days," he
wrote, "when on September 13, I awoke 'doubly downed,' having forgotten the night before to apply ointment or salve to my feet after
using an electric light on my varicose veins and eczema around my
ankles."[48] His self-medication made Solanus spend "a novena of
weeks"[49] in the hospital.

While he was in the hospital, a rumor spread that Solanus had died. To counter the many calls and to keep the people from hospital visits once they knew he was there, the "hospital sisters had to make strident rules regarding visitors since most of the people wished to see him about their troubles, having little consideration for his worn condition."[50] These rules were just what Solanus needed. Alone, he could spend more time in prayer and reflection.

Once released from the hospital, Solanus recuperated at St. Felix Friary in Huntington, Indiana. He wrote his sister that he was getting better: "The old foot is still stiff but by keeping it raised and rested, it causes very little pain. I'm resting it on the bed now and it gets tiresome sitting in one position. Well anyone over sixty need not be told how the 'rear fenders' cry for better padding."[51]

He wrote his brother James how he had been able to use the time in the hospital to grow in his relationship with God:

> While a number of my friends both in the hospital and outside, seemed to have considered my case a close call, I never felt that there was any immediate danger of collapse. Thank God. To me it seemed about ten days of the really best penance that the poor sinner Solanus had ever gone through. Therefore, since by God's grace he persevered and lived through it without complaint, we have a reason to thank Heaven for the wonderful experience.[52]

In the earlier *Chronicle* story indicating that Solanus had been taken to the hospital, it mentioned also that "he was unable to go to his help-out at St. Paul's." Capuchins called "help-outs" the weekend ministry they offered to surrounding parishes. Solanus had taken regular help-outs since 1925. Such help-outs took him all over the Detroit area.

From 1938 until 1945, Solanus ministered at one parish, St. Paul's Maltese Church on Fourth and Plum Streets in Detroit. Michael Z.

Cefai was the pastor. Father Cefai's recollection of how Solanus began at St. Paul's is worth repeating:

> I needed a priest to help at the parish and went to Fr. Marion, superior at St. Bonaventure monastery asking for this kind of help. He told me he had no one that he could send. All the priests already were assigned. He said he had some old priests. He also said, "We have Fr. Solanus, but he is not allowed to go out. He does not hear confessions; he can't speak Maltese."
>
> At that moment Fr. Solanus came in. He fell on his knees...and asked for his blessing.[53] I told Fr. Solanus why I was there and asked him if he would be willing to come if his superior approved. He said, in his high-pitched voice, "Father Superior, can I go?" Thus, it worked out that Fr. Solanus came to my parish weekends.
>
> On those weekends, many, many people came to talk to F.r Solanus and to ask his prayers. Men and women, young, middle aged, old, and very old, Catholics, non-Catholics, Jews, all sought him out. Officials of the government, thirty-third degree Masons, etc. came to see him, sometimes talking to him on his way from the church to the house where I lived. He had as much of a following among non-Catholics as among Catholics.
>
> When people asked his prayers, he would say Yes, he would pray, but they would have to pray too. As a priority he always sought the return of the person to God. He told people directly that God does not hear the prayers of sinners unless they are repentant and are converted to Him first. He used to ask the Catholics how often they went to Holy Communion. If they said three times a year, Father Solanus would tell them that was not enough; they should go every month. If they

went every month, he would urge weekly Communion. For weekly communicants he would sometimes suggest that they receive daily. He told people, "Faith alone is dead" and urged them to supplement their faith with good works.[54]

Father Cefai was indebted to Solanus not only because of his popularity with the people; he also believed that Solanus had healed his father. The two got along very well, swapping stories and telling jokes. Father Cefai was a ready audience for Solanus.

While Cefai had genuine admiration for Solanus and respected his opinions, one of his proclivities caused him concern. It revolved around Solanus's devotion to and promotion of Mary of Agreda's *Mystical City of God*.

As noted earlier, while in Yonkers, Solanus discovered the writings of Mary of Agreda. Her reflections resonated with his own spirituality, which, like much of the popular piety of that era, was influenced by private revelations. Consequently, Solanus began suggesting to more and more people that they read the four volumes of her *Mystical City of God*. This was often part of their "work" or sign to God he suggested as evidence of their sincerity in response to requests for prayers and blessing.

As he increased his suggestion that people read the volumes, criticism arose. Some of it revolved around the price of the volumes; others noted that the average person was "not ready for such writing"; still others debunked the authenticity of the *Mystical City of God* itself. For every charge, Solanus offered a counter charge. Solanus argued that popes and theologians and saints of the holiest reputation had endorsed the book. Furthermore, as indicated in a letter he wrote his brother Edward, he found it to have great value for the spiritual life: "Now in my opinion, there is hardly another book written, outside the Bible itself, more inspired-like and more inspiring than this wonderful work, *The Mystical City of God*. Its introduction alone, if read with prayerful attention, will hardly leave a doubt as to its supernatural origin."[55]

Father Solanus's unwavering enthusiasm for the *Mystical City of God* led him to difficulties involving the activities of his friend Ray Garland. Solanus met Ray around 1927. Ray often visited Solanus asking for help and counsel. In turn, Solanus enlisted Ray for car rides to get vegetables for the Soup Kitchen. When Ray was "dropped from the employ" of a certain Charles H. Chisholm, Solanus had defended for him: "I have known Mr. Garland for about ten years," he wrote Chisholm, "and I can honestly say that I doubt if I have ever met a person more solicitous to do a labor or more practical in suggesting remedies in time of difficulties."[56]

Solanus urged Ray to write the publisher of the four-volume work of Mary of Agreda, asking to work as the books' Michigan representative. Ray received the job. For fourteen years he devoted his leisure time to promoting the volumes, selling over two hundred books each year. Whether Ray benefited financially is not known. Certainly neither Solanus nor the Capuchins received any remuneration.

When Solanus began his Sunday help-out at St. Paul's, not only Ray Garland but a whole band of devotees of Solanus and Mary of Agreda came when he presided at Mass. Father Cefai had given them permission to have breakfast meetings in the church basement after Mass as long as Solanus attended (due to the excessive piety of some members). He was reinforced in this decision when he received reports that some were taking petals from flowers in the church to be blessed by Father Solanus and then insisting they saw images of Christ in the petals.

When Father Solanus was hospitalized for a time, the group met at St. Paul's without Father Cefai's permission. Upset, he banned them. They moved their meetings from St. Paul's to the Garland home. From there they would phone Father Solanus in the hospital asking for his prayers, his comments and his blessing regarding their various concerns and causes.

By the time Solanus returned from the hospital to St. Bonaventure, his superiors had been apprised of these activities. Although Ray and the group may have had the best intentions, Solanus's superiors felt they should intervene. Ray was told not to come to the monastery anymore.

Technically, Ray complied. He stopped coming, but he continued to phone Father Solanus, who remained steadfast in supporting his friend. Either because of his simple faith in the goodness of people or because he was too close to a problematic situation, Solanus could not believe anyone would try to manipulate him. However his superiors were confirmed in their decision when the chancery of the Archdiocese of Detroit noted complaints it received concerning Solanus's promotion of the four volumes. This news only made his superiors more insistent. According to Father Marion Roessler:

> Fr. Theodosius, the Provincial became very firm with Fr. Solanus and forbade any connection with this man [Garland]. Fr. Solanus told the Provincial very simply that the man was being misunderstood. Then he begged Father Provincial to give him a different position, even working in the kitchen. Fr. Theodosius told him he didn't want to take him out of the office, just to sever all connections with that fellow.[57]

Also around this time (by now it was mid-June 1945) Monsignor Edward Casey had been released from the prison camp where the Japanese had interned him during the Second World War. This release provided the occasion for a family reunion. Edward, along with his brothers Owen and Patrick, came to St. Bonaventure to convince Solanus he should visit "the West." Solanus asked, "Is Father Maurice going too?" When they said he was not, Solanus said that if Maurice did not go, neither would he.

When they realized that Solanus was serious, the three brothers went to Baltimore, got Father Maurice released from the facility where he was in residence, and went to Chicago. There they rendezvoused with Solanus and headed west. The superiors were glad to have Solanus go; it would give him a respite from the long hours at the office and the Garland controversy.

By the time he reached Spokane and Seattle for the family gathering, word spread about Solanus's presence there. Consequently, throughout the reunion, the Caseys were besieged with phone calls and visitors seeking Solanus. One recalled: "Our home was packed until his departure. I don't know where all the people came from."

Since Solanus was visiting relatives in their Washington homes, the California relatives were feeling slighted because he had no plans to visit them. After a good deal of coaxing, he decided to visit them as well.

Solanus figured that since his permission was to make a trip "West," it did not matter whether he went to Washington or California. So, even though it was not strictly part of his "obedience" or permission, he decided to travel to California.

Unfortunately, he did not anticipate the consequences of traveling in postwar time. The trains were crowded with returning troops. He soon discovered that he would not be able to return to Detroit by his deadline. He wrote Father Marion about his dilemma and the efforts of the Capuchin superior in Los Angeles who was trying to help him:

> The very best he could do—in regard to transportation, was to get reservation for next Thursday (July, 12th) instead of yesterday (9th) for Seattle, so that I may use my [clergy] "pass" to St. Paul. To get on the train as I promised, without reservation, he stressed, would be foolhardiness. So here I am still—hoping to make the best of missing the privileges of the Chapter.[58]

Solanus arrived in Detroit, on Saturday, July 21. Almost immediately Father Bernard Burke, the newly appointed superior, told him that he had been transferred to St. Michael in Brooklyn.

Bernard recalls that Solanus received the news as if he had been told it was time for the next meal. Without registering any surprise, complaint or question about the continuance of his front door ministry, Solanus immediately began to pack his bags.

He arrived in Brooklyn the following Monday.

Solanus with his priest-brothers, Father Maurice (his right) and Monsignor Edward (his left).

Solanus at the Farm of Mr. & Mrs. Ed
Bishop, near Detroit, 1935.

Solanus at his desk in the front office,
St. Bonaventure, Detroit, about 1939.

Solanus Casey at his fiftieth jubilee as a Capuchin, Third Order Hall, Detroit 1947. Behind Solanus are his sister Grace Brady and his brother Owen. Monsignor Edward is at Solanus's left.

6

BROOKLYN

JULY 23, 1945–
APRIL 24, 1946

The main reasons for Solanus's transfer involved both a desire to help create space for him to alleviate his physical ailments and provide a kind of semi-retirement for him as well as also give him distance from what the superiors considered "the harassment" of Ray Garland.[1]

Solanus seemed quite at peace with his transfer. More than a score of years in Detroit had taken its drain. Brother Ignatius Milne recalled that Solanus had once written him a confidential note saying he was tired and would like to get away.[2] Still fully functioning at seventy-four, when most men his age were retired, he prided himself on the cross-country nature of his move from coast to coast. From St. Michael he wrote his sister, Margaret:

> We'd come in from Los Angeles the night before (July 12) and offered Holy Mass in the Cathedral—and had a nice conference with the Archbishop. At 1:30 p.m. Owen left me on the train for Seattle. That was Saturday. Sunday and Monday I had Holy Mass at the Convent (in Seattle). Father Joachim served. I stopped over 24 hours in Spokane. We were on the train all day Wednesday from 7:20 am until Thursday at 10:30 when

we arrived in St. Paul. I said Holy Mass Friday in St. Paul, got to Chicago on Saturday, Detroit on Sunday, New York on Monday and Tuesday in Brooklyn. I missed two Masses from Los Angeles. Thanks be to God for all things. Praised be Jesus![3]

Once at St. Michael Solanus realized he had left various items in Detroit in his rush to arrive in Brooklyn so he could meet his deadline. He wrote Brother Leo Wollenweber at St. Bonaventure asking him to collect some of his personal belongings, telling him he looked forward to a much-needed rest from his busy schedule:

Thanks be to God, I am here in this new assignment of privileged duty just a week. Tomorrow will be the forty-first anniversary of my first Holy Mass. Deo gratias. The next day (will be) the 21st (anniversary) of my arrival from Harlem, Our Lady of the Angels, back to St. Bonaventure. 1924. How grateful we ought to be for so many graces and privileges. Praised be God in all His works and ways!

Now I hope you have not found that middle cell that succored me so long is in too hopeless a disorder. I rather fear having left you a difficult job when I asked you to pack up and forward things here. They would be of no use to anyone else and might be of quite a little convenience to me. I am not certain if I brought a trunk with me from Harlem twenty years ago. If I did, it must have been worth next to nothing, so any old box you might find would do. A box may perhaps be better than a trunk.

The "Letter" box on top of the "wardrobe" contains Father Edward's letters. These are good. The others are not important. I would like to have those few unfinished pieces in the clipper on the side next the desk, if you've not thrown them away.

I would also like to have that little prayer on modesty that we were figuring on having in the office. I started to bring it over for Fr. Provincial's approval but he was not in and then it was neglected. I hope to get a little more time for such things here at St. Michael's, although so far—what with getting acquainted, etc., I've not had much surplus time. One thing, however, I've taken a little more sleep under the great archangel's wings this past week than perhaps in three weeks before my arrival.[4]

Around the same time he wrote Brother Leo, another Michigander tracked Solanus to Brooklyn. Mrs. D. Edward Wolfe of Brighton (where Solanus had gone for many years to act as summer chaplain at St. Vincent's Home for Children) telephoned saying her infant daughter, Kathleen Ann, was dying from "early" celiac disease. She felt the doctors were not helping. So she called Solanus saying she wanted to bring the baby to Brooklyn for his blessing. Solanus would hear none of it. Not only was the baby deathly sick; the expense was too great.

Contrary to all rules he had been taught in canon law against "transmitting" blessings through mediums more than fifty feet from the hearers, Solanus said, "Kneel down with the baby and I will give you my blessing over the telephone." When he had finished praying, he asked Mrs. Wolfe to consider using the money she would have spent coming to Brooklyn to "do something for a poor family." Kathleen Ann recovered.

Soon after his arrival in Brooklyn Solanus made his annual retreat so that he might "try again to be converted for another year."[5] He took the train fifty miles to "Beautiful Immaculate Conception Monastery at Garrison on the Hudson."[6] In his retreat notebook he wrote: "Thank God! First day: Busy day; weather ideal. Arrived at the station about 5:00 P.M. Had a good hike from the station." The theme of the retreat was: "To imitate Saint Francis who so perfectly followed Jesus, our Divine Model."[7] His retreat notes, containing reflections on the vows, the beatitudes, and the "last things," filled nine pages.

Elaborating on the conference on penance, which had as its specific theme: "Unless you do penance you shall all perish," Solanus observed:

> God knows as no one else knows that we all and each need penance. God knows we need humiliations whereby we can foster humility. Hence in His love, He never fails to provide occasions for each one to practice penance, which means in other words to check self-conceit and, with God's help, to get somewhere in humility. Hence for a religious, the most practical penance is that naturally and logically connected to the Rule.[8]

While he was at Garrison (where the young Capuchins studied philosophy), Solanus also picked up some postcards of the seminary. He mentioned that he had had correspondence from Ray Garland and others in his group regarding their activities and promotion of the insights of Mary of Agreda in her *Mystical City of God*.[9] Later, in an October 1945 letter to Garland[10] Solanus commented favorably about the "interesting meeting" which the group had held a few weeks before. However, the letter also alluded to the controversy surrounding Ray and the group and implied that it was giving Solanus some concern. "Now I must tell you something that, in a way, I do not like to do," Solanus wrote. After saying he thought the devil was being kept quite busy, he said. "I have been reported as having been phoning long distance to you and the 'Agredan Society.' Whatever the source, it seems to have given important offense, if not scandal."[11]

It can be surmised Solanus was told by his superiors not to be in communication with Ray or the group. This proved to be difficult not only for Solanus to understand but to accept as well. He firmly believed Ray and the others were in the right. He also was convinced

Ray was being unduly maligned by ill-informed people inside and outside the Order.

Despite his own feelings and his belief in this cause he followed the wishes of his superiors. Therefore he wrote: "I wish that, for the present and until you be better known and your efforts recognized, you leave me out of the picture."[12] If the ministry was part of God's work, it would be exonerated, along with all its zealous workers. In this light he concluded:

> After all, if Venerable Mary of Agreda is a saint, about which I find it personally unreasonable to doubt, then in my way of thinking, it is high time that she get active in working a miracle of some kind. She needs to clear away the prejudice or jealousy or at least misunderstanding that has hampered her work—which is not hers but God's work—which has pressed on your shoulders for three years and on mine for at least seven.[13]

As noted above, upon his arrival in Brooklyn there was an almost immediate increase in letters and phone calls to St. Michael's, most from the Detroit area. Solanus tried to respond to them all. If the replies to many were similar to the one received by Mary Kenny of Detroit soon after his arrival, his answers contained words of consolation and hope as well as thoughts about God's loving care that touched all recipients:

> Dear Mrs. Kenny: God bless you and yours.
>
> I came down from Retreat in Garrison a few days ago to find quite a stack of letters awaiting opening. I just came to yours of the 23rd and sure do sympathize with you and your family. However, we've had so many decidedly worse reports than that about your Pat which turned out most reasonable after several months of suspense and anxiety, that I shall still hope for a good word about son Patrick.

At all events, I have just enrolled him in the
Seraphic Masses as requested and we shall not be surprised at any favorable report to come. We'll pray and
hope, trusting in God for the best. After all, if we look
at things in light of faith, the worst (as the world con-
siders things) is only our victory, according to our dear
Lord's words: "Greater love than this no one has that a
man lay down his life for his friends." I think that this
ought to buoy us up as it is needed in millions of sad
bereavements these days. God bless you again and give
my love to all the family and friends.[14]

Giving his love to the Kennys and other friends was typical of his way
of relating. People actually felt his love for them. They experienced
love in the way Solanus showed them his concern, interest and sincere
effort to pray for their needs. However, this love also was shared
equally with his Capuchin family at St. Michael. This endeared him to
the friars there.

The only non-endearing gesture of his care for them was connected to his violin-playing. Father Walter O'Brien recalled that, soon
after he arrived in Brooklyn:

Solanus decided to entertain the friars at their regular
Sunday recreation time. So he came in with his violin.
The friars thought, "Well, he is an old man trying to
entertain us." So they put up with his squeaking on the
violin. Their reaction seemed so positive to Solanus
that he thought he had done very well. The next
Sunday night he showed up with his violin again.

As he began to play, one of the men went to the
radio and kept turning up the volume. Without saying
a word, Solanus left the room and went down before
the Blessed Sacrament and continued his playing.

Each Sunday night after that he would go with his violin and "play before the Lord" for a half hour or so and play various hymns.[15]

The friars were not the only ones who made fun of his violin playing. It seems the altar boys did too. Walter noted that he heard from the sisters that the altar boys had been particularly mischievous. He noted:

> We have a big swivel window that separated our choir or chapel from the main altar of the church. Then I talked with the altar boys about their antics; "Oh, Father, there were some squeaks coming from your chapel that we couldn't help but laugh." There was Solanus, it seems, oblivious to everything, playing before the Blessed Sacrament. All I would say to the altar boys was, "The next time it happens just try to control yourself!" And it did happen every Sunday night.[16]

With more time available at St. Michael, Solanus not only composed letters to his family and friends; he used the Christmas of 1945 to extol the birth of Christ in verse. One of these poems (written perhaps as early as 1934) he sent to his niece Helena Wilhite. It was entitled "Always Christmas Eve":[17]

> With love and Christmas greetings to all
> Comes the Infant once more to free us from sorrow
> Whose smile and whose power and whose
>   gentleness call
> To each heart and each soul for a manger tomorrow;
> Whose love and whose goodness—whose wonders
>   proclaim
> Him, the Son of the Virgin, as promised of yore.
> Oh, may he estrange us from sin and its shame!
> And reign in our hearts, as his crib evermore!
> ...Ah, the rest of us, on Calvary

Mary conceived under the Cross
Thirty-three years later. Glory to God!
Peace to men of GOOD WILL.[18]

Other letters Solanus wrote during this time provide reflections on past incidents of God's healing power that had come to people who had visited him. One of these told of an incident that occurred in his latter days in Detroit and early days in Brooklyn. Relating what happened almost as though he were an uninvolved bystander, Solanus again credited participation in the Seraphic Mass Association as the cause for the healing:

> Now I am going to give you briefly something from my "NOTES ON CASES THROUGH THE SERAPHIC MASS ASSOCIATION," that for several years I was making and—while in Detroit. Just one case in perhaps more than a thousand—a number of them not only fearful tumors but of most positive and threatening cancer:
>
> May 25, 1945. Mrs. Catherine Nagle, 45, a mother of eight children. She was opened up for an operation two weeks ago (May 9) in Providence Hospital. She was found to be so hopelessly full of cancer that the doctors simply closed her up again saying she would "never leave the hospital alive." She has been enrolled in the Seraphic Mass Association several times. Today her husband enrolled the Poor Souls. The whole family is storming heaven by daily communion. Mother comes home today unable to take any nourishment.
>
> May 29th. Mrs. Nagle as above May 25th. Thanks be to God. The fearful pains and swelling [are] gone from [her] abdomen. She has a good appetite and is eating fine. Husband enrolls Poor Souls again in thanksgiving.
>
> Sept. 14th. Brooklyn, N.Y. Mrs. Nagle as noted above May 25th and May 29th [was] here today in perfect health....[19]

Moving from this concrete example of the power of God's healing which he had witnessed, Solanus theologized on the need for confidence in the face of human suffering. In the two paragraphs which followed, he emphasized childlike trust in the face of suffering. (At the same time, he also showed his continued support of the writings of Mary of Agreda):

> But why worry? "To worry about anything," St. Theresa, the little Flower claims, "is to indicate a want of confidence in God." She very likely speaks of excessive worrying. But why should we worry about anything? Tumors? Cancers? Death? Why not rather turn to God, whose solicitude for our individual welfare, temporal as well as spiritual puts all created solicitude out of the picture. Why not foster confidence in his Divine Providence by humbly and in all childlike humility venture to remind him in the person of our divine Brother Jesus, that we are his children. We should remind him that we are, and at least want to be reckoned as among his "little ones." Therefore, we should thank him frequently for, not only the blessings of the past and present, but thank him ahead of time for whatever he foresees is pleasing to him that we suffer. We should do this not only in general but in each particular case. We should leave everything absolutely in his divine disposal, including with all its circumstances, when, where, and how he may be pleased to dispose the event of our death.
>
> Try something like this and see if it doesn't bring you a big increase of peace and contentment. In my opinion there is hardly anything else that the enemy of our souls dreads more than confidence—humble confidence in God. The lives of the saints abound with examples of this virtue. Perhaps nowhere more beautifully than in the example of St. Joseph with Mary,

God's Living Tabernacle seeking an abode wherein to
give us salvation. What an example of confidence it
must have been to their thousand guardian angels, as
Venerable Mary of Agreda was instructed to inform us,
did Mary have from the day of her Immaculate
Conception. What an edification! And again what a
surpassing reward that followed! What a HOLY
NIGHT for them indeed! A HOLY NIGHT, the positive
dawn of humanity rescued.[20]

A reason why Solanus wrote such a lengthy letter to his niece was to
help her cope with two specific situations which were troubling her:
the sickness of her husband, Edward Wilhite, and the fact that it
seemed she would not be able to bear children. Reiterating one of his
themes about "surprising the doctors," Solanus invited his niece to do
something concrete to show her confidence in God. Possibly she could
bring life into the world in another kind of way:

> There has been something else in my mind, however,
> that I wanted to bring to your consideration. How about
> proposing to adopt one or more little ones, of whom
> Jesus assures us: "What you have done for the least of my
> brethren, you have done for me," and what if Edward
> would give the doctors a surprise and get well?
>
> I find it always practical, especially in cases where
> all human scientific help is despaired of, to just turn to
> the divine author of all good—always solicitous to be
> asked for favors—and with all the confidence we can
> muster, to promise something that we are assured is
> pleasing to him if we might only be spared (or be
> granted the certain favor). But to even raise children
> for God and society is manifestly pleasing to God. This
> applies to cases whether they are procured by natural
> generation or by adoption (which seemingly is quite a
> matter of indifference to him), that he has given a spe-

cially beautiful coloring to the love of those whose privilege it is to have become earnest faithful parents. In this song of the psalmist it can be quite appropriately applied: "Oh, the depths of the riches of the wisdom and of the knowledge of God! How incomprehensible are his judgments and how unsearchable his ways!" (Romans 11)

I am herewith enclosing a letter of Fr. Edward's…that will speak for itself. I wish to address the verse I have underlined: "God condescends to use our powers, if we don't spoil his plans by ours." Because he is always planning wonders for the patient and the humble. Hence his own blessed words: "Unless you be converted and become as little children…." Now I'll have to say GOOD NIGHT.[21]

Around this time, another woman unable to have children asked to see Solanus. Asteria Mahoney recalled the visit well:

I met Solanus Casey in 1945 while I was a Girl Scout Leader at St. Michael Church, 225 Jerome Street, Brooklyn, N.Y. I was 27 years old, married 8 years, having no children.

When my husband returned from service, W.W. II, we decided to find out once and for all the cause and the reason for our not producing a family. I was recommended to a well known gynecologist, Dr. O'Leary, and he in turn sent my husband to Dr. Griffin. The findings were that it would be very unlikely that we would have children.

This was heartbreaking news to me, having come from a large family. My husband then suggested that we could adopt a child. I was very hesitant, and it would be a first in both our families and I wondered if our children would be accepted and loved as the other grandchildren, nieces and nephews.

It was not generally known, but I had heard that Father Solanus was in our parish, that he was a very saintly man, well loved and sought after for counsel and advice by the people in Detroit from where he recently served.

One afternoon after a Girl Scout meeting, I rang the Monastery bell and asked if I could speak to Fr. Casey. Brother asked me no questions and ushered me to a small conference room when very soon Fr. Casey came in with a friendly smile. I told him about my marriage, how much I wanted a family, and my fears about adoption. His answer to me not only answered my questions, but will remain with me forever. He said, "If it wasn't for people like you, who would take care of the unfortunate ones?" When I left him, I was happy and convinced that this is what I was meant to do and shortly applied to the N.Y. Foundling Hospital to adopt a child.

On June 12, 1946 we brought our first son home. He was exactly two months old.[22]

For someone living in the 1940s, Solanus was far ahead of his time in cutting through cultural biases and barriers. Whether with the Mahoneys, whom he helped overcome stereotypes about adoption, with non-Catholics, or people of other races, Solanus evidenced a wonderful way of going beyond externals to get to the core of people and their basic needs.

In a letter written in early 1946, Solanus recalled another incident in his ministry that had taken place at St. Bonaventure involving a married couple neither Catholic nor white. And while his letter shows he was not totally free of some of the terminology that was used (which later revealed a bias), for him as well as others of that era his words were quite sensitive and sympathetic even if we now decry such expressions. "We've had several cases similar to yours, and some of them altogether more tragic and hopeless, which have turned out to have been real blessings in disguise," he wrote a woman who complained of serious headaches:

A single example: It must be ten or more years ago that a certain modest lady, having waited close to an hour, until all else had gone, introduced herself: "I's not Catholic, but I would like to get a blessin' too. I's always had headaches." Her accent rather than her color indicated something of her particular origin.[23]

Just her southern dialect was enough to coax the literary bug in Solanus Casey. He tried in his reflection to recapture the context of their dialogue, much like William Faulkner did in his novels. He recalled:

About three hours later a well-featured but very dark visitor of the same name and identical accent asked for a rosary. I told him of his namesake who had been in about 11:00. "That's my wife." He went on to explain that she had come home without any headache. Glory be to God!

They had been praying for a family for thirteen years and were naturally discouraged, or were becoming so. They believed in Christianity but had never been baptized…. It is next to "unbelievable," what difficulties they met with and, by God's grace overcame, before being received into the Church—and even for months afterwards. All Hell just seemed determined to keep them from their purpose.[24]

He told the woman receiving the above letter about his effort to get people to deepen their faith, or investigate the "claims of the Church," or for others to "get ahead of the Good God in generosity if possible." Then he concluded:

> I almost forgot to tell you that, having left Detroit, the convert[s]...returned after more than three years. There were three of them instead of two. The good God blessed them with a decidedly promising youngster, the picture of his appreciative Daddy.
>
> I hope that this may offer you an example from which you might draw a practical lesson—one case in thousands. Thanks be to God.[25]

The more people heard such stories as the above, the more the doorbell rang at St. Michael. However, it still was nothing like the droves at Detroit. After eight months, Solanus wrote his brother Edward that his coming to St. Michael had been a "decided relief" compared to the drain and strain of Detroit. He noted, "I do have perhaps hours as long but it's a change. Here it's correspondence that takes most of the time. There, I simply had to leave most of that to others [who were assigned to help him respond to requests]. And while I meet with pathetic cases to solve or try to alleviate, the strain and tension is by no means so pressing."[26]

Given the need to meet the people and answer his own correspondence, Solanus did not always get the sleep he needed, so he devised a unique way to take catnaps while portering. He would push his chair back from the desk and crawl under it. Then he would snuggle up like a little child for a quick sleep. He'd stay there until he was relaxed, or until the phone or doorbell rang. Then he'd get up, brush himself off, and put his hair in place. Like a dignified Irishman, according to Father Walter, he'd "look fresh as a daisy."[27]

With time the catnaps became less frequent as more people from the parish and beyond appeared at the friary office. As in Detroit, people began to wait in line. One of these was Ruth Keck, who then had a son at the Capuchin seminary at Garrison. He later became Father

Barnabas Keck (later a director of the Solanus Guild at St. John in New York). According to Barnabas:

> When my mother still lived in St. Patrick's (Brooklyn), she had been in a hospital. The doctor wanted her to go home and then come back for surgery. She asked him, "If I ask you straight questions, will you give me an honest answer?"
>
> He said, "Okay."
>
> "Do I have cancer?" she asked. At that he turned and walked out of the room. So my mother turned to the woman next to her and said, "What's that supposed to mean?"
>
> She left the hospital and told my aunt Agnes what happened. "Ruth," she said, "let's go over to St. Michael's and see Fr. Solanus." So she went to the friary and waited in line. When my mother's turn came, Fr. Solanus said, "And what's your problem, dear."
>
> "I think I have cancer," she said.
>
> All he said was, "Don't you know God can cure cancer just like a toothache?" So she knelt down and he put his hand on her and blessed her, praying over her.
>
> She went home and never went back to the doctor and was eighty years old when the story was repeated in 1983.[28]

As was the case in Yonkers and Detroit, when the sick could not visit Solanus, people brought Solanus to visit them. At times this created humorous incidents. Art Lohrman told of a time they took the Triborough Bridge (now the Robert F. Kennedy Memorial Bridge) to the Bronx. Returning to Brooklyn and wanting some extra time to talk with Solanus, Lohrman acted as though he couldn't find the bridge. "Oh," Solanus said, "Let's say a rosary to the Mother of God that you find it." By the time the rosary was finished they had found the bridge. "Now in thanksgiving to the Mother of God," Solanus said, "Let's say another one." After three rosaries and no conversation with Solanus, Art decided: "From then on, I never opened my mouth whether I was lost or not."[29]

Solanus didn't always pray on such drives. Often he talked about ideas, listened to people's concerns, and shared stories about his youth or friends. He considered relationships with his friends and relatives very important and tried to cultivate them, especially through such conversations and visits, as well as calls and letters.

At St. Michael Solanus made a real effort to stay in contact with his old friends and acquaintances inside and outside the Order. He went to Garrison to swim in the pool; besides enjoying it, it also gave him the chance to meet the young friars who went to school there. He made sure he didn't miss the annual Labor Day festival at Sacred Heart in Yonkers. He loved the excitement of the children, loved watching the games and eating the food. He especially enjoyed hot dogs with onions—hardly the kind of diet that reflected his later concern for eating healthy foods.

Given his various ways of reconnecting with the people, it was not long before Solanus's presence began to be known by more and more. The more Solanus came to events like this at Yonkers, or just by being available at the door of St. Michael, the more his superiors began to realize that the increasing numbers of well-meaning people would not be giving Solanus the rest they envisioned for him.

Looking around the province for a place far enough removed from the major cities the Capuchin-Franciscans served (New York, Detroit and Milwaukee), as well as having enough community presence to nourish Solanus in what they thought would be the twilight years of his life, the superiors chose Huntington, Indiana.

St. Felix in Huntington served as the province's novitiate. In a rare move for that time (which generally found transfers coming only in connection with the triennial chapter), they decided to transfer Solanus there. In addition, at the end of April, after just nine months of combining his portering with "semi-retired," Solanus was given the official status of "retirement." He was seventy-five.

His time in semi-retirement at St. Michael had made Solanus more aware of people's strengths and weaknesses, largesse and pettiness. He also realized that some people seemed more concerned about being identified with him than their stated concerns, such as taking out membership for someone in the SMA.

One such incident occurred during his last days at St. Michael and his first days at St. Felix. It illustrates the sensitive way Solanus responded to such people. The precipitating cause of this incident dealt with his "rubber stamp."

A rubber stamp had been made which reproduced Solanus's signature. The friars thought this would make it easier for Solanus to handle SMA enrollments and sign checks, since his arthritis made it very difficult for him to write and type his letters and even to sign his name—thus the stamp with his signature. However, for at least one person, receiving Solanus's signature by means of a rubber stamp rather than his own hand, was an affront. She complained quite strongly.

The complaint reached Brother Leo in Detroit. So he wrote his friend Solanus about the displeasure he had "caused" the woman by using the rubber stamp at St. Michael's. Receiving Leo's letter, Solanus immediately wrote to the upset woman, trying to placate her. He made a copy of his letter and enclosed it in a letter to Brother Leo. The letter reveals the gentle way Solanus Casey tried to deal with anger, impatience and tensions of others. It also reveals that he was beginning to be plagued by various ailments, especially with his legs.

> Dear Brother Leo:
> God bless you and all at St. Bonaventure.
> I am sending the original of this carbon to Miss Lyke. I hope it may smooth the thing off in a manner; though I am not just clear to what she really complains

about. Perhaps she expected a personal acknowledge-
ment of some kind rather than just a rubber stamp.

I've been getting so many checks—both here at St.
Felix and at Saint Michael's—that I would have to possess an extraordinary memory to recollect particulars
like this little mix-up might require. One thing I do
remember, that during the nine or ten months I was at
St. Michael it was very seldom, if ever, that I was without letters to acknowledge, even though I sometimes
worked on them until after midnight.

God be praised, however, I did not mind it and my
health kept fine. Sometimes my two faithful old sen-
tinels [his legs] would threaten to go on strike and to
quiet them down I felt I'd have to give it up.

Well, she will possibly write again. After all if she
got her checks back, she ought to know that things
were okay.

We'll hope for the best anyhow and pray for the
dear Lord's gentle guidance.

Praying in the meantime for one another's conversion, till someday we can sin no more and the angels
will be able to bear us off to eternity. There, forever,
really and truly CONVERTED, we'll be able to sing on
with the angels awaiting that blessed day: "O all you
works of the Lord, bless the Lord, praise and exalt him
above all forever."

Father Solanus Casey, O.F.M. Cap.
Praised be Jesus Christ![30]

This letter (from Huntington) would be one of the first representing
that period during which Solanus would produce the greatest volume
of writing—at least in terms of those letters that are now available.

Solanus at his favorite pastime in Huntington, Indiana. One of his favorite pieces was "Mother Machree."

Solanus, after blessing a car, 1950.

Solanus, reading the paper.

Solanus at Christmas (1952) with Frater Baldwin Beyer.

Solanus after Jubilee Mass with Monsignor Edward and other friars.

7

HUNTINGTON

The novitiate at St. Felix Friary in Huntington, Indiana, was ideal for Solanus Casey's "official" retirement. Built just before the Great Depression of 1929, the seventeen years since had witnessed quite a transformation in the once-barren land. The original novices had planted an orchard of 170 apple trees behind the friary, as well as hundreds of other of trees and shrubs. Now the fruit of their work brought a contemplative setting for those living at St. Felix.

Solanus took full advantage of Huntington's serene and peaceful atmosphere. After a life spent in the busy urban areas of Yonkers, Manhattan, Detroit and Brooklyn, the fact that Solanus could walk just a few steps outside the friary and be in the middle of nature's beauty elicited from him deep thanks. He wrote of this gratitude shortly after his arrival:

> I was strolling in the orchard and vineyard this morning. They were bountifully loaded. Deo Gratias. I knelt for a while in the little Capuchin cemetery. All of these are behind this ideal monastery. I was thrilled by the chimes of SS. Peter and Paul in their tower smiling at me less than two miles away. Thoughts multiplied of

the wonderful past. Wonderful indeed to muse over!
Thanks be to God. Still how comparatively melancholy
they are when, from the anchor of faith, we can turn to
the spring of eternal blessedness that is assured those
who persevere.[1]

After three quarters of a century of living, such a contemplative
approach—where the beauty of nature enabled him to penetrate further to the very author of that beauty—came quite easily to Solanus.
For him the only appropriate response to such beauty was appreciation: gratefulness to God: "Indeed, what is all the past, aside from the
privilege that ought to be our supreme aim, to have fostered and to
foster appreciation of our being children of our heavenly Father and
of our Blessed Mother Mary?"[2]

Solanus not only found beauty in creation; he seemed to have a
power connected to it that reflected stories told of Jesus and Francis of
Assisi. On May 13, the Huntington friary *Chronicle* noted, almost as a
matter of fact:

> Last Saturday when the daily papers announced the
> approach of frosts, the friars thought of lighting a
> smudge to save the tiny apples. Father Solanus volun-
> teered to bless the orchard instead with the oration "Ad
> Omnia" and one to Blessed Ignatius, a Capuchin
> Brother. Now it appears that only the grapes froze.
> When all around us the neighboring apples were
> destroyed—ours were unharmed.[3]

While others might see such an incident as a manifestation of God's
power uniquely working through him, as far as Solanus was concerned, it occurred because of the blessing itself. One of the friars who
lived with Solanus around that time, Father Ambrose de Groot, noted
that this humble attitude carried over into Solanus's whole life:

I am convinced that he was not aware that others held him in such high esteem. If he did, then all I can say is that he was a very good actor. But no one can put on an act for such a number of years without giving himself away. I just know he was not aware of the esteem in which others held him. Nor did he care.

He was not the kind of man who put himself on trial before anyone, nor did he reveal he was on trial. He was on trial before his God. And he loved his God and he knew that God loved him. That was all that mattered. His whole conduct showed that this must have been the case. I cannot help but marvel how God can hide such mass esteem for a person without that person being aware of it. But God does. And I'm convinced he did it in the case of Father Solanus. He was genuinely humble—without any pretense.[4]

Being comparatively unknown in Huntington, Solanus's early days there were devoted more to correspondence than doorbells. As in Brooklyn, his main form of communication with the people came through letters. However, also as in Brooklyn, he could not always answer the letters as promptly as he—and his correspondents—might like. To one of those so concerned he wrote: "It is not audiences with callers now but answering letters that is my problem. So please have charity to overlook my tardiness" in replying.[5]

Solanus's Huntington letters reveal many insights about his spirituality. In particular, some written in the latter part of his first year there offer a unique insight into his self-understanding regarding the way God's healing power was extending itself to others through his ministry. The brunt of these letters reflecting on human suffering were written within a few months of each other.

Solanus would be the first to admit the mystery of suffering baffled him, especially when it came to humans totally innocent. "I don't understand why children have to suffer,"[6] he wrote. Even though he had no sophisticated theology of suffering, the God he believed in did not want suffering (much less cause suffering), but cared about the one who suffered. Furthermore, Solanus knew that, in Jesus Christ, this God had come to heal us from our suffering, especially our sins. Therefore, while Solanus spent little time commenting on suffering he stressed a God who wanted to relieve it through healing.

On December 14, 1946, he wrote two letters to different people. These are among the best regarding his ideas about healing. In one he reflected on prayer for healings that were "successful." He believed the healings came, in part, because the petitioners had been generous to God in the way they did something like supporting the missions. In the other letter he commented on prayers for healings that had been "not successful." These had to be understood in light of God's greater designs. Whether the suffering was healed or continued, both forms demanded great confidence and abundant thanks that God was involved.

In Solanus's mind, the healings that others saw being worked through him really occurred because the people requesting the cure promised to do three things: (1) believe, (2) pray with faith, and (3) make a promise.[7] It did not matter whether the people were Catholic, Protestant or Jewish. As God's Spirit worked in the world through Jesus of Nazareth to heal "all who were afflicted," so now in the world of Solanus of Prescott, that same Spirit continued to bring healing to broken people of all backgrounds.

In the 1940s and 1950s, before Jonas Salk's vaccine, polio was a plague that struck every summer. One family visited by its crippling effects was the Abraham Trabulsys in Detroit. To encourage them, Solanus recalled a "remarkable case" which manifested God's healing power toward a Jew who enrolled his son in the Seraphic Mass Association:

> A friend of your daughter Jenny, Miss Rose Fans, writes
> me that Jenny is very low with polio and asks for

prayers that, if it be God's holy will, she might recover. I am enrolling Jenny in what we call the Seraphic Mass Association for prayers of hundreds of people.

The members of this association are asked to pray for our foreign missionaries and their work and for one another. Those members who can, pray. All those who can afford to do so are asked to help with an offering of some kind besides prayers and Masses. I am confident that this will help your Jenny. This will happen especially if you and yours do your part.

You will get an idea of what I mean by telling you of a remarkable case in Detroit about four years ago. I made note of it at the time. It is about as follows:

January 9th, Judge Healy called this evening: "...There is a certain Dr. Kleitzer in my office whose only child is very low with spinal meningitis. The doctors give him very little hope of recovery. He is not a Catholic or a Christian. He is a Jew, a good, God-fearing fellow. I wish you would enroll the boy in the Mass Association and pray for him."

"I'll be glad to do that," I answered. "Tell the parents I'd like to see them."

"I'll bring them over tomorrow," he answered.

"Next day (Saturday), I saw them—the Judge and the Doctor, waiting over in the corner. It was about 1:15 P.M. As I was introduced to the Doctor I asked, "How is the boy?"

"Well, he slept last night (the first time in a week)," the Doctor responded.

"Now, Doctor, I have a proposition I want you to make to the Good God yourself. I understand you are a Jew."

"Yes," he replied.

"That is okay, Doctor. After all, if religion can be defined us a science, and I claim it is unquestionably the greatest science of all times—in fact it is nothing less than THE SCIENCE OF OUR HAPPY RELA-TIONSHIP WITH GOD AND OUR NEIGHBORS, then, there can be but one religion, though there may be a thousand different systems of religion."

The Doctor seemed pleased but said nothing. They left.

Twenty-five minutes later the Judge phoned: "I thought you would be pleased to hear what happened. I brought the Doctor right back to the Children's Hospital and in the vestibule we met the mother of the boy. The Doctor's wife was smiling.

"She said, 'At 1:30 he opened his eyes and smiled at me.' [This was the time the Judge and the Doctor were talking about the boy with Solanus.]

"A week later (Sunday) he was brought home in perfect health."

Hoping that the above may not have been too boring for anyone and that if it be God's holy will, your Jenny may give the doctors and all concerned a favorable surprise of some kind, I remain...[8]

The same day Solanus wrote the above letter assuming a "favorable surprise of some kind" would come for all concerned, he wrote to another Detroiter trying to explain why not all prayers are answered in the way people hope:

I was pleased to receive your kind favor of the 9th even though it was not as bright, as of course, we all would like to see it. However, God knows best, and, while we'll still hope for a favorable surprise, we can hardly do better than not only being resigned to whatever

God permits, but even beforehand to thank him for
his mercifully loving designs.[9]

When people were not cured as they desired, Solanus believed this
too was somehow part of God's mysterious plan that could only work
for people's ultimate good. "I recall one day at St. Felix, I was in the
outside with some of the novices," Capuchin Ambrose de Groot
recalled. "He told the story about the time he was talking to a group
of people sitting in a car in front of St. Bonaventure in Detroit. One
of the occupants of the car was a woman who had been crippled and
unable to walk for thirty years. Solanus wanted to sympathize with
her and said: 'My, but thirty years is an awful long time to be suffering
this way.' But she replied, 'Yes, Father, but eternity is worth it.'"

Given his own advanced studies in theology, Father Ambrose
identified Solanus's insight with our need to "make up what is lacking
in the suffering of Christ":

> He saw it as having redemptive value in the life of the
> Mystical Body—that certain people are chosen by God
> to suffer as an apostolate. It recalls St. Paul's statement:
> "I rejoice now in the sufferings I bear for your sake;
> and what is lacking of the sufferings of Christ I fill up
> in my flesh for his body which is the church" (Col
> 1:24). It's the church's doctrine of vicarious or redemp-
> tive suffering. I really think he understood this well
> and was the reason why he made such statements; and
> it was the reason why he never obtained cures for his
> own brethren.[10]

Above all, Solanus believed, whether one would receive a desired cure
or not, one should always give thanks to God. Giving thanks ahead of
time—whether it be for healing or continued suffering—should
characterize true believers. "This is the way we can foster confidence
in God," he wrote in his letter to the Detroiter explaining why not all
prayers are answered in the way people might hope:

This confidence is the very soul of prayer, and consequently heightens our hopes for supernatural intervention. Not only this, but in fostering this confidence we greatly eliminate the danger of sadness, want of resignation and impatience. While these are not necessarily sinful in themselves, nevertheless, they sadly frustrate God's merciful designs. Hence the little verse: "God condescends to use our powers if we don't spoil his plans by ours...."[11]

Confidence in the God who can heal summarizes Solanus's theology of healing. As early as his novitiate, he had recalled in his notes the words of Jesus: "Ask and you shall receive." He would ask God for healing for others, because he himself deeply believed, with an almost absolute confidence, in God's promise to heal. Because of his own confidence in that God, those who experienced it in him, in turn, were heightened in their confidence in God's healing. People believed in God's healing power because Solanus believed in it. Solanus believed in God; people believed in Solanus. Somehow, in this circle of belief, wonderful things occurred through his intercession and the actions he asked them to perform.

Writing to a couple whose little daughter had eye trouble, Solanus articulated one of the best of his "give thanks before-and-after" letters:

[S]hake off the excessive worry and instead exercise a little confidence in God's merciful providence by first promising something—even a little sacrifice of some kind in thanksgiving if things go favorable. Then to show your confidence in his goodness, start and thank him whenever you think of it. Give him thanks for whatever he may see best to do for the little one and for her loving friend.[12]

The acts he asked people to perform in confident thanks varied. While these often involved supporting the foreign missions through an enrollment in the SMA or giving something to the poor, other options were suggested as well. Sometimes non-Catholics would be asked to investigate "the claims of the Catholic Church." For others, both Catholics and non-Catholics, part of the "proposition" with God might be to read more about the ways of God and religion. And, of course, some would be invited to read the *Mystical City of God*.

On February 8, 1947, Solanus wrote a man in Brighton, Michigan, noting the time when he asked the wife of a Methodist (who sought healing for her husband) to read the works of the Spanish mystic (Mary of Agreda) and how the woman did not deliver on her part of the proposition to do so:

> The case was noted close to four years ago in my own hand and runs substantially as follows:
>
> March 26, 1943. Andrew Wheeler, a Methodist of 686 Manistique Ave., Detroit, had a "brain-tumor" removed four weeks ago (Feb. 23). At first the operation seemed to have been successful. But two weeks later infection started. On March 12th there was a second operation.
>
> Last Tuesday, March 23, Mrs. Wheeler accompanied by a Catholic neighbor came weeping and lamenting: "They have just operated on my husband the third time in a month and they give me very little hope of his recovery...."
>
> "Now Mrs. Wheeler," I pleaded, "do not take it so hard. We will pray for your husband and enroll him in the Association and try to induce our dear Lord to take over the case himself." So I recorded his name, etc.
>
> Then I said, "Now Mrs. Wheeler. I have a little proposition for you to make yourself to the good God in your own honest way."
>
> "I'll do anything to please the good God," she interposed, "if he will only spare my poor, dear husband!"

"Well this is the proposition or promise I want you to make, if you choose this rather than something else, whereby to please God. It is more a suggestion, therefore, that you promise or earnestly resolve in your own mind to look into the claims of that Mother Church divinely planned and proclaimed infallible, and the claims of any other denomination or system of religion. Or I might say that you look into the connection between them."

Mr. Wheeler came home the next day, the day before yesterday. He came here with his wife and neighbor today. A patch of about three inches square was taped around his right temple. While I was noting the surprise (in the healing), he remarked to the party who had given him his place (in line): "It is great to feel normal again, although I feel a little weak. The doctors in Ann Arbor, Peet and Wood call it miraculous…that a patient should talk intelligently inside of twenty-four hours after such an operation."

"Thanks be to God!"

I had not heard from them for over a year and a half, when Mrs. Wheeler came to lament that her husband was not very well of late. I asked her if she had kept her promise as I had suggested and if she had read the book I lent her, *The Mystical City of God*. She humbly admitted that she had not. She had come without him, as she said, because she wanted to tell me about him first.

I told her without hesitation, "The whole trouble is in your failure to keep your promise, or your proposition, whatever it was."

She promised to return next night with her husband and in the meantime to do something to show her good will. It was a very stormy evening, the next night, so she phoned her inability to come as promised but that they would come the following evening. Following is the note that I made under the original:

> October 18, 1944: Thank God they are both here today. He has started to read the wonderful life of the Blessed Virgin, *The Mystical City of God* and is quite enthused about it.

Among other things in praise of the wonderful work. *The Mystical City of God*...he remarked: "I find so much in it that I have often wondered about."

I hope, dear Mr. Taylor, that I have not bored you overmuch with the above. If I were an experienced typist I would do the whole letter over. Under my circumstances, however, that is out of the question. I am enrolling yourself and Mrs. Taylor in our emergency list and will hope for a favorable surprise of some kind—and a favorable report.[13]

In his letter to the Taylors he added a postscript which made it clear that, as far as he was concerned, God's healing could come to people of all faiths as long as they truly professed and acted on their belief:

> P.S.: Incidentally, I think it is slightly an error for one who is a Christian (as I presume you are), or who believes in Jesus our Redeemer, to intimate that he does not belong to the same faith as another who, though believing in Jesus Christ and professing Christianity, happens to differ with him in some details, possibly not even essential. Because I claim that there is really but one Christianity, as scientifically there can be but one religion, though there be a thousand different systems of that "Greatest science of all times and all generations—THE SCIENCE OF OUR HAPPY RELATIONSHIP WITH GOD AND OUR NEIGHBORS."

"Thus says the Lord: Let not the wise man glory in his wisdom and let not the strong man glory in his strength, and let not the rich man glory in his riches. But let him that glories, glory in this, that he understands and loves me, for I am the Lord that exercises mercy and judgment, and justice in the earth. For these things please me, says the Lord" (Jeremiah 9:22–23).[14]

Solanus had begun the above letter noting that "for the present" he was "no longer at St. Bonaventure." The reason why he couched his letter in such a way was that, given his need for doctoring as well as the desire of the people in Detroit for this return, discussions had taken place about transferring him again to Detroit. For his part, Solanus was indifferent. Commenting on the rumor that he might go back to Detroit, Solanus wrote his brother Edward:

There is a possibility that I might be sent back to Detroit or elsewhere, though I hardly think it is at all probable. I have not the least worry about whether I remain here or be transferred. It is after all, essentially quite the same. It is such a surprising privilege to know definitely that one is doing God's will by keeping the rule and obeying. Sorry to say, if we can use the word, it is so little for any one of us to possibly appreciate such privileges.

Indeed, just herein seems to me to be humanity's great weakness—WANT OF APPRECIATION. But again, how fortunate for us that God's mercy is above his works—and his patience is essentially one with his mercy.

Blessed and praised be his holy Name![15]

Part of the rumor regarding the possibility of Solanus's return to Detroit was connected to his return there to celebrate his golden jubilee of religious vows on Sunday, January 26, 1947.

The people of Detroit were not being told where Solanus was. However, when *The Detroit News* ran a January 25, 1946, story about his jubilee thousands came to celebrate with him—and, as in the former days, to share with him their problems and requests for prayers.

Solanus had been asked to write a message on the back of a "holy card" which could be given to the people as a memento of the occasion. Solanus wrote and rewrote his thoughts until they finally reflected his inmost thoughts about his ministry, God and God's people:

PAX ET BONUM
IN MEMORY OF MY
GOLDEN JUBILEE IN RELIGION
St. Bonaventure's Monastery
Detroit, Michigan
Thanks be to God for uncountable mercies—for every blessing!
Thanks be to my neighbor for his charitable patience.
Fifty years in the Order—almost unnoticed—have slipped away from me into eternity. Thither I hope to follow before half another fifty: trusting in the merciful goodness of God!

Father Solanus, o.f.m. Cap.
DEO GRATIAS

If his superiors wondered whether they should return Solanus to Detroit, the number of people converging upon him at his jubilee there confirmed them in their original decision to send him to Huntington. Staying at St. Felix was best for him. It would be wrong to move him again.

Solanus returned to Huntington a week later laden with many gifts, including money, a chalice, vestments, an alb and altar linens. There he began the task of writing thank-yous. High on the list was Father Simon Hesse, the spiritual director of the Third Order of Saint Francis Fraternity (Secular Franciscans) at St. Bonaventure. He and the fraternity had hosted the celebration. Solanus could not be more thankful:

My Dear Confrere Simon: More than simply to say, "A thousand times many thanks" for your practical help in the elaborate preparations and actual celebration of the golden jubilee at dear St. Bonaventure a few weeks back, I want to congratulate you and your dear tertiaries…and the members of the privileged Eucharistic Mission Band, on their beautiful, artistic generosity. One could hardly feel other than convinced without a second thought that they must all have worked in real Franciscan harmony. They masterly "put over" a fraternal, loyal display. May our dear Lord bless all and each who helped along.

I am sure that, even aside from the solemn holy Mass itself—whose very ceremonies, etc. I am assured brought tears to many a non-Catholic eye—was the mutually fraternal simplicity of the whole proposition. It was a source of much happy edification. Writing later on, when the tension of excitement had gone (if there had been such), a certain Jew who attended and understood the beautiful prayers with the epistle and Gospel, assured me that he could not restrain his tears.[16]

Having returned to Huntington for the foreseeable future, Solanus developed a regular pattern at St. Felix: following the provincial-wide plan for prayer, meals and recreation and answering the letters in the 9:30 AM mail.

Because of the increased correspondence, it had been decided to give Solanus a secretary to help him respond to the many letters coming to him. However there was another reason as well—the superiors had discovered many letters containing money for various requests had not been filed in the correct places. Furthermore, some letters with money for various intentions had gone unacknowledged. In trying to figure out why requests were not being answered, the superiors found money all over Solanus's room. There was need for better accountability.

One of the first secretaries was the newly ordained Father Blase Gitzen. As a boy he had served Mass for Solanus in Detroit. He was a good counterpart to the more easygoing Solanus, especially when it came to the money that often accompanied the letters he received. He recalled:

> In some ways he offended my Prussian regularity and orderliness. He had money on him (which he just stuffed into his habit pockets) and money all over his room (which he stuffed into the cubbyholes of his desk, or used as page markers). And he didn't know to which account that money was to be credited.
>
> So one day, with the blessing of the superior, I went through his room and collected $153. He never said anything, but I got the impression that he wasn't very pleased that I cleaned up his room. Not that he cared about the money. He never took care of it because he just couldn't care less. But I lost his place in many a book![17]

Blase noted that while he respected Solanus deeply, he did not stand "in awe of him," like some others. Consequently he would not be willing to allow the former ways to continue. He recalled:

> Generally, Father Solanus received from 30 to 40 letters a day. Since most of the letters contained money, it was my duty to open all his mail, find out what the money was for (Masses, Seraphic Mass Association, alms) and record these. Naturally, in looking through these letters I came across four or five in each mailing that were particularly pitiful cases. In my heart, I prayed that Fr. Solanus would answer these himself, and almost invariably, those were the letters he chose to answer

personally. The rest I would acknowledge with a short note. In the course of the day, I would receive the answers he had crashed out on an old battered typewriter. They were typed, mostly, on three by five cards. The spelling was bad, pure fifth-grade stuff, but the contents simply amazed me. With a few words he was able to come to the heart of the problem. His understanding of people, his sympathetic response, his grasp of theology just astounded me. He may not have passed his examinations, but his wisdom was far beyond mine.[18]

Many times Solanus would be interrupted in his room with telephone calls from people in need. Brother Pius Cotter recalls that, while he might initially show frustration when told of a visitor at the front parlor or a call on the phone, within a second or two, Solanus's initial emotional reaction would turn to his broad Irish smile. He then would get up and go to talk to the person in need.[19]

Other times, after such telephone calls or visits, he would go to the choir and kneel in prayer. "At times he was so absorbed in prayer that it seemed he was in some sort of mystical state," Father Blase Gitzen recalled. "At such times one could not get his attention by motioning or calling to him; he had to be shaken."[20]

Not only did the problems of individuals need to be brought to God, the problems of society did as well. Thus, as the arms race developed after the Second World War, so did Solanus's concern about its potential for destruction.

For him the invention of the atomic bomb seemed to be saying that somehow God was permitting "men without faith to be preparing the fearfully poisoned lightning fires, with which he will arm his angels of wrath on an adulterous, defiant, atheistic generation."[21] As he looked at the United States, Solanus believed that the nation was becoming increasingly consumeristic and materialistic. He noted:

> What I'd like to stress is the very insanity of trying to
> reckon on anything material these days as amounting
> to anything of importance aside from its use in pro-
> moting the glory of God and charity toward lifting
> humanity—and the necessarily very short time such
> material things hold their value.[22]

Rather than condemn the nation for its materialism and militarism,
he dreamed of a world where people would use the world's resources
to better humanity, especially those in need. This would be the way
that the reign of God could be revealed in contrast to a generation
which was "running after these things" (see Matthew 6:32). In contrast
to the ideology of materialism, Solanus stressed the value of being
concerned about its victims, the poor.

The poor were not very evident at Huntington except for the
occasional "knight of the road." However when beggars did come, they
often were greeted kindly by Solanus and taken to a special room that
they might eat in dignity. In this way he was doing his part in bringing about God's reign, as envisioned by Jesus. Thus he wrote: "What a
marvelously different society we would have here and what an ideal
world we would have to live in if we all would keep in mind the assurance of Jesus, 'What you have done to the least of my brethren, you
have done to me.' "[23]

On January 12, 1949, around the time Solanus wrote this
reflection, the house *Chronicle* for St. Felix friary notes, "Father
Solanus received the sad news that his priest brother Fr. Maurice
Joachim passed away this morning."[24] The fact that he could go to
Maurice Joachim's funeral brought Solanus much peace.

While he believed his brother finally found peace, Solanus did not
find the same in the world. Indeed it was headed toward even more
violence and evil.

One particular form of that evil, in Solanus's eyes, had been
personified in the Soviet Union's trial of Cardinal Mindzenty in

Hungary for alleged espionage during the early days of the Cold War. Reflecting on the trial of the Hungarian primate, Solanus showed the same indignation regarding injustice against the innocent which he had shown twenty-five years earlier regarding British injustices against the Irish.

Cardinal Mindzenty's trial garnered front-page copy in papers around the world. However, Solanus interpreted it from the wider perspective of his understanding of discipleship and the cross. Only from this perspective could one find encouragement and meaning. He said as much in a reply to one of his correspondents:

> I hope this finds you well, which means of course hopeful too. This latter is something that is sadly overlooked (these days) to the great detriment of spiritual progress as well as physical.
>
> Probably the all-outstanding example of proof of this is the historical scandal that some of the disciples took at Jesus' choice of the CROSS AND CALVARY. There he establishes his Reign of Love rather than any other. This "scandal" drew from St. Peter himself, "Master, far be it from thee...!" This drew the alarming response: "Get behind me, satan.... You are not serving God."
>
> It is well to remember that such scandal was never intended to be confined to the Apostolic Age. Hence, S. Bernard, the outstanding Doctor of the Middle Ages wisely reminds [us]: "Since the scandal of the Cross, it is never reasonable to take scandal." Another occasion of the first disciples taking scandal is the detailed insistence of his giving us himself for our own life of soul: "I am the bread of life. Your fathers did eat manna in the desert and are dead. This is the bread which comes down from heaven; that if any man eat of it he may not die." (Jn 4:48)

> Of course it is only natural for honest, upright
> people to resent falsehood and injustice as was St. Peter
> in striking off the brutal Malchus' ear. The same can be
> said of the wave of international indignation that the
> damnable hypocrisy manifest these days in the sacrile-
> gious treatment of Cardinal Josef Mindzenty.[25]

Solanus's feelings about society's lies and injustices were strong, arguing that it was "natural for moral integrity to resent falsehood and
injustice."[26] For Solanus, the trial of Cardinal Mindzenty revealed the
diametric opposition to that reality upon which he founded his whole
life—the existence, power and love of God. Since this God was so real
for him, he could not imagine how any reality except insanity or evil
incarnate could believe in or promote atheism.

Around this same time, Solanus also had written a reflection
called "THINK OVER." It elaborated on his thoughts about knowing
God versus atheism. He wrote:

> If the primary purpose of my creation is to know my
> Creator, so that I may be happy in his loving service,
> and if no one but a fool can say in his heart, "There is
> no God," then the conclusion would seem to be that
> God's existence must be manifest, one way or other, to
> everyone that is not a fool, that every normal person
> able to think can and ought to recognize his
> Creator....[27]

Solanus did not realize it then, but there are different ways of knowing;
this refers especially to knowledge of God. For him, religion itself was
the science of our knowing and relating to God. However, trained by his
Thomistic background to believe that all experience must be rational,
Solanus merely concluded that all experience of God had to be equally
rational. By linking experience with rationality, Solanus actually was
evidencing his own contemplative grounding and, therefore, his mystical understanding of God. Since his experience of God was so real to

him, he considered such to be simply rational and normal. It followed, then, for him, that only a fool—one without rationality—could say there was no God.

At its depths authentic religiosity cannot be reduced to the simply rational. At the same time, neither can religion be irrational. The "religion" of Solanus was beyond simple identification with things intellectual. His notion of religion involved something beyond the rational: another level of reality, the mystical. Solanus had come to know God so intimately and mystically that he simply believed any rational person would have to be convinced of God's existence in the world and their lives.

For Solanus, there were two ways of knowing God. The ultimate way could only be reserved for the Beatific Vision. The second reflected the first and greatest commandment—to know, love and serve God. Knowing God in this second way and acting on it laid the foundation for the beatific knowing to come.

Knowing this God, for Solanus, was the essence of life. However, knowing God in this way also revealed Solanus's "knowing" to be mystical. Without using the term "mystical," Solanus believed that, what we would call "knowing God" in the mystical life, had to be available to all:

> Self-understood there can be no thought of our knowing God in our present state directly and as he is known in heaven. Our privilege here is to start such knowledge as can be perfected only in the great, blessed Beyond. Nevertheless, if we stop to think as we ought to do, there must be ways and means close at hand whereby, according to the lives of the saints, we may if we try, to ascend to great sanctity and to an astonishing familiarity with God even here as pilgrims to the Beatific Vision.[28]

The "astonishing familiarity with God" which Solanus experienced "even here" was so real for him that he could not possibly believe that anyone but "the fool" could say there was no God. For this reason, reacting so negatively to the rise of atheism in the world, he decided that, once and for all, he would try to spearhead an effort open to all atheists to prove that God did not exist. The effort would constellate around a contest with a million-dollar prize to whoever could write the convincing essay which proved that God did not exist.

The more he thought about the idea, the more excited Solanus became. He pitched his "essay proposition," as he called it, with the Provincial and wealthy benefactors, including Mrs. Montgomery Ward Thorne. "Without effort" he noted, she "could donate the whole Prize ($1,000,000) and possibly will do as much."[29] Quite a few people showed interest, including wealthy friends, like the O'Donnells in Chicago and the provincial of the Milwaukee Province of the School Sisters of Notre Dame, Mother Mary Fidelis.

Solanus decided to further discuss his plan with the O'Donnells and Mother Mary Fidelis on a trip to Milwaukee in April 1949. The trip to Milwaukee was occasioned by ceremonies connected to his former friend and coworker, Father Stephen Eckert, O.F.M. CAP. Solanus and Stephen had lived and worked together during Solanus's assignment at Sacred Heart in Yonkers.

Stephen Eckert had left Sacred Heart to begin a boarding school, St. Benedict the Moor, for blacks in Milwaukee. Soon after Stephen's death, people began to press for his canonization as "The Apostle of the Colored Race." Solanus himself promoted Stephen's cause at least since 1935.

When Stephen's cause for sainthood had begun, his body was exhumed from Mt. Calvary Cemetery in Wauwatosa, Wisconsin. The province used the occasion to relocate his body to St. Benedict. Solanus wanted to be in Milwaukee for this and the dedication of the statue of Stephen that would mark his new grave.

After the ceremony, all went next door to a ham dinner. However, the ham was tainted. In very graphic terms Solanus described how the illness hit him as he was visiting Mother Mary Fidelis, explaining his "million dollar essay Contest" at the School Sisters of Notre Dame motherhouse, then a mile from St. Benedict:

> I mentioned the proposition to Rev. Mother Mary Fidelis, helpless invalid at the time, and afterwards to about fifty of her nuns.... Well, Mother Mary Fidelis and her nuns seemed quite interested and promised to pray the good God to bring it to success. I had hardly come to the parlor after blessing them with several relics and a little visit in the Chapel when I urged, "Sister, please get me a vessel quickly. I'll have to vomit. I'll wait right here on the floor."
>
> Luckily nothing came but strenuous wrenching 'til the vessel arrived, and then very little, with quite a relief of very short duration, again and again. Then the ambulance came and took the patient to St. Michael Hospital where he stayed about forty hours.[30]

"The patient" spent two days at St. Michael Hospital before returning to St. Felix.

Upon his return, some friars noticed Solanus rubbing his legs. He also seemed to be taking the stairs much more gingerly than before. It was a pace very unfamiliar to the man who—at more than seventy-five years old—was known to take the stairs at a run. For years Solanus had been having problems like this with his legs. Some doctors called his disease "weeping eczema;" others some kind of psoriasis. At any rate, the open sores caused by the disease gave Solanus great pain, especially in the last decade of his life. This was one of those times.

"I noticed something was wrong with his feet and legs," Father Blase recalled of his condition:

So, after quite a bit of persuasion he finally let me look at them, and they were as raw as a piece of meat. We bathed the socks off and sent him at once to…the hospital in Fort Wayne. There the doctors recognized the seriousness of his condition. Fearing the loss of blood circulation, they prepared an operation room for probable amputation. Every three minutes a nurse checked his circulation.

It was decided by the friars that word of his hospitalization would not be mentioned. We knew he was seriously ill, and we wanted him to get some rest. To my utter surprise, despite a big "DO NOT DISTURB" sign on the door, I found fifteen people in the room the next day when I visited him. Some had come from as far away as Detroit. How they found him, I'll never know. But here he was, propped up in bed, with a white canopy over his legs, amiably chatting with his visitors. And sure enough, every three minutes, a disapproving nurse came in to check the pulse in his legs.

His attitude toward his illness was one of such lack of concern that I was curious whether he knew how seriously ill he had been and brought up the subject on the way home from the hospital. Yes, he knew that his legs might have to be amputated, but he had the attitude: "If they came off, it was all right; if not, that was all right, too." He showed absolutely no shock, surprise, worry or upset. He knew, and said calmly, that it was caused by his allergy to ham.[31]

Reflecting on his stay, Solanus wrote that, "according to the way one looks at difficulties and crosses, I was one of the dozens of unfortunate ones, although I would rather say fortunate ones. It was surely to nature a very unpleasant experience. But, thanks be to God, I feel that my soul profited greatly by the experience of about a month in the hospital…."[32]

His sickness led him to think of others who had to deal with such difficulties as well:

> It was a "bitter pill that turned to sweetness of soul and body," as St. Francis tells us in the Holy Rule, about his personal experiences with the poor, dear lepers of his day, and as many chaplains and soldiers tell of what they went through in the Second World War.[33]

Christmas 1947 found his skin problem so serious that he remained in bed most of the day. At other times, the house *Chronicle* simply notes that Solanus "again" was having problems with his legs. Because of its proximity to Huntington, Solanus usually went to Fort Wayne for medical treatment. Once in a while, however, he would go to Detroit, and use such occasions to reconnect with old friends.

Father Cefai, pastor of St. Paul Maltese Church, loved to tell how Solanus would sometimes "telephone my sister telling her he was on his way to St. Bonaventure's Monastery." Then, "as simply as a child he would ask her if he could have some of her spaghetti on the way. He liked a glass of wine. He also liked Maltese cheese cakes.[34]

On one 1950 visit to Detroit, a young man named James Allen Maher paid him a visit:

> I went to see him at the Monastery on Mt. Elliott, and I told him I was thinking of going into religious life as a Franciscan Brother. I had quite a conversation with him. He asked me where I worked and when I told him I worked for the railroad, he said he always liked the railroad, and then we got off on a conversation about Jesse James and his gang. He said that while he was a prison guard in Minnesota he had met Jim and Cole Younger who had been with Jesse James. He said he befriended Cole Younger, and Cole had given him a chest or clothes trunk for him to keep and he said, "I still have it."

Maher first talked to Solanus about his wonderment as to whether he might have a religious vocation: "I asked him whether he thought I had a vocation to the religious life, and he started asking me questions to see how much I knew about the Bible." Then, Maher recalled: "He told me as I was leaving he thought I should wait awhile before I made a final decision to go into the monastery."[35]

Young Maher's visit provided him the next day with the chance to pump Solanus for more thoughts. This occurred in the unique way he ended up driving Solanus to Huntington:

I had gone down to see Fr. Solanus with a Franciscan Brother from Duns Scotus College. He wanted to talk to Fr. Solanus about some problems he was having. While he was in talking to him he asked Fr. Solanus if it was true he was going to Huntington, Indiana, the next day. Fr. Solanus said he was. Br. Romuold asked him if he had a ride down there and Fr. Solanus said he had a ride with a couple who said they would be happy to drive him, "but they are Protestants and I would rather go down with some Catholics, because I would like to say some prayers on the way down there, especially the rosary and it would be kind of awkward if I went down with this Protestant couple."

So Brother told him he had a friend who had a car and that we would be happy to drive him down. As it turned out the Brother couldn't go. His superior wouldn't let him take the day off. So I drove him down myself. We left on Wednesday afternoon. I was supposed to pick him up in the morning, but about 10 o'clock in the morning, my car was not working right. The brakes needed fixing. I took it to a service station and had to wait a few hours for it. I called Fr. Solanus and told him. He said, "Get the car fixed and give me a call when it is ready." The car wasn't ready until about 3 o'clock in the afternoon. So I called Father again and he said that he would meet me at the service station.

When he got there he asked me if there was a Catholic Church nearby. I told him we were near the church I went to (Presentation Church on Pembroke and Meyers). So he said, "Let's go there and say some prayers before we leave for Huntington."

We drove over to the church and when we got inside he took out his rosary and said, "Let's say the rosary."

We left the church and started for Huntington about 4 o'clock. Father said he wanted to be there about midnight. So I thought we had better go pretty fast as I figured it would take about eight hours to get there.[36]

Once on the road, an encounter with a man hitchhiking brings a wonderfully human dimension to Solanus. Maher noted:

On the way we came upon a hitchhiker. We were going so fast that by the time Fr. Solanus told me to stop and pick him up, we had gone quite a distance. Father said, "Well, we missed him. But if we come across any more hitchhikers, stop and pick them up." We had not gone very far when we came upon another one. I stopped the car.

When the hitchhiker came over to the car, he looked pretty downcast. Father got out of the car and let him get into the back seat. As we started out, Father began asking him questions. He asked the hitchhiker where he was coming from. He said that he had just left Detroit and was on his way to Chicago to look for a job. Father asked him what happened in Detroit. The hitchhiker said, "I lost my job and couldn't seem to find another one. So I am going to Chicago. Maybe I'll have better luck there." Father asked him if he went to church. He said, "Yes, I am a Catholic."

The next town we were coming to was Niles, Michigan. Father said, "We had better stop to get something to eat." I said, "OK." Then Father asked the hitchhiker if he was hungry. He answered, "Yes. I haven't eaten for two days."

We stopped at a restaurant and pulled into the parking lot. Father had a cardboard box and a valise in the back seat of the car, so I locked the car.

We sat down in the restaurant. The hitchhiker ordered a hot beef sandwich. I ordered the same. Father ordered a plate of fish. While we were eating I noticed Father had pushed some fish toward the back of his plate with his knife. He seemed to be taking his time eating the fish that was in front of him.

The hitchhiker ate his hot beef sandwich up in no time at all. In fact, I hadn't eaten more than half of mine by the time he was through.

Father noticed this and asked him if he was still hungry. He said, "Yes, a little bit." So Father said, "I have this fish you can have. Hand your plate over." Father took his knife and put the fish on the hitchhiker's plate.

As we were leaving the restaurant. Father asked the hitchhiker if he had any money. He answered, "No." So Father gave him about $5.00, and I bought him some cigarettes.

Father said to the hitchhiker, "We are going to Huntington, Indiana, and you are going to Chicago, so we will have to separate here." The hitchhiker said. "Well, I sure appreciate your helping me. I wish I could repay you for what you've done." Father answered, "Well, we are happy to do it. But there is one thing that you can do for us. When you get to Chicago, will you go to the nearest Catholic church and say a prayer for poor sinners." The hitchhiker responded, "Yes, I'll do that!" We then went to the car.

When we got to the car I took the keys out of my pocket to open the door. Father reached in front of me and opened the locked door. I stood there thinking I must be going crazy. I said to Father, "That's odd, I thought I locked the door," and he said. "Oh?" I dropped the subject, but still was puzzled and wondered about it for years...[37]

Once on their way, Maher "asked him a lot of questions on the trip, such as, 'Why is it some people have told me you have powers to cure people?' He said, 'I don't cure anyone, God does it.' I said, 'Well, people say you bless them and they are cured of different ailments.' Solanus answered, 'I have a relic of the true cross and the apostles which I bless people with. If God wishes to cure them, they will be cured if they have the faith.'"[38]

When they arrived at Huntington, another dimension of Solanus's humanity revealed itself in an equally wonderful way. This time it dealt with the hungry Maher, who would be given food even if it was past midnight and he wanted to "go to Mass and Communion in the morning:"

When we got to Huntington it was about 12:30 a.m. Thursday morning. We first went to chapel. Father wanted to thank God for being with us on the trip. After praying, Father bent down and kissed the floor in front of the altar. I might add that we also said the rosary about three times on the way down.

After we left the chapel, he asked me if I was hungry. "Yes," I said. "But it is after 12:00 o'clock and I wanted to go to Mass and Communion in the morning." Father said, "Oh, that's all right. It's only after

11:00 o'clock Detroit time and that's the time we are going by."

Father cut some homemade bread for me and gave me some milk and honey for the bread. After eating he showed me where I was to sleep for the night.

Thursday morning I was awakened by one of the brothers and I went to Mass at 6:30 a.m. in the chapel. Father was celebrating Mass at a side altar. He was like he was in another world.[39]

After breakfast, before returning to Detroit, Maher had the chance to continue his visit with Solanus, along with his recollection of Solanus's thoughts on a subject that had been occupying his thoughts for some time, aggravated by the rise of communism throughout the world:

Father gave me this definition of an atheist and an agnostic. He said, "An atheist is a person who knows there is a God, but denies it, as he wants to live life his own way. He continually tells himself there is no God and finally convinces himself there isn't, and eventually gets to the point in life where he has completely convinced himself there is no God." He said that this is a form of insanity.

"An agnostic is a person who is looking for God and can't see him nor can he establish any reasoning to prove there is one. But eventually this person will find proof there is a God. It may take him some time but he will eventually find the proof there is a God."[40]

While people continued to come to Solanus about their own problems for relief, his own skin ailments gave him no relief. On June 16, 1950, he was taken again to St. Joseph Hospital in Fort Wayne. Somehow such ailments and hospital visits didn't seem to bother him one bit. Rather, upon his return to the quiet of St. Felix he found real peace in its quiet environment. He wrote nostalgically, recalling days on the farm many years before:

> I was in St. Joseph Hospital, Fort Wayne, a couple of weeks myself recently. Thanks be to God for the same and thank him doubly I am back at St. Felix since last Friday. It is quiet here just about a mile from town. With other birds that entertain, I am listening to the simple call of the turtle dove and the quail, so familiar more than seventy-five years back. Their old "bob white" call is musical now. Perhaps because, like an old-time song, it brings back memories of innocent days, maybe, happier dreaming. Deo gratias.[41]

Solanus's union with God, the Creator, naturally found him connecting with all of God's creation. An evening sunset could bring words of deep praise to the source of such beauty. The wonders of nature could hold him wrapped in deep thanks for long periods of time. Of all God's creatures great and small, bees, especially, were Solanus's love. Often on his strolls through the orchards and vineyards of St. Felix, he would stop at the beehives, reflecting on the beauty of the bees.

Now and then bees would alight on his hand. As he watched them move about his hand and fingers, Solanus became utterly fascinated by their intricate construction and operations. He would often then proclaim some words of praise, such as: "My dear God, how could you have created such a marvelous thing!" Other times he would play his harmonica for them.

Because of his love for the bees (who sometimes did not reciprocate, and stung him), Solanus was asked to become the assistant bee-keeper. Each novitiate class had its own story about the credulous soul who would come upon Solanus talking to a bee as he held it in his hand in his room or the corridor. Invariably the novice would be asked by Solanus (who, like other professed friars, was not to talk to novices) to take the bees outside. Inevitably the story would conclude with the novice being stung.

Father Elmer Stoffel, the novice master, also cared for the bees. One day, around this time (1950), he was stung severely. He fell to the ground in great pain. Seeing his coworker in such agony, Solanus gestured a simple blessing toward him. Immediately, Father Elmer recalls, the pain left; he had no ill effects whatever.[42]

That evening, at the time when the friars could talk, the incident of Solanus's blessing of Elmer quickly made the rounds. When Solanus entered the recreation room, they chided him as to why he would go back on his word about not healing the friars because of their need as Capuchins to suffer. When they asked why he cured Elmer (who also had been a regular nemesis to him), Solanus simply said: "But he was dying."

Solanus's easygoing nature often came through, even when he might otherwise have had strong feelings about an issue. One such case dealt with the decision to construct a swimming pool in the backyard. In order to build it, some of the apple trees had to be cut down. This decision created a problem for Solanus both for aesthetic reasons and because he felt it conflicted with the friars' vows of poverty. He judged the pool to be unnecessary and un-Franciscan. However, when it was explained that the novices (who never were allowed out) might get a little release for their pent-up emotions, and that the novices themselves would be building the pool, Solanus actually came to see merit in the idea. He made a point of being one of the building "inspectors" at the construction site each afternoon during his "jog" outdoors.

Besides his jogging (actually fast walking), Solanus regularly practiced the regular schedule of the Capuchins. At noon he ate with the community. Then he went to the priests' recreation room (in those days the brothers and novices each had their own recreation rooms). There he sometimes told tales about his family and childhood (often repetitious) and listened to others' such stories. Other times he would play billiards. "He was no hot shot, but he joined me often in playing billiards," Father Blase recalled. "He didn't make it obvious, but he was trying to make me feel at home, especially since none of the other priests were interested in billiards."[43]

At 1:30 he would take a siesta until 2:00 or 2:30. If he had finished his mail, he would often walk outside, watch the construction of the swimming pool, do some pruning in the orchard, or hoe the garden or ground paths. Other times he walked back and forth praying the Little Office of the Blessed Virgin. He would say the Office with the community at 5:00. At 6:00 he would join the community for supper, followed by a short recreation and night prayer at 7:15. His evenings were usually spent in his room, reading and praying.

If he had had no exercise during the day, he would run around the paths of the friary and orchard, so that, as he said, he could "keep in trim." Father Blase remembers, "He loved to run, especially up and down stairs. After a while, we were able to judge the state of his health by the way he managed the stairs. If he ran, he was feeling well; if he walked, something was wrong."[44]

Other ways Solanus "kept in trim" were by playing tennis and volleyball. He did so into his eighties. In everything he did, he enthusiastically played with all his energy. If he'd stumble or fall, he'd pick himself up and continue as intensely and concentrated as ever—a sign of a healthy competitiveness he never abandoned. Such energy and enthusiasm applied not only to sports but to his life in general.

In 1952 the Province of Saint Joseph split between its eastern and midwestern sections. The New York–New England branch took the name Saint Mary's Province. The Detroit-to-Montana branch kept the name Saint Joseph's. Solanus chose to remain in Saint Joseph's Province. Thus, after the split, it was decided he would stay at Huntington.

With fewer novices, the novitiate for the priest-candidates returned to Detroit. St. Felix became the college of philosophy.

Whether there as novices or philosophy students, recollections of the young Capuchins who spent time at Huntington while Solanus was there have helped balance the image of Solanus from one who never showed negative human emotions to a person who periodically got agitated at their pranks, overly critical about small matters (such as registering his concern in a Midnight Mass sermon to the novices that some friars were trimming their beards), or insistent that Mass start on time because the people "who made a great sacrifice to come in the first place, might not be further inconvenienced." However one thing generally elicited strong reactions from him came when some might question whether God would really forgive sins or answer prayers for needs. Then Solanus's eyes would either flash or well up in tears. Then he'd ask, his voice a tone or so higher, "Aren't we going to let the Lord do anything?"

In June 1953 Brother Booker Ashe (a relative of tennis player Arthur Ashe) replaced Blase as Solanus's secretary. When Booker had come to Huntington as a postulant in 1951, Solanus wrote: "Thank God we have a very promising bouquet of brother-candidates, including a very carefree, happy darky."[45] Even then the term "darky" was insulting and derogatory but many white people remained ignorant of the fact. Solanus's words were certainly meant positively, even if they were paternalistic.

The two struck up a relationship of mutual respect and trust. Booker, who entered the Order with a good educational resume, found that Solanus's effect on him was prophetic:

> In those days the young brothers were sort of lost at Huntington, and we did not receive much instruction. I personally went through a great deal of trepidation and indecision within my own self. I think it was through his encouragement that I was able to persevere. He told me that I would make solemn profession, that I would see my twenty-fifth jubilee, and that I would help to

bring about a lot of changes in the Province. Now I think that many of those things have really come to pass. He even told me that I would do things that no brother had ever done.[46]

Solanus's prophecies about Booker proved true in all cases. After various assignments around the province, Booker helped found and direct the House of Peace in Milwaukee, a large direct-ministry and service program for the inner-city poor. He served on many government commissions. He became the first brother in the history of the modern Capuchin Franciscan Order to become a provincial councilor, serving for two terms. He was president of the clergy group of the National Office of Black Catholics and represented the North American Capuchins at the plenary council of the Capuchin Order which dealt with the theme of "Prayer" at Taize, France. He won numerous awards for his service and talents (such as directing various high school plays for years [often Broadway shows] which brought accolades). Certainly he proved Solanus's prophecy true that he would "do things that no brother has ever done."

In hindsight Booker believed that Solanus influenced him in the uncanny way: he could answer people's letters saying the right thing in the right way at the right time, as Solanus would do himself:

> Every day, I opened his mail, read it and informed him as to what people were writing about and he usually had a word or so to say to people and somehow I was able to get them out. I think it was sort of a miracle in itself, because I certainly was never experienced in that. The letters just came off. And, they were, I must admit, rather beautiful. I'm not an experienced typist but I used to sometimes get out a hundred or two letters a day. And around the various holidays like Christmas, Thanksgiving, Feast of St. Francis, his name day and other days like that, mail would just double or triple.

If I asked him a direct question that someone wrote, he usually would tell me what to write back. Otherwise he would tell me just a word or two to write. He would sometimes say, "Well, you tell Mrs. so and so that she doesn't have to worry about that. She doesn't have to see the doctor again, or, when she sees him again, he will discover there was nothing wrong. But she really doesn't have to because it may be a waste of money since she had to pay a price to see him."

Sometimes people would write back in reply to those kinds of prophecies. At one time, I kept a separate file of such replies. What happened to them after I left, I don't know. But I would say that during the time I worked for Fr. Solanus, there must have been five or six hundred such letters from people who were helped through his words of encouragement, through his prayers, and so on.

It made me very humble, too, because people would write back and thank him for the beautiful letters and words of encouragement. It was what they really needed to resolve the problems they wrote about. Even though I typed it, I looked upon it, certainly, as Fr. Solanus's words.[47]

Besides answering letters for Solanus and helping care for the many guests who came to see him, Booker also acted as Solanus's driver. He recalls:

Whenever I had to drive him anyplace, we always said the rosary. Then we always talked about Christ "in Francis." He very seldom ever talked about Francis without Christ. Christ was always there. Whenever he would relate something to Francis, it was always turned to Christ. And he sort of impressed that upon you, and

> always so beautifully done. It was always important to
> Fr. Solanus to get Christ in everything.[48]

The earlier 1950 proclamation of the dogma of the Assumption of
Mary meant a great deal to Solanus. To him it represented "unprece-
dented progress in the blooming and ripening these later decades and
generations in 'Devotion to Mary,'"[49] It also confirmed him in his
commitment to promote Mary of Agreda's *Mystical City of God*.

Solanus loved jokes; however if they involved impiety, especially
about the Blessed Virgin or the saints, he would take affront and didn't
hesitate to correct those who made them. One who experienced his
fraternal correction was his own local superior, Father Thomas
Aquinas Heidenreich. "One time we were in the recreation room," he
recalled. "I jokingly referred to 'Mary O'Grady!' He said, 'We should
never speak disparagingly of people, especially holy persons. Mary of
Agreda has been recognized by the Church as a holy person.'"[50]

For Solanus devotion to Mary could be an important antidote to
what he considered to be the increase in atheism. Like many in the
1950s (the era of Joe McCarthy), Solanus believed atheistic communism was insidious and pervasive. Being from Appleton, Wisconsin,
Senator McCarthy had many supporters among the Capuchins. That
he often worshipped at St. Joseph (where Solanus celebrated his first
Mass) only made his rhetoric and anticommunism all the more convincing to someone like Solanus. Solanus's support of the anticommunism of Charles Coughlin in the thirties shifted easily to McCarthy.
McCarthy found communists in movie studios, the halls of Congress
and all sorts of places in between.

Given such paranoia around the omnipresence of communists
Solanus's natural naiveté and gullibility could be exploited with stories
about communists penetrating the ranks of the church as well. He
wrote a Grand Rapids Dominican Sister:

There is such a thing as "red communism" stealing into convents and monasteries. Very clever young men have been known to offer themselves as candidates for the Order who have turned out after months, sometimes after years, to have been nothing more than secret promoters of unrest and red communism. Such candidates, I have heard of and in one case at least have known to show themselves very clever and experienced and naturally older than real promising candidates. They are in their late 20's or even middle 30's and, of course, are not too fervent at all, even though they keep the rule fairly to the letter.

Of course, to suspect anyone deliberately without a conscience [sic] observance and prayer, is a rather dangerous course. Nevertheless, self-preservation and "charity begins at home" where right order and charity always must begin. Superiors especially are expected to be on the alert concerning any subject who persists in refusing to speak to, or associate with any other member of the religious family.[51]

Whether Solanus's convictions about such matters was true will never be known for sure; only a history not yet written will reveal the degree to which communists had become as significant as McCarthy and Casey believed them to be.

The early 1950s also found no abatement of Solanus's physical ailments; this demanded ever-more visits to Fort Wayne and Detroit. During 1951, he spent much time in Fort Wayne getting relief. In 1952 he went to Grace Hospital in Detroit and made a great impression on its staff. The fact that he made his bed himself contributed to his popularity. When he left, "doctors, nurses, patients and visitors all formed two lines from his room to the entrance door all seeking his blessing."[52] In 1953 he referred to himself as a "poor, clodding, stupid brother—just at the present a stumbling, three-fourths invalid."[53] In May 1954 blisters

broke out all over his body when a doctor gave him the wrong medicine for an infection.

Despite his failing health and "semi-retirement," Solanus continued to actively promote the missionary activity of the Capuchins
through the Seraphic Mass Association. By now his success had
reached Father Benignus, the head of the Capuchin-Franciscans in
Rome. He wrote a letter of commendation for Solanus's untiring
effort on behalf of the Capuchin missions around the world:

> Dear Father Solanus,
>
> We have heard, through Our Secretary General for
> the Missions, Very Rev. Fr. Tiziano of Verona, of your
> magnificent work for the Seraphic Mass Association.
> Fr. Tiziano was very eloquent in your praise; and when
> We Ourselves examined the details of your work We
> realized the justness of his words. Further, knowing
> that you are no longer young in years We could not but
> marvel at your tremendous zeal and energy, both of
> which reveal a heart and will still youthful.
>
> If your marked success in that work gives Us a pater-
> nal joy and pride, must it not be for you, in the inner
> recesses of your heart, a source of great consolation.
>
> We feel that you, dear Father, will deplore even this
> little publicity, making your own the counsel of Our
> Lord: "when you have done all these things, say we are
> unprofitable servants." Yet, whilst respecting that senti-
> ment, We wish to thank you very sincerely for your
> grand work, and We pray the Lord of the harvest to
> grant you many more fruitful years.[54]

In the first part of 1954, Solanus eagerly prepared for his fiftieth
jubilee of ordination to the priesthood. In mid-July, *The Detroit
Times* ran a feature story about the upcoming celebration. It noted
that the jubilarian:

> ...at 83 stands amazingly erect, although his tall frame is gaunt in its brown homespun habit from many decades of fasting and self-denial.
>
> But his most striking characteristics are his eyes and his voice. The eyes...are the eyes of a man 50 years younger. At times they are shrewd and penetrating, but when he speaks of his faith they shine like the eyes of a child.
>
> His voice is low and warm and somehow it can make his simplest remark sound like a benediction.[55]

Responding to a question as to why God had been so powerful in others' lives through his fifty years of ministry, Solanus shared his conviction that God really wanted to do the same though everyone, not just priests. "One need not be a priest to be an instrument in God's hands," he said. "If a man lives as he should, he will be given the knowledge to aid people. And if we are interested in saving souls we must have an interest in others."[56]

On the jubilee day, Solanus was feted along with the house superior, Thomas Aquinas Heidenreich and Cuthbert Gumbinger (later archbishop of Smyrna, Turkey). Due to the large crowd, the Mass was celebrated at St. Mary in Huntington. The dinner took place a couple blocks away at Sts. Peter and Paul. The meal began at noon and did not conclude until 3:00 "due mainly to the number and length of the after-dinner-speeches."[57] Solanus gave his thank-you by stressing again his main theme: the need to show gratitude and thanks to God.

To celebrate his jubilee, a "purse" was presented to Solanus totaling six thousand dollars. As Solanus read the list of hundreds of donors—who had given donations from 25¢ to $100, tears of thanks glistened in his eyes. Nothing like this, he managed to say, had ever happened to him before. The money was used to redecorate the chapel at St. Felix.

The day after his jubilee, as Solanus and Brother Pius Cotter were talking, Solanus let slip an underlying rationale for his seeming bravado in inviting people to "thank God ahead of time" for favors they requested. Pius had asked Solanus why he always urged people to "thank God in advance for the grace you are about to receive." Solanus explained: "It's like putting God on the spot." Because Jesus promised: "Ask and you will receive" (Matthew 7:7). Solanus, in his simple, direct faith, took Jesus at his word. Because of this promise, he reasoned, people could always "put God on the spot," on the assumption that God would be faithful to what Jesus promised.[58]

While it might be expected that someone celebrating his golden jubilee as a priest might slow down, this was not true of Solanus Casey. While Solanus's leg problems definitely curtailed him, his counseling by letter as well as in person via visits and phone calls never abated. Neither did the reports of wonderful things happening. One of these Solanus recalled in a letter he wrote his sister Margaret in October 1954:

> Last Palm Sunday we had quite the cause for celebration here. It came from Wyandotte, Michigan. A certain Mrs. Magolan called from that suburb of Detroit, saying, "Father, we were figuring on coming down to Huntington next Sunday. But my husband had like a stroke this morning and we don't know where we're at. He is not himself."
>
> That was Thursday, about 9:00 A.M. This family for several years had been bringing at least one bus load of people down to the Corpus Christi celebration. They have wonderful faith.
>
> "Oh, Mrs. Magolan!" I answered. "Where is your faith? I'll tell you. Get your friends to start a triduum of Holy Communions for the glory of God on that day and at the same time in thanksgiving for his answer to

our prayers. We will all be helping tomorrow, Saturday and Sunday."

"Oh!" she exclaimed. "That is grand."

I could almost see the tears in her voice. I said nothing to anyone further about it. But in the meantime I was appointed for the High Mass at 8:00....

Mr. Magolan was the first to receive Holy Communion. He had driven himself about half way, 175 miles. Deo gratias. I'd never seen him before look so well. He's been 100 percent himself ever since.[59]

Another "stranger" who sought Solanus's help but who became a good friend was Frank J. Brady, the president of Frank J. Brady Company of Huntington Woods, Michigan. He noted:

My wife, Katherine M. Brady, was seriously ill approximately in 1955 or 1956. She was in traction in the hospital waiting surgery on a calcified disc in her neck between the fifth and sixth vertebrae. She was in constant pain and could not sleep nights because of it. Her condition had developed into degenerative arthritis due to a whiplash injury incurred when she was a young girl and was in an accident in which her head had gone through the windshield. She had been to a neurosurgeon. The operation had been decided upon as a last resort. Because the operation was so close to the brain, chances of survival were slim.

I had heard of Fr. Solanus for years, but I had never met him. He was then stationed at St. Felix Friary, Huntington, Indiana. A friend of mine, Clarence C. Wetzel, suggested a telephone call to Fr. Solanus. I talked to Fr. Solanus and told him my wife was in the hospital and was going to have the operation. We had four children. He listened for a minute and then said, "Oh, no, she won't have the operation.

She'll be all right. She'll be out in a few days. She'll be
back with those children. Now, tell me how the Tigers
are doing."[60]

It was as uncomplicated as that: Mrs. Brady would be healed. The next
item of business was to get the latest score for the Detroit Tigers baseball team and their rank in the standings. Never abandoning his
enthusiasm for baseball, Solanus followed the Tigers. Whether a healing or baseball—everything could become a source of praise. Mrs.
Brady came home without the operation and gradually improved. "As
far as I am concerned," Frank Brady noted, "It was miraculous."[61]

As he had heard of Father Solanus from others, so Brady told
others about the power God being manifest to many through the
Capuchin at St. Felix. One of these was a nurse whose mother was
seriously ill. Brady noted: "I suggested that the nurse call Fr. Solanus.
She did telephone him in Huntington. Fr. Solanus said, 'Your mother
is quite old. God wants her.' The mother died two days later. The
daughter, being prepared by Fr. Solanus, was reconciled to her
mother's death."[62]

The St. Felix house *Chronicle* (July 21, 1955) noted that "Fr.
Solanus, although 85, is still as busy as ever, consoling all the people
that come to him. Despite the fact that he receives many calls every
day, he is a model to all in his faithfulness to religious exercises. His
favorite pastime is killing the weeds on the lawn and of course he is
never without his gracious smile."[63]

Yet that smile covered tremendous suffering. At times the pain
from his "weeping eczema" and varicose veins became so unbearable
that, in unguarded moments, attentive friars could see him wincing
in pain. Indeed, by January 1956, his ailments had become so severe
they were impossible to hide. Since relief could not be found in
Huntington nor Fort Wayne, it was decided that Brother Gabriel
Badalamenti, the infirmarian, should drive him to Detroit.

They left on January 12.

Solanus praying the Little Office of the Blessed Virgin in the garden, St. Bonaventure Monastery, 1956.

Solanus blessing student friars leaving Huntington for Garrison, N.Y., 1951.

Solanus giving priestly blessing, St. Bonaventure Friary
Chapel, 1956.

Last known picture of Solanus. At
St. John Hospital, summer 1957.

8

THE LAST YEAR

JANUARY 12, 1956–
JULY 31, 1957

Within a week of his arrival in Detroit, Solanus received a diagnosis of skin cancer. A resulting operation seemed successful. As to the rest of his problems, it was concluded that, for a man of his age, he was in quite good shape. As a precaution it was decided he should stay longer in Detroit for recuperation.

On February 15, 1956, Solanus received the news his brother Patrick had died in Seattle. Only a few months before, another brother, Owen, had died in Seattle as well. Now only he, his brother, Monsignor Edward, and two sisters, Margaret (LeDoux), and Genevieve (McCluskey) remained of Bernard and Ellen Casey's sixteen children.

Despite his awareness of life's passing, Solanus was not willing to sit around counting his days. His energy was as great as ever. As far as he was concerned, he could return to counseling in the front office of St. Bonaventure as he had done for so many years before.

However, the local superior and doctor had other thoughts. They thought him to be too weak to bear the burden of the continual stream of people who would come to St. Bonaventure once they knew he had returned to Detroit. Consequently they told the friars not to mention his presence there. The superior, Father Bernard Burke, also told Solanus not to tell people he was in Detroit. "We had to limit his acceptance of phone calls and visits to the monastery office because of his feebleness," he explained: "He was asked not to go to the phone or the Front Office without special permission in order to save his strength. To my knowledge, he complied with my wishes in this regard."[1]

Complying with such orders was not easy. "Why won't they let me see the people?" Solanus asked Brother Ignatius one day.[2] His question was not so much an undermining of his superior's decision but a genuine confusion as to why they would not let him be about his ministry. Nonetheless, he obeyed.

At that time, the assistant superior of St. Bonaventure was Father Lawrence Merten. He noted that efforts to implement these decisions were not always easy because "some people came to the monastery and were very insistent on seeing Fr. Solanus. Sometimes, however," he recalled:

> [T]he Superior had granted permission for limited visits. In the absence of the Superior, I was the Vicar. Once when an insistent visitor continued to ask to see Fr. Solanus, I followed the precedent set by the Superior and granted permission for Fr. Solanus to visit for thirty minutes.
>
> Now the people were always inclined to overstay the allotted time and Fr. Solanus paid no attention to time. He just wanted to help people. So I went in at the end of thirty minutes and concluded the visit. Although it was hard for Fr. Solanus to say goodbye, as his natural inclination would be to spend a longer time, he nevertheless very readily acceded. There were never any arguments. His attitude toward authority was always marvelous.[3]

While the friars kept him from being inundated by the people, their efforts were not assuaging Solanus's ever-failing health. After consulting Solanus's doctors, his friend and provincial, Father Gerald Walker, decided not to return him to Huntington. On May 10, 1956, he was officially transferred from St. Felix to St. Bonaventure.

It happened that Father Elmer Stoffel—whom Solanus had blessed when he got the bee stings at Huntington—had come to Detroit in 1952. With the novitiate again at St. Bonaventure Elmer had moved there in his capacity as novice master.

In those days, all seating in the dining room, in the choir and for all other formal functions was ranked according to class (priest, seminarian and lay brother) and seniority. For this reason Elmer always sat next to Solanus. Because Elmer was in charge of the novices and because some of them had come to Solanus for help, Elmer came to believe Solanus was giving them bad advice. He also thought that, at least to a degree, Solanus liked the accolades that had come his way. As a result, when talking was allowed, Elmer told Solanus his feelings. At times these got expressed as jokes and at other times they came as barbs. No matter the form, the message was clear: Solanus did not measure up to Elmer's expectations.

When he would see Solanus not eating very much, he'd comment: "Are you trying to be a saint?" Or when people would talk about the many wondrous things done through his prayers and presence, he'd say: "You're trying to work miracles and taking the honor for them while the Seraphic Mass Association is doing the work."[4]

Since he sat on the other side of Solanus at meals, Father Lawrence heard these comments:

> These accusatory remarks got a little strong at times, but Fr. Solanus just looked down and continued eating. He would never in any way be grieved or get mad. He took it. Sometimes he laughed, and other times you could see it hurt a little. Other friars kidded him a lot

about many things, even mispronouncing a word. Some would say that he was bluffing the people, but they couldn't get him angry.[5]

In his earlier days, a keen observer of Solanus could sense that he was sensitive to such criticism. While the accusations and barbs no doubt stung, by now Solanus had moved to that point in his spiritual journey that he could be free of others' criticism, especially when it came from the likes of Elmer.[6]

While Solanus had to contend with Elmer, another friar at St. Bonaventure treated him in exactly the opposite manner. Father Gerald Walker, having known and revered Solanus since he was a child in Detroit in the 1920s, was now provincial at St. Bonaventure and one of Solanus's greatest supporters. Where Elmer questioned the motivation underlying Solanus's ministry, Gerald only found deep faith.

One such manifestation of Solanus's "total faith," Gerald loved to tell, came while he was the provincial:

> Faced with what seemed to me would be a tragedy, I asked him to pray that God would spare me from it. He promised that he would. A week passed by. The situation seemed more threatening. I went to see him again to ask if he was praying, as he had promised. He assured me that he was. I went back to my room.
>
> Soon there was a knock on the door, and there was Father Solanus, the tears pouring down his cheeks. Evidently hurting very much, he said, "Gerald, I am so disappointed in you."
>
> Paining to hear that from him, I asked, "Why?"
>
> He said, "Because I thought you had more faith than that!" Then, referring to Jesus' words in the Gospel, he said, "Remember that Jesus said, if you ask, you shall receive."
>
> It was a lesson in faith I needed.
>
> By the way, I then received what I asked for.[7]

While people like Gerald were absolutely convinced about Solanus's faith and holiness, the novices wanted to make sure. Consequently some decided to test him to make sure, for instance, that his prayer was authentic. Identifying contemplative or mystical prayer with freedom from distraction, Capuchin Dan Crosby recalls being in chapel where he appeared to be "completely absorbed in the Lord." This invited a test. So, on his way to his place in chapel a novice would deliberately detour to walk directly in front of Father Solanus. As they knelt they would watch to see if Solanus's eyes would open or at least flutter distractedly. To their amazement, Solanus always passed the test.[8]

While Solanus might appear to be totally "otherworldly" when at prayer, he was very concerned about that world and its events. With the Korean War just ended and the growing threat of nuclear war and the arms race, Solanus became ever more convinced of the need for world peace. Furthermore, he was convinced peace would come only through justice among peoples and prayer.

In one of his letters he enclosed a "Prayer for Peace." He mentioned that, as he prayed it, he sensed that someone with a saddened heart had written it. He noted that "My own heart filled up, at my first official praying thereof."[9] The "Prayer for Peace" which he had typed read:

> Almighty and Eternal Father, God of Wisdom and Mercy whose power exceeds all force of arms and whose protection is the strong defense of all who trust in Thee; enlighten and direct, we beseech Thee, those who bear the heavy responsibility of government throughout the world these days of stress and trial. Grant them the strength to stand firm for what is right and the skill to dispel the fear of discord. Inspire them to be mindful of the horrors of atomic war for victor and vanquished alike, to seek conciliation in truth and patience. Grant the strength to see in every man a brother—that the people of nations may, in this our

last day, enjoy the blessings of a just and lasting peace. Conscious of our own unworthiness, we implore thy mercy on a sinful world in the Name of Thy Divine Son, the Prince of Peace and through the intercession of his Blessed Mother and all the Saints. Queen of all Saints, pray for us. Queen of Peace, pray for us.[10]

While Solanus was very concerned that nations come to new ways of establishing just relations and peace with each other, he spread the same message to husbands and wives, religious in communities, and individuals with their God. As Father Lawrence remembered:

Sometimes those with troubles were told that this was the first requisite to gain God's help—to make their peace with God. Oftentimes he enrolled people in the Seraphic Mass Association so that they might benefit from the Holy Sacrifice of the Mass. Then with the spiritual uplift and the faith inspired by Fr. Solanus, things did go much better. And at times God did grant extraordinary favors. He was so understanding of human hearts and minds, yet he could not understand how it was possible for anyone not to believe in God....[11]

This incredulity regarding the possibility of anyone in their right mind being an atheist was highlighted by another incident recalled by Father Lawrence:

A professed atheist was brought to him. The latter with a bold and flippant front said, "Father, what would you say to a man who does not believe in God?"

Solanus's immediate response was, "I would say that such a man is a fool. The height of insanity is not to believe in God, for only the fool says in his heart that there is no God when the heavens and the earth proclaim his glory."[12]

In a beautiful expansion on the Psalmist's recognition of God's glory throughout creation, Lawrence found the source of such an insight in the way Solanus discovered God's presence within his very being:

> Fr. Solanus discovered God in all the beautiful things he had made, in the grass on which he trod, the flowers he admired. He found God in his own soul. He found him in Divine Providence. "God is so good!" he often said. Even sufferings helped him to unite himself to God. He could say "Thanks be to God" even for pain.[13]

On December 2, 1956, all efforts to shelter Solanus from the people were shattered. A feature article on the one hundredth anniversary of the Capuchins' establishment in the United States ran in *The Detroit Sunday News*. While purportedly highlighting various Capuchin ministries in the midwest province since its 1856 foundation, the house *Chronicle* noted, "Fr. Solanus was spread all over the front cover of the Rotogravure section."[14] Consequently, the real story became the news that Solanus Casey had returned to Detroit. The only quote featured in the article came from Solanus. Responding to a question about the Capuchin Franciscan life of prayer, study, and work: "Fr. Solanus Casey, who is 86 and in his 60th year in the order, said, 'It's like starting heaven here on earth.'"[15]

The article brought a deluge of calls on Monday morning. The house *Chronicle* stated: "The Brothers at the front door office desk were suffering a headache from answering the avalanche of telephone calls from the people who wanted to know whether Father Solanus was available for consultation and blessings."[16] Trying to protect him, the answer to the people's requests was a gentle, but firm, "No." Generally, the people accepted this explanation and then asked simply to be remembered to Solanus.

When Christmas came in 1956 many wondered if it would be Solanus's last. While it turned out to be so, Capuchin Dan Crosby remembered it as very special:

Christmas evening I was on my way to community recreation and stopped in the friary chapel for a visit to the Blessed Sacrament. While kneeling there I heard a familiar squeaky noise coming from the larger church, which I immediately knew was Fr. Solanus playing his violin. I wanted to see the sight, however, and so opened the door from the friary chapel to the main church. There I saw Father Solanus alone in the choir-loft playing Christmas carols on his violin and singing them to the Christ Child.[17]

On January 14, 1957, Solanus celebrated the sixtieth jubilee of his investiture in the habit of the Capuchin Franciscans. That he had found in the province a way to "start heaven on earth" became very evident when it came time for Solanus to renew his vows. The further he went into the vow formulary, the more choked-up he became. By the time he came to the words where he would rededicate his life to "live in obedience, without property, and in chastity," the sense of God's overpowering goodness enveloped him. With his eyes full of tears and his throat too choked-up, Father Giles Soyka stepped in to finish the vows for Solanus.

Solanus renewed his vows that day near where he had also knelt in 1897 to receive the habit, committing himself to begin living the Capuchin Franciscan way of life. In describing the latter 1957 ceremony to his brother Monsignor Edward, Solanus wrote:

I would hardly know how it could have been more beautiful, under the simple circumstances. ...I had come to the holy novitiate Christmas eve. It was six months ahead of the seven other students who joined me the following July. They are all gone to Heaven now, we hope, with the senior of them all, Father Damasus, in his 90th year. Had he waited five months longer, he and I would have had our golden jubilee together. He was patient and joyful to the last. May he be privileged to await in the peace of the saints, the inconceivable glory of the general resurrection.

Please pardon the digression. Today, Deo Gratias, it is sixty years and sixty days since I was invested.[18]

While his life as a Capuchin Franciscan had been lived without the faculties to formally preach or hear confessions his way of embracing its evangelical witness probably reached more people than had any other friar in the one hundred–plus years of the Capuchins' presence in the United States. His humble acceptance of his superiors' decision to keep him from hearing confessions had been embraced throughout his life in a spirit of equanimity. This was made clear from the recollection of Father Michael Dalton, a priest of the London, Ontario Diocese, who visited St. Bonaventure during Lent of 1957:

> I said Mass in the monastery chapel and a very elderly friar served my Mass. I did not know then that he was a priest. I was quite impressed when I saw him kneel and kiss the floor when he passed in front of the tabernacle. I thought it very devout and humble.
>
> After Mass he took me in for breakfast. Taking me down a long monastery hall, he went into a room with the name "Fr. Solanus" over the door. When I saw who he was I asked him to hear my confession. He is the only priest in seventy-five years who refused absolution saying, "I'm only a simplex priest—no faculties to absolve."
>
> He told me, however, that his work in the office, meeting troubled humanity, was similar to confession. He talked at breakfast of being a streetcar operator in his youth.
>
> At eighty-six years he was my oldest altar boy.[19]

That Solanus could serve at the Mass celebrated by Father Dalton, as well as kiss the floor in reverence to the Blessed Sacrament (which was a Capuchin custom in those days), attests to the fact that, during late winter and early spring, Solanus had experienced some welcome respite from his various ailments.

Feeling more strength, Solanus was able to be more available to others in their pain. As he did so, he often (as he had done with Father Dalton) spoke about his childhood and the happy memories he recalled about his family. In the case of Earl and Adeline Striewski and their son Tommy, such a visit spanned two hours. He brought up many things about his boyhood and life on the farm. He spoke about his brothers and sisters—all fifteen of them—whom he said were all "bright." "But," he said, in words that indicate he had accepted the notion of himself being intellectually challenged: "I was not very bright; all the others were more brilliant than I." To support this reasoning, he recalled the difficulties he had in school. And then he added, "But God was good to me."[20]

The statement about God's goodness brought Solanus to a rare moment of candor. He started telling the Striewskis about the many favors people had received. Interspersed with such stories he would say: "Oh, God is so good," as tears rolled down his cheeks. He spoke about people who had come to him and the trials and troubles they brought and how they had found relief. Even though the dinner bell rang, Father Solanus seemed compelled to talk about God's goodness and power to heal.

Another person who considered herself fortunate to communicate with Solanus during the spring of 1957 was Mrs. Edward Klimczak. In March she called St. Bonaventure. "When I called, I asked to speak to Father. The priest who answered the phone told me Fr. Solanus was too ill to come to the phone. I asked Father if I could tell him what I wanted and then he could ask Fr. Solanus to pray for this intention." Hearing this, the friar said, "Just a minute." She recalled:

After a short wait I had the joy of hearing the words, "Fr. Solanus speaking." Fr. Solanus then asked me to tell him my problem. I have often thought since that time that only God and those very close to him knew what it had cost him to answer that phone call, being as ill as he then must have been.

His voice sounded weak but one of the things I remember most about it was the sound of joy in his voice and his fervent and joyous phrases praising God.

In a unique account of their conversation, she recalls that Solanus made it clear that, if the request she sought would be answered, she would have to respond by seeking to know more about Christ. In her case this involved examining the mysteries of Mary and her Son, as contained in the writings of Mary of Agreda. Even if told not to be connected with Ray Garland, Solanus never stopped promoting the *Mystical City of God*:

I asked Fr. Solanus's help for my mother, a good practicing Catholic, who after many years of hardship and an extremely distressing trial was at the point of despair. After speaking with Fr. Solanus, I sat down immediately and wrote down our conversation while it was still fresh in my mind. The only thing I have added to the notes was to put in (Mrs. Klimczak) and (Fr. Solanus) at the beginning of each quotation. I recopied the notes as the original copy is quite faded and battered....

Mrs. Klimczak: "Fr. Solanus, did Father tell you what I had just told him?"

Fr. Solanus: "No, I was just finishing my prayers."

I repeated what I had said to the priest that answered the phone ending with, "I thought you would tell us what to do, Father."

Fr. Solanus: "Have you heard of *The City of God,* the volumes written by Mother Mary Agreda?"

Mrs. Klimczak: "Yes."

Fr. Solanus: "It was dictated by the Holy Mother herself, written at her command. Do you know what I mean?"

Mrs. Klimczak: "Yes, Father, it's a book, isn't it?"

Fr. Solanus: "Yes, it is four volumes. You need not get all of them at once, just the first volume."

Mrs. Klimczak: "Yes, I know right where I can send for it."

Fr. Solanus: "Yes. Well get the first volume and begin reading it, all the family together and promise the Blessed Mother that if she will take all into her hands, you will read this book. I am sure if you read this first volume you will want to read the rest. You will be amazed at the wonderful change that will take place in your family. I am sure everything will turn out all right. God be praised. It will all work out for the greater honor and glory of God. Glory be to God!"

Fr. Solanus asked about my family and I told him a little about my husband, our children, and my mother, two brothers and sister with whom we were living. He then asked:

Fr. Solanus: "Do you receive Holy Communion regularly?"

Mrs. Klimczak: "Yes, Father, every Sunday."

Fr. Solanus: "Try to go more often, Where are you?"

Mrs. Klimczak: "I'm calling from Alpena, Michigan."

Fr. Solanus: "That's hm-m-m."

Mrs. Klimczak: "It's 250 miles from Detroit. North."

Fr. Solanus: "Yes, I want you [all] to come to see me. I would like to see you."

Mrs. Klimczak: "Oh, yes. Father, we would like very much to see you. Maybe I could bring my father." Fr. Solanus: "Yes, come to see me. I have received many great favors. On the 8th of this month I received a call from Oakland, California, from my niece, my oldest sister's daughter. She said her mother's palate had been bothering her and she went to her dentist and found she had cancer. Her husband is an invalid, the result of a heart attack. She has had a hard time to get along. Just last week a lady came to see me, very distressed and at the point of committing suicide. I told her about my sister and asked her to pray for her (Father's sister). She said, 'Why don't you call your sister now? I'll pay for the call.' I did. The thought of suicide passed in a moment like a shadow. God is never outdone in generosity. He will always take care of you. All will be well again. Don't delay. Do your part right away. Don't wait. It may be too late. Begin right away. If you do your part the Blessed Mother will take care of everything. Don't worry. Everything will be all right. Don't worry anymore. What is your name?"

Mrs. Klimczak: "Mrs. Ed. Klimczak, Mary."

Fr. Solanus: "Mrs. Klimczak, (here he paused and then said) God bless you. (Then added) As sure as the sun is now rising, things will change today. Come to see me. Promise you will come."

Mrs. Klimczak: "Yes, Father, we will come."

We did not visit Fr. Solanus while he was still alive, but I did not forget my promise to come and see him. So when we were able to go to Detroit, my husband, my sister and I visited Father's grave. It was a completely overcast day. As we knelt at Father's grave the sun broke through the clouds briefly almost as though

Father was letting us know he knew we were keeping my promise to visit him.

Yes, I did get the books *The City of God*. I sent out an order for them that day explaining that I needed my books right away to fulfill the request Fr. Solanus made. I enclosed all the money I could spare, $7.00. They wrote back saying that I would have to buy the set of books (4) and that since my situation was unusual, they would accept payments, whatever I could send, until the books were paid for—something they just did not do normally. In the meantime so as not to lose any time in beginning to keep our promise to do our part if the Blessed Mother would take all in her hands, I asked the Sister at our parish convent if they had a copy of the first volume of *The City of God* that I could borrow until our books arrived. They had the abridged copy and lent it to us. And we, as a family, mother, brothers, young sister, husband and son read the book each evening.

Fr. Solanus had said that we need only read the first volume of *The City of God*, but he was sure that once we began reading it we would want to read the others as well. And of course we did.

Mother was able to take courage and go on after I told her everything Fr. Solanus had said. We did all that Fr. Solanus told us to do, beginning that same day. Our prayers were answered. My Father, who was living a sinful life was given the grace to turn away and begin the long road back to Jesus.[21]

In early May, when Solanus's skin eruptions appeared again, his doctors diagnosed the lesions as severe erysipelas. On May 15 Solanus was taken by ambulance to St. John's Hospital. Once there his condition worsened; it appeared he was close to death. He was anointed, and an oxygen tent was placed over him to help him breathe. With the oxygen he rallied. He began singing a hymn of thanks to the Blessed Virgin. Brother Gabriel, assigned to care for Solanus, had told him to stop singing lest he use up the little strength he had left. Though he thought Gabriel's way was somewhat officious, Solanus stopped. Even though Gabriel was a Third Order Brother and Solanus a priest, Gabriel was given authority to care for him. Thus, for Solanus, obeying Gabriel was obeying God.

With his strength renewed, his humor became more evident. When one of the nurses, Sister Arthur Ann, came into his room, she said, "Father, throughout the years I have so often heard people speak of you."

"Yes," he replied, "people often speak of Jesse James too,"

"But these people, Father, spoke of wonderful things that occurred through your prayers for them."

"Ah," he conceded, "many wonderful things have happened—but the people had faith."

Another day Sister Arthur Ann came into his room and asked, "How about a blessing, Father?"

"All right," he smiled, "I'll take one!"

After blessing her, he began talking about the rise in materialism and consumerism. He said, "So often people hope to find happiness in money or the things money buys. If only they would stop running around, acquiring this and that, instead of seeking happiness only where it can be found—in love of God. They are so foolish."

Improving daily, Solanus enjoyed being taken in his wheelchair to chapel. There he enlisted various people to read for him *The Mystical City of God*. Others would pray the rosary with him. When he was strong enough, he would celebrate the liturgy.

Whenever he went to chapel the word quickly spread. People would come into the corridors asking for a blessing, or would come to the chapel to participate in his celebration of the liturgy. At the end, they would ask Solanus to bless them or pray for their intentions. Even though he did not like the personal attention that he was receiving, he would always respond gently and as generously as he could.

One day he asked Sister Arthur Ann if she would pray the rosary with him. Taking her own rosary, she said, "Father, will you use my rosary? Then I can regard it as a keepsake associated with you." Instead of protesting, he reluctantly reached out saying: "All right, give it to me."

Solanus went between St. Bonaventure and St. John two times. However, on July 2 he went to St. John and would not return.

Even though the erysipelas was creating severe discomfort, another nurse, Sister M. Margretta, recalled:

> A Sister companion and I often read to him—always from *The Mystical City of God.* Always, too, he would precede the reading by asking us to recite with him a prayer to the Holy Spirit. As we read, he would close his eyes, and seem to doze. But let the word be misread, and he would open his eyes, and we'd note a twinkle in them as he corrected us. Or some passage would strike him, and he would exclaim—"Glory to God."
>
> He told us that he had "prayed" the four volumes of *The Mystical City of God* through three times, kneeling.
>
> His sickness brought excruciating suffering. He developed a skin reaction that enveloped his entire body. This alone caused intense pain. Tubes, needles, examinations— these added to his discomfort.
>
> Yet there was never a complaint from him, and he was rational at intervals even on the morning of his death.
>
> In his presence it was impossible not to feel his Christ-likeness, his genuine simplicity and humility, his great love for mankind, his selflessness. Even in his pain, he wanted to continue working to bring more

people closer to God. "I can't die," we overheard him say, "until everyone loves him."

...He frequently spoke of God's mercy with such childlike tenderness that tears came into his eyes. "God is so good," he would say, and then repeat slowly and quietly, "Glory be to God, Glory be to God."

The Sisters realized that he was suffering intense pain, and sought to alleviate it. "Where do you hurt, Father?" one compassionately asked.

"Oh, I hurt all over—thanks be to God," he responded.

Because of poor nutrition and continuous intravenous feedings, his hands had become red and raw. "Your poor hands," said Sister Arthur Ann, as she prepared to remove a needle. "I hate having to remove the adhesive tape."

"Well, Sister, don't feel badly about it," he comforted her. "Look at our Lord's hands."

Sister Carmella, one of those who read to him, noted that one would go in and out of the room, and he wouldn't know it. His mind was elsewhere. He seemed to be thinking continuously of the love of God. "The love of God," he would say, "is everything." As he said this, his face would shine with an inner light.[22]

Once, when Brother Ignatius Milne entered his hospital room, he saw Solanus scratching himself. "Gee, Father, you must be hurting quite a bit," he said. Without hesitation Solanus replied, "Would to God it was 10,000 times worse."[23] When Gerald Walker visited, he asked, "Where do you hurt, Father?" Solanus said simply: "My whole body hurts. Thanks be to God. Thanks be to God." Then he added: "I am offering my sufferings that all might be one. Oh, if I could only live to see the conversion of the whole world."[24]

Gerald remembered how Solanus explained to him the day before he died how he found his suffering fitting into his life's purpose:

> I looked on my whole life as giving, and I want to give until there is nothing left of me to give. So, I prayed that, when I come to die, I might be perfectly conscious, so that with a deliberate act I can give my last breath to God. I looked at him there on his deathbed, clothed only in a little hospital gown, a rosary in one hand and a little relic in the other and felt like crying out, "My God, there is scarcely anything left of him to give."[25]

Before he left, Solanus said to Gerald, "Tomorrow will be a beautiful day." They both knew that Solanus was not talking about the weather.

Knowing that Solanus had little time to live, Monsignor Edward had come to Detroit, as had his sister-in-law, Martha, the recently widowed wife of Owen. She arrived on the feast of Saint Martha and Solanus was alert enough to make the connection. As the administrator of a nursing home in Seattle, Martha used her expertise to keep visitors at bay.

On Wednesday, July 31, Monsignor Edward celebrated an early Mass. Around 8:00 he visited Solanus. Solanus seemed his old self; better than Edward had observed the last few days. Though he tried to stop him, Solanus seemed compelled to talk about something that had come to dominate his thinking and conversation—in the same way the Fourth Gospel recalls of Jesus' last day: his passionate desire for the world's conversion and need "to be one."

Feeling that Solanus seemed so much better, Edward went to his room in the hospital to write the relatives that things were improving.

Around eleven o'clock, a nurse came to bathe Solanus. She took away his rosary and the relic he was holding and then slipped off the hospital gown from his frail body. While bathing him she could hear Solanus whispering in a voice too weak for her to catch the words. As she held him in this way he suddenly opened his eyes widely and stretched out his arms, saying very clearly: "I give my soul to Jesus Christ." Falling back, he died.

It was 11:00 AM, July 31, 1957. Fifty-three years before, to the hour, Solanus Casey began celebrating his First Solemn Mass in Appleton, Wisconsin. Now his own sacrifice of praise was complete. He had given his very body for the life and unity of the world. God now had accepted his offering.

The friars had prepared for this day. Knowing the numbers of people who would want to come to his wake and funeral, it had been determined that it would be better to have the wake for Father Solanus at a funeral home rather than the friary chapel. So his body was taken to Van Lerberghe Funeral Home. His death was announced over the radio and television with the word that mourners could come to the mortuary at 10:00 the next morning.

At 6:30 AM, people began to gather. When allowed to file by the open coffin they touched his body or touched religious articles to it. People came with infants; teenagers approached the coffin with the deepest respect and awe. There were many priests and religious. One after another, they told the Capuchins story after story of Solanus's impact on them and their families. One said to Father Gerald:

> "...meet my son. Fifteen years ago he was dying of polio, Fr. Solanus blessed him, and today he is in the best of health." Someone else would introduce an elderly lady, saying: "Father, meet my mother. She was dying of cancer and Father blessed her, and she is here tonight." Others would tell us that they themselves were here because he (allegedly) had cured them of some serious illness when they were doomed to die.... One lady began to cry and pointed to him saying, "He was the best friend I had in the world. Some years ago I was in utter despair and just wanted to die. I spoke to him and began to live again."[26]

One of the five thousand coming that day was Bernadette Nowak. After her first child she had lost three babies by miscarriage and was desperate to have a second child. Her blood type was RH negative—a serious problem in those days for a woman hoping to have children.

In December 1956, she began to suspect that she might be pregnant. So she immediately wrote Solanus a letter, recalling the fact that he had helped her fifteen years before:

> I addressed it to the Monastery with a note attached saying that if Father was too ill, not to bother him with my problems. In the letter I asked him to pray that I could have a living, normal baby. I also explained my previous medical history. Shortly after, I received a reply saying Fr. Solanus had been very happy to have the letter and would indeed pray for such a good intention. He urged me to name my child now after two of God's saints, enroll the intention in the Seraphic Mass Association along with enrolling the Poor Souls. I did so. I also promised God to call my child, if a boy, Anthony Joseph. I cannot remember the girl's name I chose, but I think it was Mary Anne. My pregnancy progressed uneventfully and the baby grew. Fr. Solanus died a month before the baby was due. I went to Van Lerberghe Funeral Home to view his body. The baby had lain so quietly within me the past few days, and when I approached the casket, the baby seemed to leap inside. I could see my dress moving and I was embarrassed. I felt sad because I wanted to tell the good news to Fr. Solanus and now I could not do so…. During the labor I, indeed, felt a comforting presence although I was in the "preparation room" all alone the entire time except for an occasional visit by a doctor or nurse. It was a swift, easy, uncomplicated delivery. Joseph was born with the cord around his neck, twice, and it had a knot in it. Despite all these things, the baby was fine

and I never felt better. I was up and around and at home in three days.[27]

At 10:00 the next day, Friday, the body of Father Solanus returned to St. Bonaventure chapel. People were already lined up to pay their last respects. For twelve hours, until the doors closed at 10:30 that night, people—at least ten thousand that day—filed past the coffin where the thin old man laid in his rough brown habit, a rosary in his hands, a stole around his neck, and the Franciscan Rule and Capuchin Constitutions at his side.

On Saturday after the regular 8:00 AM Mass, the crowds were asked to leave the chapel that it might be prepared for the funeral liturgy. Upon reopening, the pews filled immediately. Loudspeakers were set up for the people who now lined the sidewalks of both sides of Mt. Elliott Street. A squadron of police had been sent to keep order and to make sure there would be no disruptions of people seeking a relic or remembrance of the man whom people were already calling a saint. However, they need not have worried. "I was present for his funeral." Father Bernard Burke recalled: "The calm and the order that pervaded the crowd, to my mind, was a miracle itself. Even the police officers were surprised at the calmness of such a large crowd."[28]

Monsignor Edward Casey, now the only surviving brother of the Caseys, celebrated the Mass. Bishop Henry E. Donnelly paid a final tribute on behalf of the clergy and people of the Detroit archdiocese. Father Gerald Walker preached the funeral sermon.

Gerald spoke not so much as the provincial superior of Solanus, but as his spiritual son and disciple: "Fr. Solanus was a man I loved dearly," he began. He stopped often, choking back his tears. In concluding he recalled the "two loves" of Solanus—the sick and the poor—and said:

> His was a life of service and love for people like me and you. When he was not himself sick, he nevertheless suffered with and for you that were sick. When he was not

physically hungry, he hungered with people like you. He
had a Divine love for people. He loved people for what
he could do for them—and for God, through them.[29]

After the funeral liturgy, the friars carried the body of their brother to
his resting place in the friary cemetery next to St. Bonaventure
monastery. Solanus often had gone there to pray for other deceased
brothers who had preceded him. Now he would be with them sharing
in their eternal reward. As he never saw himself as any different than
these brothers in life, so in death, his grave marker would be no
different than these and those who would follow him:

Overlooking his and the others' gravestone was a large granite slab
covered with a bas-relief of Saint Francis. He is represented proclaim-
ing the words he added near his own death from the Canticle of
Creation: "Praised be the Lord for Our Sister Bodily Death." Toward
the bottom of the monument is the motto of the Capuchin
Franciscans: the dream Solanus Casey spent trying to experience in his
life and express in his living:

"MY GOD and MY ALL!"

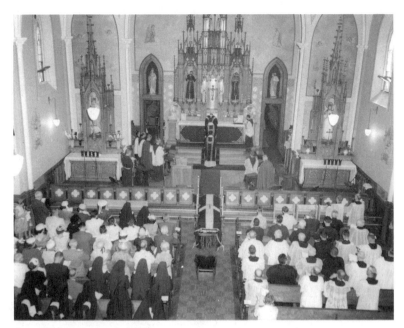

Funeral Mass, August 3, 1957.

Funeral procession from the chapel to the friary cemetery, St. Bonaventure, August 3, 1957.

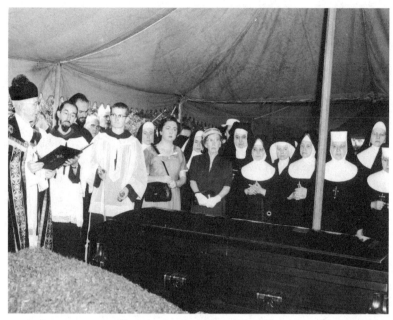

Monsignor Edward Casey saying Prayers of Commitment, at the burial of Solanus Casey in St. Bonaventure Friary cemetery, August 3, 1957.

People praying at gravesite of Solanus Casey, 1957.

9

THE SPIRITUALITY OF SOLANUS CASEY

Solanus Casey died in the last half of the twentieth century. That century also gave birth to one of its greatest Catholic theologians, Karl Rahner. Rahner once noted that "the Christian of the future will be a mystic or he will not exist Christian at all."[1]

Solanus Casey would never have considered himself a mystic but, paradoxically, his very insights about atheism point to his being so. Furthermore, he was not only a mystic, but a mystic in action: one who combined in himself the contemplative and active dimensions of the God-experience in such a way that he became a Christ-figure for many people.

The twentieth century called for such a mysticism in action. On the feast of the Transfiguration in 1945 it witnessed history's most horrific release of negative energy: the atomic bombing of Hiroshima, followed by Nagasaki. Solanus saw atomic weapons and the resulting "Cold War" not only as manifestations of people's lack of faith and the rise of de-facto atheism among Christians who professed to believe; he found such infidelity as evidencing a crisis of cosmic consequences. "And just these days of atomic invention," he wrote in apocalyptic imagery, "it would seem that God might be permitting men without faith to be preparing the fearfully poisoned lightning fires with which he will arm his angels of wrath on an adulterous, defiant, atheistic generation."[2]

Solanus Casey interpreted the conflicts of his time as grounded in theoretical or practical atheism. Theoretical atheism involved one's denial of God's existence; practical atheism stood for the lack of faith-in-action in people who embraced their culture's patterns to the detriment of their professed beliefs. The antidote to both he found within his notion of religion.

For him, religion was the core of one's psyche—it represented our natural attraction to God and others. This is evident in a response he made to a policeman named Mack. When he said he had become an atheist, Solanus wrote, with tongue in cheek:

> Many a time, however, I have wondered if "big W. Mack" ever tried to realize in any way what he has been missing in refusing to believe in RELIGION.... Of course, the very fact that I respect you as I do, ought to be proof sufficient that I am confident that you cannot be a true atheist, except possibly such a one as have been heard to thank God for their atheism![3]

No single topic preoccupied Solanus more than "religion." He called it: "The science of our happy relationship with and our providential dependence on God and our neighbor."

Solanus's convictions about "religion" were not defined by its meaning in the middle ages as referring to "religious life" nor by its latter application to the "religions" that populate our world. Rather he used the image equally with Protestants as well as Catholics, along with Jews and other Christians, who acted on their beliefs in good conscience. In this approach, his use of the term means what is known today as faith or "spirituality."

Spirituality is the experience and expression of the nature and activity of a supreme reality. Solanus experienced this supreme reality as God and expressed the demands (or invitation) connected to that experience in his life in ministry and community. Solanus considered religion to be a science, but not in the sense of an academic study. It was the way people experienced God and expressed that experience in their life with others.

In effect, Solanus's definition of religion involved the two key components of what Jesus said constituted the fulfillment of "the whole law and the prophets" (that is, all religion): "You shall love the Lord your God with all your heart, and with all your soul, and with all your mind. This is the greatest and the first commandment. And a second is like it: You shall love your neighbor as yourself" (Matthew 22:37–39). This insight was echoed years later when Pope Benedict XVI declared that "True religion consists of love of God and love of neighbor."[4]

Given the theology of the time, it is not surprising that Solanus considered religion a science. After all, he had been taught that theology is faith seeking understanding. Furthermore he found understanding relating to reason and rationality, which he considered the realm of science. Consequently, for Solanus, what could be more reasonable and rational than God and our response to God by love? "There is nothing more rational in reason than to love God," he wrote. "By stifling reason and gratitude, sin begets atheism—atheism, the unqualified climax of intellectual insanity, of moral degeneracy, of diabolical blasphemy."[5]

To better understand how Solanus's thoughts about rational knowledge of God revealed his own mystical knowledge, we need to consider five possible ways people come to know all reality, including their understanding of God. The first deals with the material world outside ourselves which we acknowledge through our senses. The second arises from the reflections we have about this sensed world. The third form of knowing deals with the application of reason to what we sense and how we reflect on these sensations. The fourth level adds intuition to the first three levels; consequently intuition and rationality combined reveal a highly developed mind. The fifth level of knowing goes beyond the other four to the level of mystical experience. At this level, such a person has a direct and highly personalized experience of that which simply is; this experience convinces them of the rightness of the experience. This experience becomes the lens through which the mystic views life. For the mystic this experience grounds all ways of knowing; it is ultimate rationality. We see this in the call of Isaiah found in Isaiah 6; once he experienced God's holiness all previously understood notions of God were viewed as ungodly or sinful. Given his own experience of God, Solanus could not possibly fathom how anyone could say there was no God. Consequently only the fool—an irrational being—could say there is no God.

For Solanus, knowing God demanded a threefold response: appreciation, love and service. He wrote that everyone's "purpose as a rational creature, is to recognize and to know his Creator, so as to be able, intelligently to love him, confidently to hope in him, and gratefully to serve him."[6] Through knowledge, love, appreciation and service, Solanus found realized his definition of religion: the science of our happy relationship with and our providential dependence on God and our neighbor. In another elaboration on this theme he wrote: "Our Faith—Religion, is the science of our happy dependence upon God and our neighbor—of our living in his grace and dying in his love."[7]

An examination of Solanus's definition of religion (or faith) reveals two equally important elements. First, it is the science of our happy relationship with God and our neighbor. Second, this religion reveals our providential dependence on God and our neighbor. Besides witnessing to these two poles of all spirituality (as well as in the testimony of those who knew him), these elements of the great commandment found their unique articulation in Solanus's convictions regarding what he called thankfulness, gratefulness or appreciation. In his continual stress on the need for gratitude, Solanus indeed shows himself to be a mystic-in-action and, in the process, a living embodiment of the words of Meister Eckehart: "If the only prayer you said in your whole life was, 'thank you,' that would suffice."

The rest of this final chapter will discuss how these themes come alive in his spirituality.

1. RELIGION IS THE SCIENCE OF OUR HAPPY RELATIONSHIP WITH GOD AND OUR NEIGHBOR.

Religion is about life and life involves our relationships with self, God and others. For Solanus religion could never be limited to one's personal experience of God or self; it also had to be communal.

As early as the novitiate he realized that religion deals with our way of being connected to God as well as others. Thus his novitiate jottings contain a brief entry into his notebook after the phrase Pater Noster, stressing the "noster." In a special way, being Catholic, he also found in the "our" the "*totius ecclesiae*," the whole church.

At a time when people arranged and ranked various callings according to a God-ordered hierarchy in the Roman Catholic church, Solanus did not consider his vocation any greater or lesser than any other Christian's. "We should be grateful for and love the vocation to which God has called us." Solanus wrote. "This applies to every vocation, because after all, what a privilege it is to serve God—even in the least capacity."[8] Fidelity to one's call, he believed, was the invitation to Christians and non-Christians alike. As Pope Benedict XVI would say years later: "to become a saint is the task of every Christian, and what's more, we could even say it's the task of everyone!"[9] While it is clear he did not consider his own call as better than others', he did value it deeply. "How can we ever be grateful as we ought to be for such a vocation in the Order of the Poverello of Assisi?,"[10] he once wrote. Novices often heard the same thing from his lips ink a slightly different way: "If only we'd appreciate what it means to be a Capuchin!"

Next, authentic religion (or spirituality) involves a certain way of being connected: "our *happy* relationship with God and our neighbor." All personal happiness begins with acceptance of oneself in a way that includes others. Solanus Casey was a happy man. His happy demeanor with himself evidenced itself in his deep equanimity and peace. His positive sense of himself was based in an awareness and sense of call and purpose. The source of this happiness came from his discovery of God's reign or life within himself; this was the pearl of great price Jesus talked about in the Gospel (Matthew 13:46). Having found this pearl, he could joyfully "sell" whatever undermined his happy relationship with God and others.

Solanus's positive relationship with himself and others evidenced the fruit of the Spirit at work in him, especially in his charity, joy and peace. Through this Spirit, God was not beyond his experience— "out there" or beyond himself. Rather he found God deeply within himself, others and everything in creation.

God was the very ground of his being, the source of his power. He referred to this relationship as a kind of "blending" of God's existence to his.[11] So "blended" with God, he was empowered to continue God's work of creation which began in Genesis and continued in Jesus of Nazareth. Now, in the twentieth century, the God "in heaven" had come on earth in the person of Solanus of Prescott, Wisconsin. What Jesus did in Capernaum and Jerusalem, Solanus was to imitate in Detroit, New York and wherever obedience to his superiors might take him.

Solanus believed that God had given every human being the divine grace of power to become a cocreator with God. "In his divine economy," Solanus wrote, "God has honored his creatures—most especially rational ones—by giving them each according to his ability, a part of his own work to do—by participation in his own divine activity."[12] "We are continually immersed in God's merciful grace like the air that permeates us," he wrote.[13] Consequently, he believed that fidelity to this grace was a sure path to holiness: "Were we only to correspond to God's graces, continually being showered down on everyone of us, we would be able to pass from being great sinners one day to be great saints the next."[14] The God that Solanus continually talked about was not the Father, the Son or the Holy Spirit of the Trinity. His faith was simply, generically, in "God." Believing with almost a "certain" belief in this God, his faith in this God was characterized by another key virtue promoted by Saint Paul: thanksgiving.

As Solanus looked at his times he discovered much unhappiness, worry and anxiety. For him, such alienation spelled the absence of sufficient faith. "Humanity's sad weakness," he wrote, is "lack of faith and, consequently, want of confidence in God."[15] Solanus connected peoples' worry and sadness with their lack of faith and lack of confidence. Thus he continually urged people to nourish their faith and confidence in God. "In fostering confidence," he noted, "we greatly eliminate the danger of sadness that frustrates God's merciful designs."[16] The confident faith that Solanus talked about represents what people refer to today as the result of having a personal relationship with God that leads to confidence and commitment. No worry was worth the erosion of that confidence in God which anxiety represents. In fact, the only worry Solanus might allow in others was to be directed at their commitment regarding "the little progress we make in conversion and perfection."[17]

No friar ever recalls Solanus's manifesting excessive worry, anxiety or depression. Rather they continually heard words from Solanus that manifested a deep sense of gratefulness for God's many gifts received in the past and the future. In a unique way, love and service of God and neighbor were cohorts of a life defined by appreciation, thanksgiving and gratefulness. Capuchin Dan Crosby recalls:

> The word I heard more often than any other on Solanus's lips was "appreciate." To me it sums up his whole spirituality, so much akin to that of Saint Francis who was constantly filled with praise and gratitude to God for his blessings. Frequently he would say, "If only we would appreciate our faith" or "If only we would appreciate what it means to be a Capuchin." The word "appreciate" came from his lips like honey, in the same

way that Celano describes Saint Francis' saying the
word "Bethlehem."[18]

Dan recalls a humorous incident that reinforced this notion, while, at
the same time, bringing out "as well his deep contemplative attitude:"

> One Sunday morning in 1956 the novices gathered in
> the choir loft at Saint Bonaventure's in Detroit for the
> 9:00 o'clock High Mass. Father Solanus sat directly in
> front of me. I was a novice. Father Cuthbert Gumbinger
> celebrated the Mass. In his sermon he told a story about
> a farmer and his donkey, except that he used the term
> "ass." Hearing this unaccustomed word the novices
> broke into laughter. My laugh was more of a loud snort
> and so Solanus turned around to say to me: "The trou-
> ble with us is that we don't appreciate what he is trying
> to tell us. If we did appreciate it, we wouldn't think it
> was so funny." At this I only laughed the louder, but I
> have never forgotten this and have come to appreciate
> deeply his meaning of appreciation.[19]

This humorous incident reveals much about core elements of the spirituality of Solanus Casey. First of all, his mystical grounding is evidenced in the way he listened to Cuthbert's homily that he might be
"formed by the Word" and that he might deepen his "happy relationship" with God. His desire to get beyond the surface words of the
homily to its deeper message is clear from his suggestion to Dan that
he try to discover "what he's trying to tell us." Secondly, Solanus's own
happy relationship with neighbor appears in the way he did not shame
or ridicule the young novice but acknowledged that they both shared
a common lack: "the trouble *with us*." And, finally, their shared problem was revealed further in that nobody can appreciate deeply enough
God's multiple forms of revelation in our lives—even if it comes in
words like Cuthbert's!

How did Solanus cultivate his own happy relationship with God? By prayer (personal and communal), the celebration of the sacraments, devotion to the saints, especially the Blessed Virgin, the practice of discipline through bearing crosses and the practice of charity toward all.

First of all, prayer connects us to God. The greater our relationship with God the greater our confidence in God. Authentic prayer generates confidence, and confidence gives rise to gratitude and thanks. Because these attitudes of gratitude and thanks characterized his own personal and confident relationship with God, Solanus invited many others (besides Dan the novice) to deeper faith and prayer that would give rise to these attitudes as well. In a remarkable letter he wrote to a woman experiencing anxiety and a deep sense of failure:

> Why do we have discouragement as long as we have a spark of faith left? What a different view we get by exercising and by fostering the "triune virtues of FAITH, HOPE, CHARITY!" In the first place "life" here in this world is so short—comparatively so momentary—that in regard to its success or failure one is inclined to think: "…After all, what is the difference"—"Life" so short, that worldlings are so inclined to worship as the only LIFE—as worth everything.
>
> How is it possible that man can be so shallow-minded and still be considered "rational"?
>
> Your failure, yes, is an indication of weakness of some kind somewhere. But if "the weak things of this world hath God chosen to confound the strong…" as Saint Paul so wonderfully assures us—and the history of religion abounds in examples and all creation says Amen—then why ever be discouraged: unless it be that our faith, more or less, weakens?

Why dear sister, you ought rather thank God for having given you such an opportunity to humble yourself and such a wonderful chance to foster humility—and by thanking him ahead of time for whatever crosses he may deign to caress you with, CONFIDENCE in his wisdom. Confidence in God—the very soul of prayer—hardly comes to any poor sinner like we all are, without trials and humiliations, and your failure, though simple and possibly single, has no doubt been quite a little cross, at least for a "little soul" to carry. There is a little verse I am sure will profit you to keep in mind and ought to help you foster confidence in God: *God condescends to use our powers, if we don't spoil his plans by ours.* God's plans are always for the best: always wonderful. But most especially for the patient and the humble who trust in him are his plans unfathomably holy and sublime.

Let us therefore, not weaken. Let us hope when darkness seems to surround us. Let us thank him at all times and under whatever circumstances. Thank him for our creation and our existence, thank him for everything—for his plans in the past that by our sins and our want of appreciation and patience have so often been frustrated and that he so often found necessary to change. Let us thank him for all his plans for the future—for trials and humiliations for as well as great joy and consolations; for sickness and whatever death he may deign to plan; and with the inspired Psalmist let us call all the creatures of the universe to help us praise and adore him who is the Divine Beginning and the everlasting Good—the Alpha and the Omega.[20]

Solanus's counsel to others about confidence being at the heart of prayer did not arise from textbooks on prayer or spirituality. It flowed from his own experience of God and his resulting mystical life. He grew in confidence in God because of the many hours he spent in the public prayer of the church and his private prayer, especially his contemplation, and in the way he confided in God when he took the concerns of the people to his prayer.

Another form of prayer that was expressed in Solanus can be found in his involvement in charismatic prayer. However, because he lived at a time when charismatic phenomena were seen as "Protestant," his contemporaries in the Catholic church had no name for the way they observed a certain way he often prayed.

When it came to seeing the Spirit work through him charismatically in healing and prophecy, people could make the connection. They also could identify the way he would so often say: "Deo Gratias" with the way many charismatics say: "Praise the Lord!" However, they did not know how to describe the phenomenon they witnessed when they found him late at night in chapel lying on the floor. Some would call this being "slain in the Spirit," or "resting in the Spirit." If it was not that form of charismatic prayer, it did express an intense form of adoration and obeisance before the presence of God. For his part, Father Benedict Joseph Groeschel is convinced that this form of Solanus's prayer revealed ecstasy.

As noted previously, Groeschel, like the other young Capuchins at Huntington, were intrigued by Solanus's prayer life. He recalls that, on a very hot night he was unable to sleep:

> About three o'clock in the morning I decided to walk around the cloister a few times and came to the side door leading into the friars' chapel. After a few moments kneeling in the dark I became aware that someone else was in the chapel quite close to me. Slightly startled, I reached over and put on the spotlight which flooded the sanctuary with bright lights. About ten feet in front of me, kneeling on the top step of the altar with his arms extended in an attitude of

profound prayer was Fr. Solanus. He appeared to be totally unaware that the lights had gone on although his eyes were partly opened and he was gazing in the most intense way at the tabernacle on the altar. I am sure that he did not know that I was there because it would have been totally uncharacteristic of him to remain in this extraordinary posture if he knew he was being observed. I watched this scene for three to four minutes. He never moved at all and seemed to be scarcely breathing. After thirty years, I recall the profound sense of presence I observed in his fixed stare at the tabernacle. I do not recall ever seeing anyone in such fixed attention, although I had observed something remotely similar at a great moment in a musical presentation or as an effective preacher reached the high point of a sermon. I have never seen a human being more absorbed in anything in my life. After a few minutes, I felt that I was intruding on an event so private and intimate that I should not have been there. I put out the light and left. I later learned that it was not uncommon for the first brothers down in the morning to find Father Solanus already in the chapel either praying or sometimes asleep curled up at the foot of the altar.[21]

Besides his personal prayer, which took various forms, and the regular communal prayer which was part of Capuchin Franciscan living, Solanus cultivated his confident, happy relationship with God through the celebration of the sacraments. For him these signs of faith flowed to and from the heart of religion; as such they were gifts of God that must be appreciated. "How little we appreciate our incalculable privileges—the blessings of our holy Faith,"[22] he noted. Because he considered life "the vestibule of heaven," the sacraments were the stepping-stones that would get us there: "When we were baptized, we became candidates for heaven," he wrote, "and every time we receive the sacraments of Mother Church, we take another step forward. How wonderful and legion are our privileged opportunities!"[23]

The most privileged opportunity to celebrate the sacraments involved full participation in the Eucharist, including communion. Communion not only deepened one's happy relationship with God, it promoted one's relationship with others: "Frequent Communion brings peace into a family and into the soul. It also fosters faith in God and heavenly relationships with all God's dear ones in heaven."[24]

Solanus's understanding of the doctrine of the communion of saints reached its peak in the eucharistic banquet. There he was at one not only with God but all his dear ones. He could call on these dear ones in heaven as much as he had called on them when they were on earth. Among God's dear ones, he said, were our parents, relatives, friends. Also remembered were the special people the church called saints. Now that Thérèse of Lisieux, Conrad of Parzham, and Francis of Assisi were in heaven, they could help him and all others on their heaven-bent journey as well. This was especially true of the Blessed Virgin. "Learn to know Mary," he wrote, "that you may love Heaven and heavenly things."[25]

By learning about Mary, he believed, one could grow closer to the way of Jesus. "How little we realize what a benefit it is that we taste sorrow now and then. Get acquainted," he urged, "with the Queen of Martyrs—God's Mother suffering—and you will learn something of how we ought to love sorrow and pains in this life."[26]

As we have seen, Solanus felt he had become personally acquainted with Mary through his regular reading of the four volumes of the *Mystical City of God*.

Its author, Mary of Jesus (of Agreda [1602–1665]), was the foundress and first abbess of the Franciscan Recollects at Agreda. She was known for her virtue and for her prolific writing. Among the latter *The Mystical City of God* has proved to be the most important[27] and most controversial. Solanus adamantly believed that the four volumes reflected Mary's deepest thoughts about redemption and salvation. Given this conviction it was very natural that Solanus would want to share these reflections with others that they might draw closer to Christ, their Redeemer and Savior and, ultimately, to God. Solanus also believed it was God's will that Mary receive special honor. "There is no one else on earth or in heaven, that God himself loves as he loves his ever Virgin, Immaculate Mother, and wishes her to be known and loved."[28]

Through prayer, fasting and the traditional forms of ascetical discipline that were practiced in the province, Solanus developed an approach to people and things that facilitated his relationship with God. If anything or anyone got in the way of that relationship, he would try to avoid it not because it might not be good, but because of that God whom he wanted to experience more deeply. "Oh, if we would only learn to keep an eye on ourselves, e.g., on our inordinate inclinations to pamper our own whims and desires," he wrote, "so that we might be like Jesus, catering and adjusting himself to the will—not only of his Father, but to the meanest of men...even to death on the Cross!"[29]

Solanus Casey believed that the easiest way to imitate the Crucified Jesus was by faithfully and happily "taking up our crosses." Crosses were "the best school wherein to learn appreciation for the love of Jesus Crucified."[30] Such daily sufferings could lead people more closely to a deep relationship with God. "If we only try to show the dear Lord a good will and ask him for resignation to the crosses he sends or permits to come our way," he wrote, "we may be sure that sooner or later they will turn out to have been just so many blessings in disguise."[31]

In light of his experience of that God who "blended" with his life, Solanus was able to place human suffering in a salvific context: "If we were to get a glimpse into the infinite depths of eternity and the glory reserved there for those who suffer patiently; or at least resignedly," he wrote, "the momentary joys and sorrows of time would seem like nothing."[32] In fact, viewing suffering from the perspective of eternity made it even more salvific: "How merciful is the good God in letting us now and then run up against a snag of some kind, halts us for at least a moment of reflection on the real purpose of our existence as rational creatures: ETERNITY IN GOD."[33]

Solanus viewed suffering as redemptive with cosmic implications. "In the crosses of life that come to us, Jesus offers us opportunities to help him redeem the world," he would say: "Let us profit by his generosity."[34] Or again, "We do well to remember how very short after all, it is till our suffering and our time of merit too, will be over. Let us offer everything, therefore to the divine Spouse of our souls, that he may accept it as helping him to save immortal souls, our own included."[35]

Because, through Jesus Christ, God has blended the divine with the human, Solanus's faith in God involved an almost absolute conviction that God's power was without limit within every human, especially those who believed. He was not about to set restrictions on what God could do for others, whether those "others" lived at the time of Jesus or in the twentieth century. Setting limits was a sign of weak faith. "We are so weak in faith," he would say, "setting limits to God's power and goodness."[36]

In suffering, rather than resorting to "whys," he urged over and over: "Let us turn to God whose solicitude for our welfare—temporal and as well spiritual—puts all created solicitude out of the picture."[37]

The solicitude and care of God for us was echoed in Solanus's solicitude and care for others. Probably the most moving tribute about how his concern for so many brought them wonderful healings came from the Chancellor of the Archdiocese of Detroit, Monsignor Edward J. Hickey:

> He heard more of the ills, of the sufferings, of the worries and fears of people of our city, perhaps more than

all the priests in any one parish or more than two or three parishes combined. From morning to night he would be listening to persons with worries and cares and disturbances and with all the humility and all the patience in the world he would give them fatherly advice and often enkindle their courage and hopes and reassure them in a brief time their troubles would be finished or counsel them to be resigned to suffer with Christ. "Tomorrow at 9 o'clock," "in two days at 3 o'clock," or "within a short time" if you have faith these troubles will disappear.[38]

He concluded with remarks that set Solanus's gift of healing within the pattern of Jesus as well as other places identified with the miraculous:

It is my conviction that after reading his biography and the records of cures which seemed to have resulted from his prayers, perhaps there were more cures reported in these notes, which he kept by order of his superior, than were reported in the Gospels, than were reported perhaps at Lourdes, at Saint Anne de Beaupré or at Fatima, in the same length of time.

Now that would be a very surprising record if the dear Lord was working more supernatural cures through the prayers and faith inspired by Father Solanus here in our city on Mt. Elliott Avenue than in all the notable shrines of Christendom combined.[39]

Besides the gift of healing which brought happiness to many, Solanus also used his gift of prophecy to encourage, challenge and bring hope to others. Usually his "prophecies" took the form of dealing with the future and what would happen to people. Yet somehow, as early as his years in Yonkers, people felt he could tell the future. The sisters of Saint Agnes at Sacred Heart, his first assignment, had a saying: "If, in June when you go back to the Motherhouse in Wisconsin, Father

Solanus says, 'See you in September,' you will be coming back; if he just says, 'Good-bye,' you will be transferred."

Even when his prophecies indicated continued suffering or even death, people received in his words the strength to approach their pain with greater peace. One of these people was Mrs. Eva Dugall. She lived in Windsor, Ontario, and suffered from tuberculosis. She was in her late thirties and had two children. She had been on the verge of dying for many months, but struggled to live because of her children. Someone drove Solanus across the river from Detroit to visit her.

When he entered the house, the first thing she said was, "Oh, you look just like Jesus Christ himself." His dark beard and his tall, lean frame in the brown habit, combined with his gentle blue eyes and peaceful composure had often brought such a response. Solanus had learned to take such comments in stride.

"Well, I'm taking his place," Solanus replied. "I was sent here by him. I came here because the Lord has a crown waiting for you. Why don't you resign yourself to go to heaven and forget about your children? The Lord has a lot of good mothers, especially the Blessed Virgin, and she will take care of your children."

"Oh, I feel so different now," the woman responded, sensing a calm which so many others seemed to receive in Solanus's presence and words. "Well, if you do," Solanus said, "let's all pray for you and you pray with us."

Everyone knelt down and Solanus led a decade of the rosary. There was not a dry eye in the room. When he finished, Solanus said, "I promise you the Lord will help you today."

By eleven o'clock that same night the woman was dead, relieved from her pain.[40]

At other times, Solanus had ways to imply that people would receive healing. He used terms such as, "the doctor will be surprised," "have the doctor look again," or "I don't think there is a need for that." Such responses would often be made after people approached him for prayers and his blessing. He would often look away as though he was thinking deeply, or close his eyes for ten or fifteen seconds. Then he would say something like, "She'll be better in seven days."

Far from attributing such marvelous powers to himself, Solanus simply believed they should be expected in our age as much as in the age when Jesus said, "[T]his scripture has been fulfilled in your hearing" (Luke 4:21). "To doubt the truth of miracles in any age of history," he noted, "would be nothing less than to fall in line with the ideas of the unbelieving world—deaf, dumb, and spiritually blind."[41]

While the gifts of healing, prophecy and wisdom were extraordinary in his life, the greatest of all these gifts shown in Solanus's eighty-seven years was charity. Charity not only characterized his happy relationship with God, it overflowed in the warm, caring, fraternal and even humorous way he related to his neighbor. "Charity is always good; always to be commended and fostered," he wrote. "But after all, rightly ordered charity begins at home. To my mind, that means it should begin right in one's own heart—to be practical, in my own soul."[42]

Whether it was in the ways he ministered to outsiders or his own fellow Capuchins (like the gentle way he tried to help his aging classmate Father Damasus, in his blindness or the newest novice like Father Dan) or his nonthreatening demeanor which seemed even to quiet noisy babies when he touched them, charity defined his life. This characteristic, even more than his purported healings and mystical phenomena, witnesses to the evangelical perfection he sought and promoted. Since charity is that which makes us most like God, his self-giving love or charity was his greatest virtue.

As noted above, for Solanus, "charity, properly ordered," begins at home. In a loving way he referred to himself as "this poor sinner...who more than anyone else gives me the most trouble." Then he would add, "I consider it a mercy that we need examine one conscience only!"[43] When it came to judging others, charity demanded that we "be as blind to the faults of your neighbor as possible, trying at least to attribute a good intention to their actions."[44]

Those who lived and worked with him, including his own confreres (some of whom could be very critical of him) cannot remember a time when Solanus spoke negatively of another human being. Somehow, it seemed, he tried to act on his belief that each person was a spark of God's goodness and, in response to that goodness, he could only be grateful.

And, again, gratitude or appreciation was the unique way Solanus manifested the "happy" part of his relationship with God and neighbor. Because "gratitude is the first sign of a thinking, rational creature,"[45] ingratitude, whether it be toward God or neighbor had to be "poor humanity's sorrow, or unhappiness."[46] "Be sure," he warned, "if the enemy of our souls is pleased at anything in us, it is ingratitude of whatever kind. Why? Ingratitude leads to so many breaks with God and neighbor."[47] Because any break with God or neighbor reflected a break in charity, gratitude would be the way to preserve not only a happy relationship with God and neighbor, but union with both as well. Thus he wrote: "How wonderful are all God's designs for all who confide in him. How fortunate! How humbly grateful we ought to be!"[48]

2. RELIGION IS THE SCIENCE OF OUR PROVIDENTIAL DEPENDENCE ON GOD AND OUR NEIGHBOR.

Solanus viewed "our providential dependence on God" as having two elements. The first implies passive abandonment or trust in God's will for us at all times. "Trust in God," he often urged: "his providence governs all things sweetly, even though we cannot see it immediately. This is where we must have faith and confidence."[49] The second element involves active abandonment or the willingness to be cocreators with God in history in the way(s) we allow God to act in us. Such active abandonment also involves asking confidently and thankfully.

The heart of Solanus's spirituality flowed from his passive abandonment. Solanus's faith convinced him there was a God. Solanus's joyful life evidenced his experience of God as one who wills to bring order from disorder, healing from pain, abundance from poverty and loving union from sinful alienation. For him, the only things that could place obstacles to the power of God at work in the world were doubt and fear. Thus his conclusion that "one of humanity's greatest weaknesses is setting a limit on God's power and goodness."[50]

Unshakable confidence earmarked his whole approach to God. In "fostering confidence, we greatly eliminate the danger of sadness that frustrates God's merciful designs,"[51] he wrote. Solanus's stress on confidence reflected a key element of the spirituality which is found in many writers of his era. It was encapsulated in the work of the eighteenth-century Jesuit, Pierre de Caussade. In his *Abandonment to Divine Providence*, de Caussade taught that the height of perfection can be achieved by lovingly and confidently fulfilling the simplest of common duties, believing such to be God's will. Probably the most well-known interpreter of that insight was Thérèse Martin of Lisieux, France.

"The Little Flower" died when Solanus was twenty-six. When her autobiography was released, it touched something deep in the spirit of Solanus. "She makes sanctity really attractive and so beautifully simple,"[52] he wrote to his sister in 1915 (little aware that his own confidence was already at that time beginning to help people in their path to God).

Because God's care for us is deeper than the greatest of our cares for ourselves, Solanus reasoned that we should abandon ourselves to God's care, confident that all things will work out for the good. Reflecting Jesus' words in the Sermon on the Mount, Solanus urged people to "Shake off excessive worry and exercise a little confidence in God's providence."[53] His experience of God's loving providence assured him that nobody would ever be asked to bear more than could be borne. "How merciful the good God is," he once said with his Irish wit, "always fitting 'the back to the burden,' if not vice-versa, as often is the case!"[54]

"How wonderful are all God's designs for all who" have confidence, Solanus would say over and over again. He saw God's designs unfolded both in the manifest and the hidden events of life. With confidence, a hope-filled person should be able to see beyond these manifestations to a God by whose grace we are "fortified to profit by them all."[55]

In his mind the chief obstacle to living providentially dependent on God was grounded in worry. Just as Jesus said, "Do not worry," because he knew there was a God whose very nature as parent demanded that our needs would be met, so Solanus advised others to think about that same God-parent, rather than being controlled by fear and anxiety. "Why worry? Rather foster confidence in his divine providence by humbly and in all childlike humility venturing to remind him—remind him in the person of our Brother Jesus—that we are his children."[56]

Even though the psychologist in him wisely realized that "worry is a weakness from which very few of us are entirely free," the theologian in him saw that worry could also indicate lack of faith. We should "be on our guard against this most insidious enemy of our peace of soul," he wrote. We maintain our guard when we "foster confidence in God, and thank him ahead of time for whatever he chooses to send us."[57] He also offered sound psychology (or perspective) to people: "Shake off anxiety," Solanus wisely urged. "Last year it was something that you now smile about. Tomorrow it's about something that will not be serious if you raise your heart to God and thank him for whatever comes."[58]

While Solanus seems to have been faithful to a caution he wrote to himself in his novitiate—"Beware of congratulating thyself on the blessings wrought through thy medium"[59]—it also seems his own reflections on any healings that might have come to others linked to his belief in the power and value of the sacraments and sacramentals of the Catholic faith. As outward expressions of the deeper reality of God's

Word and the church's promises, he believed these latter were actually the instruments of healing the theologians and indulgence-givers said they should be. Invariably, he connected healings with various blessings of the true cross, membership in the Seraphic Mass Association, feeding the hungry or caring for the sick, the blessing of a priest, or some spiritual or corporal work of mercy. Referring to these sacraments and sacramentals of the church, he noted, "If we could only learn to appreciate the holy Faith and the innumerable blessings flowing from it and the blessings otherwise surrounding us; we should never have time to worry about anything."[60] And again, on Good Friday, 1955, speaking of his desire to have "a spark or two more of holy Faith," he wrote: "Do we appreciate the little faith we do have? Do we beg God for more?"[61] Solanus just could not appropriate such divine power to himself; it all came from the spark of faith that needs constant rekindling through humility. Indeed, as he would say so often: "God condescends to use our powers, if we don't spoil his plans by ours."

Another way passive abandonment to God's designs may be cultivated is connected to our intelligence itself. Memory enables us to recall; recollection empowers us to make connections. Both facilitate that knowledge by which rational creatures become aware of God. "What a wonderful gift of God is memory! But what is it compared to hope?" Solanus asked. While they were different, they were far from exclusive. He concluded that "they cooperate together to glorify God, along with the other two triune virtues of faith and charity."[62] Memory also helps develop gratitude.[63] "When we think of past blessings and the merciful providence (not withstanding our sins), whereby God has blessed us," he asked, "why should we not foster confidence by thanking him for the future?"[64]

Solanus's active abandonment to God or cooperation with grace evolved from his conviction that he was not only dependent on God; he was in awe that God was providentially dependent on him as well. God depended on all creatures to be who or what they were created to be to fulfill their part in God's original plan. "Who can fully appreciate the privilege that God has given us of the possibility of our helping him in the work of redemption," he marvelled, "thus saving our own 'destiny for eternal glory.'"[65]

Probably the words of Jesus in the Gospels that most influenced Solanus's particular way of participating in God's provident plan for the world involved "asking." Scores of years before Rhonda Byrne's *The Secret* became one of the bestselling self-help books of all time, Solanus preached the gospel of confident asking. Both he and Byrne based their philosophy of life on Matthew 21:22 (and, for Solanus, 7:7). Where Rhonda Byrne based her self-help book on the "law of attraction" found in "the universe" that demanded that we (1) know what we want and ask the universe for it, (2) feel and behave as if the object of your desire is on its way and (3) are open to receiving it, Solanus believed that (1) God is the one who must be asked (2) with confidence in God's promises, along with (3) the willingness to become open to what we ask for, even if we have to change our lives to be able to receive it.

Besides being the science of our providential dependence on God that is revealed in the confident way we can ask God for what we need, like all good children, religion also involves our mutual dependence on each other. "How wonderful, in the promotion of mutual and common charity," he wrote, "that next to our happy dependence on God himself, he has made us mutually dependent on one another."[66] In responding to others in their needs, as God has responded to us in our needs, we actually become images of God. In the process, we not only reveal God's care or pathos, but experience ourselves cared for by God and part of God's reign or reality. In doing a favor for our neighbor, Solanus reasoned, the favor is done for God; thus we become favored or blessed by God.[67] If more people would only live by this basic principle of the Last Judgment, Solanus believed, the world could be transformed: "What a marvelously different society we would have here, and what an ideal world to live in if we would all keep in mind the assurance of Jesus, 'What you have done to the least of my brethren, you have done to me.'"[68]

Given this conviction of humanity's interdependence, Solanus could not imagine a me-and-God approach to spirituality that was limited to an inner, personalistic dimension. On the contrary, he clearly stated that any spirituality controlled by individualism was incomplete: "If we are interested in saving our souls, we must have an interest in our brothers and sisters."[69] Such a statement places Solanus's spirituality in absolute synch with *Spe Salvi*, the encyclical of Pope Benedict XVI, wherein he stated: "salvation has always been considered a 'social' reality." He explained that authentic life, toward which we continually reach, "is linked to a lived union with a 'people,' and for each individual it can only be attained within this 'we.' It presupposes that we escape from the prison of our 'I,' because only in the openness of this universal subject does our gaze open out to the source of joy, to love itself—to God."[70]

Faithful to this insight about salvation being communal, Solanus's greatest concern was for helping (or saving) others in need. Much of this compassion was expressed in his healing ministry. But to many, even more than healing, Solanus's concern about providing "the food" for others, is what made his virtue heroic. Unfortunately too many people have remembered Solanus Casey for the former gift and not the latter; yet he often said, "I have two favorites: the sick and the poor." Not everyone might be so gifted with Solanus's unique healing powers, yet all can imitate him in his concern for the poor. In Solanus's eyes, all baptized people, including all religious, should be concerned about the poor. Among all the baptized this should be the special concern of those who follow Francis of Assisi. "Our lot," he said, referring to the Capuchin Franciscan vocation, "has been cast among the simple lives of the poor."[71]

One person who seems to remember Solanus more for his concern for people in need than for healing, was a person who was on the receiving end of Solanus's care. Andrew Lawrence was not a person in need of daily bread; this priest of the Holy Trinity Mission Congregation was in need of funds that would enable his congregation to survive. Andrew Lawrence first met Solanus in 1930. Desperately in need of monies to continue the fledgling Congregation's ministry among the poor in southeastern Alabama, he and a companion had come to Detroit trying to raise money but they had no place to stay. They mentioned their plight to a man on the elevator as they went to visit the diocesan director of the Congregation of the Doctrine of the Faith. He recalled:

> This man said, "Well, if you have need, why don't you go and see Fr. Solanus?"
>
> We said, "Who's Fr. Solanus?"
>
> He said, "Oh, he's a very holy and wonderful Capuchin priest. He's very good to the poor and helps so many people."
>
> The man spoke with such deep conviction that Brother and I found out where the Monastery was located…. We found our way out there and this very sweet, kind, wonderful gentleman welcomed us. He was an older man at the time we met him, and had a long beard covering a very ascetic face. We thought he was a lay brother and we asked to speak to Fr. Solanus.
>
> He said. "Well, what can we do for you? Come in."
>
> So, the first thing he did was bring us in and give us some coffee and some bread and some food. He was so very kind. He made us feel very much at home. Then we told him we were Trinity Missionaries and that we were working with the poor in our own country but that we just had no place to stay and no money to go to a hotel.

"Well," he said. "I'm sure that Father Guardian will be happy to have you stay here. We are delighted to welcome those who work with the poor."

He was so fine and friendly. He not only got Father Guardian and pleaded our cause for hospitality, but he took the bags we had and carried them. He wouldn't even let us carry our own bags. He took us upstairs. He was…very solicitous about these two beggars who came in unannounced.[72]

Solanus did not limit his ministry to try to alleviate "the cry of the poor" who came to him; he also spent a good amount of his time trying to alleviate the causes of poverty by his work for social justice. Thus he wrote: "Only lovers of justice and truth can possess the kingdom of heaven…. And to be children of God we must be lovers of justice, truth, and peace."[73]

Solanus had a passion for what he believed to be true or a matter of rationality. Faithful to his continual linkage of religion to rationality, he once wrote, "Disregard for the claims of justice—under whatever pretext—has always been a manifestation of, to say the very least, shallow thinking—or rather a betrayal of real thinking."[74]

Whether it was his concern that the truth be told to his provincial about a Capuchin confrere whom he believed had suffered injustice at the hands of his local superior in Harlem or the articulations of "the facts" related to the British subjugation of the Irish, he made it very clear to whatever "powers that be" that truth and justice were absolutely necessary for authentic human relationships. At the same time, when he himself would be slighted by others' untruths or injustices, especially by the very few fellow Capuchins who could mock him or slight him, he never, to anyone's memory, tried to justify himself or retaliate. He accepted corrections patiently, even when accused of mistakes that were not his fault.

While not at all keen on defending his own rights, his concern for the rights of others and for various justice issues at different times might raise some eyebrows today. For instance, faithful to his Irish heritage, he wrote such a stinging reply to the *Catholic News* about an apparently (to Solanus) pro-British article that the paper rejected his letter to the editor. It was subsequently printed in *The Irish World* and *Industrial Liberator*. Another indiscretion in justice efforts was shown in his early support of Father Charles Coughlin. While Solanus had the gift of prophecy to deal with some situations and people, his reference to Coughlin as "our prophet,"[75] shows it was not necessarily applied to all people and situations!

At times he used harsh words against groups of people whom he thought were violating basic principles of truth and justice. Yet, while he spoke out against those politicians or leaders directly responsible for such wrongdoing—such as England's leaders vis-à-vis the Irish— he loved the British people themselves. Similarly, he could condemn atheists as a group; however, he could find only compassion for individuals who said they were atheists.

The Thomas Aquinas whom Solanus had studied so diligently as a student wrote that courage is the virtue that is needed in the promotion of justice. Whether it was for this reason or because he linked courage so closely with confidence in God and building God's reign on earth, Solanus made courage one of his major themes. For him confidence was the very soul of courage; at the same time confidence was courage divinely reinforced.[76]

Courage is the stuff of martyrs. Recalling the victims of oppressive regimes who were suffering persecution for the sake of justice, Solanus wrote,

> It is hard to reckon the extent of modern martyrdom the Church has suffered these several decades, and probably less possible to surmise what seems still shortly to follow—the judgment awaiting enemies of

truth, as well as the glory reserved for those who will
have persevered—suffering for justice and truth.[77]

Because truth is the foundation of justice and justice is the foundation of peace, perhaps the greatest "Pauline weapon" Solanus used in
his defense of the gospel was his inner peace and effort to bring peace
to others.

First of all, Solanus possessed the gift of peace personally. From
this source of peace Solanus was at rest with God. He thus could communicate a calming effect to others even in the midst of very trying
circumstances. "Peace is an outstanding characteristic of charity," he
wrote. "They accompany each other and must begin if really genuine,
between God and the individual soul."[78] For Solanus, no human could
achieve this peace except "in the willing service of his Creator."[79]
Remaining true to his definition about religion vis-à-vis God and
neighbor, Solanus's peace had to extend beyond his own relationship
with God into his service of others, with whom he led a mutually
dependent life.

By natural disposition (of all the sports he played as a youth, he
never took up boxing), Solanus was nonviolent. Though he was com-
petitive and found it easy to debate issues, he had tamed his anger and
directed it positively toward a passion for justice. Such discipline
demanded continual, ongoing conversion. Aware of his tendencies, as
well as his real human feelings, Solanus continually asked others to
pray for his conversion. He said we should be "praying for one
another's conversion, till some day we can sin no more and the good
angels will bear us off to eternity, forever really and truly converted."[80]

For Solanus Casey, conversion was not connected just to his bap-
tism or his entrance (and perseverance) into the Capuchins; it was a
process demanding continued, ongoing and radical transformation.
He knew this process was life-long, ending only in death. Thus he
wrote that, "only in heaven can we be satisfied as being fully and really
converted."[81]

What we have done on earth, the "vestibule of heaven," will be the basis for our reward in heaven. Heaven, to Solanus, was "where love of God and our neighbor is the life and the very soul of society and association, where hopeful faith has merged into eternal charity."[82] Since these triune virtues of faith, hope and charity are the "trace of the Holy Trinity in our immortal souls,"[83] and because the Trinity is the basis for our lives on earth, we should have no fear of passing over to fully experience God at the moment of our death. For him death was "the happy transition to the heavenly promised abode, where gratitude ripens into perfect love of God and neighbor."[84] Thus he said, "if we prepare for the moment of our passing from time to eternity, it can be like that of a tired child confident in the arms enfolding it."[85]

This attitude should be expected of all people at death's door whose religiosity manifests a provident dependence on God and our neighbor. Yet the actual way Solanus prepared to die shows something more. While he died peacefully, turning his life consciously and rationally over to God, his last days reflected that preoccupation which often accompanies mystics as they prepare to pass over to the Lord. This preoccupation rests in their almost obsessive desire for unity for all people still on earth. Coming closer to that blessed vision of unity wherein one sees the Trinity face to face, that experience and understanding makes one preoccupied with all the forms of disunity which still exist on earth, especially among humans.

In describing his last hours Gerald Walker, Solanus's provincial, recalls:

> It happened during the last night of his life on earth. I was visiting him in the hospital. He seemed to be in utter spiritual darkness, but there was the same love of God and of Christ's members. There was the same faith, the same trust, the same zeal for souls. At one point he began to writhe in pain. I bent over him and asked, "Where does it hurt, Father?"

> I wish that all the world could have seen the gleam of utter joy on his face and heard his words, "My whole body hurts. Thanks be to God. Thanks be to God. I am offering my suffering that all might be one. Oh, if I could only live to see the conversion of the whole world."[86]

He had lived a life of renunciation. Now at the point of death, Solanus was ready to renounce an immediate entrance into heaven, if only more people could experience that God to whom he was so united mystically. At the point of being one with God's own being in a new and unimagined way, there is almost a bittersweet feeling; the work is not yet done. As long as a breath is available one's efforts must be oriented to this goal of unity. However, even here and despite this bittersweet feeling, the feeling itself must be oriented to God's will. To that goal all life must be directed. Thus at the point of entrance into final union with God, Solanus freely dedicated the depth of his being to be at one with his maker: "I give my soul to Jesus Christ."

Twenty years before, Solanus wrote his sister, Margaret, about this day: "I console myself occasionally with the thought that sooner or later the day will come when they will say of poor Father Solanus: 'He's gone.' Please God, the struggle for existence will then be over. I just hope that by that time I'll be able to exclaim with Saint Paul: 'I long to be dissolved and to be with Christ.'"

Indeed, in giving his very life—body and soul—to Jesus Christ, he became dissolved into Christ. In the process he fulfills for us today what he said could be found in the task of all saintly people: "As manifested in the lives of the saints," Solanus once wrote, never believing anyone would ever apply his own words to himself, as we have tried to do in this book, "if we strive and use the means God has given us, we too can ascend to great sanctity and to astonishing familiarity with God, even here as pilgrims to the Beatific Vision."[87]

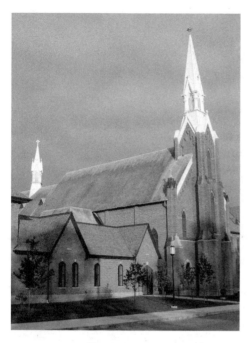

St. Bonaventure Monastery and
Solanus Casey Center, Detroit.

Creation Garden and entrance to Solanus Casey Center, Detroit.

Tomb of Solanus Casey and Chapel, St. Bonaventure, Detroit.

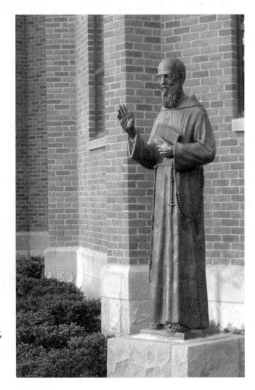

Bronze sculpture of Solanus Casey, by Ferenc Varga, Solanus Casey Center, Detroit.

NOTES

INTRODUCTION

1. *Congregatio de Causis Sanctorum.* "Decretum super Virtutibus: Beatificationis et Canonizationis Servi Dei Francisci Solani Casey, sacerdotis professi Ordinis Fratrum Minorum Capuccinorum (1870–1957). *Acta Apostolicae Sedis Commentarium Officiale* 88 (1996), p. 118.

2. *Congregatio de Causis Sanctorum,* p. 118.

3. Gustav Niebuhr, "One Man's Life of Virtue Earns the Papal Spotlight," *The New York Times,* August 5, 1995.

4. Kenneth L. Woodward, *Making Saints: How the Catholic Church Determines Who Becomes a Saint, Who Doesn't, and Why* (New York: Simon and Schuster, 1990).

5. Sandro Corradini, Promoter General of the Faith, in *"Super Dubium"* Report and Votes of the Congressus Peculiaris on the Virtues, April 7, 1995, *Congregatio de Causis Sanctorum,* P.N. 1400 (Roma: Tipografia Guerra s.r.l., 1995), p. 114.

6. Solanus Casey, "Think Over," in *Collected Writings of Father Solanus Casey, O.F.M. CAP.* (hereinafter *Collected Writings*), volume two, p. 253.

CHAPTER ONE

1. Solanus Casey (hereinafter Casey) "Letter to Margaret T. LeDoux," April 1930, *Collected Writings,* volume one, p. 142. Solanus used abbreviations and many dashes in his writings. I have adapted these for the sake of clarity.

2. For much of the data referring to the childhood of Solanus Casey I am indebted to the interviews James P. Derum had with Solanus's brother, Monsignor Edward J. Casey. These were the foundation for Derum's *The Porter of Saint Bonaventure's: The Life of Father Solanus Casey, Capuchin* (Detroit: Fidelity, 1968). When a statement is made that seems to need documentation that is not given, such statement can be found in Derum's book from his personal interviews with members of the Casey family.

3. Casey, "Letter to Margaret T. LeDoux," April 30, 1930, *Collected Writings,* volume one, p. 143.

4. Casey, "Letter to Edward Casey," April 23, 1953, *Collected Writings,* volume one, p. 190.

5. Casey, "Letter to Margaret T. LeDoux," *Collected Writings,* volume one, pp. 143–144.

6. Casey, "Letter to Margaret T. LeDoux," *Collected Writings,* volume one, p. 143.

7. Casey, "Letter to Father Maurice E. Joachim Casey," April 2, 1946, *Collected Writings,* volume one, p. 158.

8. Casey, "Letter to Margaret T. LeDoux," *Collected Writings,* volume one, p. 144.

9. Casey, "Letter to Margaret T. LeDoux," *Collected Writings,* volume one, p. 144.

10. Casey, "Letter to Margaret T. LeDoux," *Collected Writings,* volume one, p. 145.

11. Casey, fragmentary note c. 1949, *Collected Writings,* volume one, p. 162.

12. Casey, "Letter to Miss Margaret Shavey," October 3, 1949, *Collected Writings,* volume two, p. 282.

13. This paragraph is from Edward Casey's reflections shared with James Derum and noted in his book, p. 26. See note 2, above, for other references from this source.

14. Casey, "Letter to Edwin Wilhite," c. October 4, 1950, *Collected Writings,* volume one, p. 128.

15. Casey, "Letter to James M. Casey," July 18, 1938, *Collected Writings,* volume one, p. 111.

16. In an effort to better understand some of the inner dynamics of Solanus Casey, his handwriting was submitted to analysis. Today businesses, among other entities, include handwriting analysis to better determine people's characteristics. The Library of Congress now includes the subject of handwriting under psychology. Selections from various periods of Solanus's life were submitted to two expert graphoanalysts. Sheila Kurtz, MGA, CGA, of New York has been featured in *Forbes* (May 9, 1983) and in United Airlines' *Mainliner* magazine (June 1983). Richard Stoller, PH.D., of Milwaukee wrote his doctoral dissertation on graphology. Where the reader may question the basis for statements regarding the inner dynamics of Solanus, such are grounded on the perceptions of others as well as the results of the graphology.

17. Marion Roessler, O.F.M. CAP., *Written Reports Concerning Father Solanus Casey, O.F.M., Cap.,* June 4, 1984 (hereinafter *Written Reports*).

18. Recollection of account by Solanus Casey to Shirley L. Jarosik, 1955, *Written Reports.*

19. Record of Classical Department, September 1891–June 1924, Milwaukee: Saint Francis Provincial Seminary archives, pp. 1, 7, 11, 16, 20, 25, 30, 36, 41. Thanks to Reverend Thomas Fait, Archdiocesan Archivist, for providing these records.

20. Students' ledger, 1887–1893, Saint Francis Seminary, p. 171. Materials courtesy of Reverend Thomas Fait.

21. Bonaventure Frey, O.F.M. CAP., Documents File. Vice Postulator's Archives, Detroit, Michigan.

22. Casey, "Letter to Maurice E. Joachim Casey," December 15, 1938, *Collected Writings*, volume one, p. 147.

23. Casey, Notebook 9, c. 1909, p. 27, *Collected Writings*, volume one, p. 18.

24. See testimonies of Father Lawrence Merten and Father Marion Roessler, O.F.M. CAP., in *Written Reports*.

25. Years later Solanus would book back at the founders and thank God for the decision that he made that December 8, 1896. Recollections of Father Solanus noted in Casey, "Letter to James M. Casey," January 29, 1943, *Collected Writings*, volume one, pp. 232–234.

26. Casey, "Letter to James Casey," July 18, 1938, *Collected Writings*, volume one, p. 200.

CHAPTER TWO

1. Casey, notes written on a page of Solanus Casey's copy of the *Rule and Testament of Saint Francis*, January 13, 1897. Documents File, Vice Postulator's Archives, Detroit, Michigan.

2. Until the adaptation of the Capuchin-Franciscan way of life after the Second Vatican Council, those studying to be priests were called "Frater" (*Frater* is Latin for "brother"). The lay brothers were called brother. With the changes which attempted to return to the spirit of brotherly equality which Saint Francis of Assist envisioned for his followers, all members of the community, especially those in formation, would be called brother.

3. Casey, unfinished letter to Rev. Edward Casey, March 14, 1957, *Collected Writings*, volume one, p. 195.

4. Casey, Notebook 9, c. 1897, p. 2, in *Collected Writings*, volume one, p. 2.

5. Notebook 9, p. 5, in *Collected Writings*, volume one, p. 5.

6. Latin reference to Saint Bonaventure, March 20, 1897, Notebook 9, p. 7.

7. Notebook 9, p. 7.

8. Solanus Casey had a problem with scrupulosity earlier in his life. He confided that he was free of the problem as he became more abandoned to God. See Mary Therese Bernadine Goodman in *Written Reports*.

9. Casey, Notebook 9, c. 1898, p. 14, in *Collected Writings*, volume one, p. 10.

10. Notebook 9, p. 7.

11. Casey, "Attestation," July 20, 1898. Document in Documents File, Vice Postulator's Archives, Detroit, Michigan.

12. Official vow formulary for the Capuchin Franciscans.

13. While it is true that Fathers Francis and Bonaventure had successive terms by reason of special exception, the exception could have been requested for Father Anthony but was not. This seems to reinforce the general impression that the Chapter delegates had reason for not reelecting Anthony.

14. Father Boniface Goldhausen, O.F.M., CAP., 1970, in *Written Reports*.

15. Casey, Notebook 9, c. 1899, p. 19, in *Collected Writings*, volume one, p. 12.

16. Notebook 9, c. January 1900, p. 21, in *Collected Writings*, volume one, p. 14.

17. Notebook 9, April 12, 1898, p. 16, in *Collected Writings*, volume one, p. 11.

18. Casey, Radio Talk, June 11, 1937, in *Collected Writings*, volume one, p. 94.

19. Cardinal Ganganelli, quoted in Casey, Notebook 9, c. 1899, p. 19, in *Collected Writings*, volume one, p. 12.

20. Casey, "Letter to Mrs. Ella Traynor," February 21, 1904, in *Collected Writings*, volume one, p. 71.

21. "Academic Record of Father Solanus (Bernard) Casey," Chicago: Province of Saint Joseph of the Capuchin Order Archives.

22. Casey, untitled statement. July 5, 1901. Documents File, Vice Postulator's Archives, Detroit, Michigan.

23. Notebook 9, c. 1903, p. 21, in *Collected Writings*, volume one, p. 15.

24. Notebook 9, p. 22, in *Collected Writings*, volume one, p. 16.

25. Notebook 9, p. 22, in *Collected Writings*, volume one, p. 16.

26. Casey, "Letter to Mrs. Ella Traynor," Notebook 9, p. 22, in *Collected Writings*, volume one, p. 16.

27. Father Boniface Goldhausen, O.F.M., CAP., February 11, 1963, in *Written Reports*.

28. Recent studies have been able to ascertain one's IQ within five points of the Stanford-Binet reading from an analysis of handwriting. While this is not definitive, it consistently correlates. The study of Solanus's handwriting was done by Richard J. Stoller, PH.D., author of *Write Right: Change Your Writing to Change Your Life* (Milwaukee: n.p., 1978).

29. Casey, "Letter to James M. Casey," January 29, 1943, in *Collected Writings*, volume one, p. 228.

CHAPTER THREE

1. Casey, "Letter to Father Maurice Joachim Casey, O.F.M. CAP.," August 16, 1937, in *Collected Writings*, volume one, p. 146.

2. Casey, "Letter to Mr. William Spring," March 27, 1935, in *Collected Writings*, volume one, p. 88.

3. Casey, "Letter to Mrs. Margaret LeDoux," January 3, 1916, in *Collected Writings*, volume one, p. 5.

4. Casey, "Letter to James M. Casey," January 29, 1943, in *Collected Writings*, volume one, p. 234.

5. Casey, "Letter to Br. Leo Wollenweber, O.F.M. CAP.," February 28, 1943, in *Collected Writings*, volume two, p. 119.

6. James Lawless, January 13, 1977, in *Written Reports*.

7. Casey, Notebook 9, c. 1909, p. 27, in *Collected Writings*, volume one, p. 18.

8. James Lawless, January 13, 1977, in *Written Reports*.

9. Casey, Notebook 9, c. 1909, p. 27, in *Collected Writings*, volume one, p. 18.

10. Casey, Notebook 9, c. 1909, p. 27, in *Collected Writings*, volume one, p. 18.

11. Sister Dolora Brogan, C.S.A., interview with Michael H. Crosby, O.F.M. CAP., January 11, 1983.

12. Walter O'Brien, O.F.M. CAP., interview with Michael H. Crosby, O.F.M. CAP., January 11, 1983.

13. Sister Agrippina Petrosino, C.S.A., interview with Michael H. Crosby, O.F.M. CAP., January 11, 1983.

14. Petrosino, January 11, 1983.

15. Casey, "Rev. Father Stephen Eckart, As I Remember Him," unfinished manuscript, 1948, in *Collected Writings*, volume two, p. 251.

16. Casey, notes on volume three of *The Mystical City of God* in *Collected Writings*, volume one, p. 286.

17. Casey, "Letter to Mrs. M. LeDoux," April 1, 1915, in *Collected Writings*, volume one, p. 3.

18. Cletus McCarthy, O.F.M. CAP., interview with Michael H. Crosby, O.F.M. CAP., January 11, 1983.

19. Sister Dolora Brogan, C.S.A., Interview with Michael H. Crosby, O.F.M. CAP., January 11, 1983.

20. Casey, sermon on John 2:1ff. in Notebook 2, c. 1915, p. 43, in *Collected Writings*, volume one, pp. 35–36.

21. Casey, sermon on John 2:1ff. in Notebook 2, c. 1915, p. 43, in *Collected Writings*, volume one, pp. 35–36.

22. Casey, sermon on Matthew 13 for the 10:15 AM Mass, November 11, 1917, in Notebook 2, p. 47, in *Collected Writings*, volume one, p. 50.

23. Casey, Sermon on Luke 15:2ff for the 10:15 AM Mass, 1917, in Notebook 2, p. 48, in *Collected Writings*, volume one, p. 52.

24. Casey, Sermon on Luke 15:2ff for the 10:15 AM Mass, 1917, in Notebook 2, p. 49, in *Collected Writings*, volume one, p. 50.

25. Casey, quoting Pope Leo XIII, in Notebook 2, c. 1917, p. 96, in *Collected Writings*, volume one, p. 54.

26. Casey, "Letter to Rev. Mother Lurana S.A.," April 17, 1912, in *Collected Writings*, volume one, p. 72.

27. Casey, "Letter to Sister of the Atonement," December 4, 1917, in *Collected Writings*, volume one, p. 73.

28. Casey, "Letter to Sister of the Atonement," December 4, 1917, in *Collected Writings*, volume one, p. 73.

29. Casey, "Letter to Brother Leo Wollenweber," September 7, 1945, in *Collected Writings*, volume two, p. 125.

30. Casey, "Letter to James Casey," July 18, 1938, in *Collected Writings*, volume one, p. 199.

31. Casey, "Letter to Margaret LeDoux," July 24, 1921, in *Collected Writings*, volume one, p. 9.

32. Casey, "Letter to Mrs. Margaret LeDoux," July 16, 1918, in *Collected Writings*, volume one, p. 7.

CHAPTER FOUR

1. Casey, Notebook 9, August 16, 1918, p. 28, in *Collected Writings*, volume one, p. 19.

2. Casey, Notebook 9, December 12, 1918, p. 29, in *Collected Writings*, volume one, p. 20.

3. Casey, Notebook 9, c. 1919, p. 35, in *Collected Writings*, volume one, p. 20.

4. Sister Rose Cecilia Ascherl, O.P., "Letter to Michael Crosby," April 12, 1983.

5. Casey, Notebook 3, August, 1919, p. 2b, in *Collected Writings*, volume one, p. 69.

6. Saint Bernard of Clairveaux, in John S. Maddux, "When You Pray," *The Way*, volume XVII, issue 3 (July 1977), p. 236.

7. Casey, "Letter to Mrs. Margaret LeDoux," July 16, 1937, in *Collected Writings*, volume one, p. 18.

8. Casey, "Letter to Mrs. M. C. LeDoux," July 24, 1921, in *Collected Writings*, volume one, p. 9.

9. Book of Minutes of the Friary Discreets at Our Lady of Angels, March 1, 1921 to November 5, 1924, October 25, 1921. New York: Our Lady of the Angels Friary.

10. Casey, "Letter to Mrs. Abraham Trabulsy," December 14, 1946, in *Collected Writings*, volume two, p. 195. As the date of the letter notes, Solanus did not

write this letter while at Our Lady, Queen of Angels, but while he was at Huntington, Indiana. However, it best reflects his sentiments while he was at New York.

11.   Casey, Notebook 1, November 8, 1923, p. 17 in *Collected Writings*, volume one.

12.   Casey, "Letter to Mr. Raymond T. Taylor," February 8, 1947, in *Collected Writings*, volume two, p. 214. Again, although written later, this letter reflects Solanus's attitude while at Our Lady of the Angels.

13.   Casey, "Notebook 1," *Collected Writings*, volume one.

14.   Book of Minutes, January 14, 1922.

15.   Casey, "Notebook I," *Collected Writings*, volume one, p. 5. Until the new understanding which accompanied the Second Vatican Council in the 1960s there was a practice in United States' Catholicism to "adopt pagan [heathen] babies" through donations of various amounts of money. It was a way of supporting foreign missionaries in the form of evangelization that was prevalent at that time, besides the actual "adoption."

16.   Father Laurence Lisotta, O.F.M. CAP., September 11, 1978, *Written Reports;* His report slightly adapted.

17.   Father Justin Joos, O.F.M. CAP., interview with Michael H. Crosby, O.F.M. CAP., January 11, 1983.

18.   Father Justin Joos, O.F.M. CAP., interview with Michael H. Crosby, O.F.M. CAP., January 11, 1983.

19.   Casey, letter to the editor, *The Catholic News*, September 27, c. 1922, in *Collected Writings*, volume one, p. 74.

20.   Casey, letter to the editor, *The Catholic News*, September 27, c. 1922, in *Collected Writings*, volume one, p. 74.

21.   Casey, letter to the editor, *The Catholic News*, September 27, c. 1922, in *Collected Writings*, volume one, p. 74.

22.   Casey, letter to the editor, *The Catholic News*, September 27, c. 1922, in *Collected Writings*, volume one, p. 74.

23.   Casey, "Letter to Very Rev. Pater Benno, O.F.M. CAP.," January 25, 1924, in *Collected Writings*, volume one, p. 83.

24.   Casey, "Letter to Mr. James M. Casey," July 18, 1938, in *Collected Writings*, volume one, p. 198.

CHAPTER FIVE

1.   Casey, Notebook 1, p. 14. Solanus made a habit of returning to his original entries that he might make follow-up comments about developments in the various cases. Thus the range of dates. Also, for the sake of easier reading I

have tried to make sentences from the phases and code words that Solanus used. Abbreviations have been extended to the full word and corrections have been made to spelling mistakes. The notations from Notebook 1 dealing with those items requested by Father Benno will not be footnoted unless for some special reason.

2. Sometimes, as in this case. Solanus noted the "cure" on the day it was announced to him. He then referred back to previous encounters, as in this case.

3. Father Marion Roessler, O.F.M. CAP., March 11, 1980, in *Written Reports*.

4. Casey, "Letter to Mrs. Belle Lyke," May 22, 1946, in *Collected Writings*, volume two, p. 175.

5. Casey, "Letter to Mrs. Margaret LeDoux," July 16, 1937, in *Collected Writings*, volume one, p. 18.

6. Casey, "Letter to Sister Cecilia Eagen," November 7, 1947, in *Collected Writings*, volume two, pp. 240–241.

7. Casey, "Letter to Sister Cecilia Eagen," November 7, 1947, in *Collected Writings*, volume two, p. 241.

8. Casey, "Letter to Margaret Therese LeDoux," October 19, 1954, in *Collected Writings*, volume one, p. 35.

9. Father Herman Buss, O.F.M. CAP., July 19, 1977, in *Written Reports*. Brother André was beatified on May 23, 1982, by Pope John Paul II.

10. Father Lawrence Merten, O.F.M. CAP., March 21, 1980, in *Written Reports*.

11. Casey, "Letter to Mr. Merrick O'Laughlin," June 28, 1947, in *Collected Writings*, volume two, p. 233.

12. Casey, "Letter to Mrs. E. Nettyk," July 18, 1949, in *Collected Writings*, volume two, p. 280.

13. William Tremblay, March 15, 1979, in *Written Reports*.

14. William Tremblay, March 15, 1979, in *Written Reports*.

15. Father Blase Gitzen, O.F.M. CAP., taped interview with Michael H. Crosby, O.F.M., CAP., January 1983.

16. Bernard Burke, O.F.M. CAP., August 9, 1973, in *Written Reports*.

17. Father Herman Buss, O.F.M. CAP., July 19, 1977, in *Written Reports*.

18. Father Cosmas Niedhammer, O.F.M. CAP., March. 16, 1980, in *Written Reports*. The time Father Cosmas spent in Detroit with Solanus was from 1938–1952. However, almost from the beginning, the routine described by Father Cosmas was Solanus's pattern.

19. Maurice Casey, quoted in Casey, "Letter to Father Maurice E. Joachim Casey," December 15, 1938, in *Collected Writings*, volume one, p. 148.

20. Casey, "Letter to Mrs. Margaret LeDoux," April, 1930, in *Collected Writings,* volume one, p. 142.

21. *Chronicle,* St. Bonaventure, Detroit, February 19, 1928.

22. Father Marion Roesslerf, O.F.M. CAP., March 11, 1980, in *Written Reports.*

23. The Blessing of Saint Maurus can be found in many old prayer books and rituals.

24. Mrs. Bernadette M. Nowak, March 28, 1970, in *Written Reports.*

25. Casimera Scott, March 2, 1977, in *Written Reports.*

26. The description of the Soup Kitchen and Solanus Casey's role in it relies heavily on the written report of his coworker Father Herman Buss, O.F.M. CAP., in Father Herman Buss, O.F.M. CAP., July 19, 1977, in *Written Reports.*

27. Al C. Billard, April 16, 1977, in *Written Reports.*

28. Father Herman Buss, O.F.M. CAP., July 19, 1977, in *Written Reports.*

29. Casey, "Letter to Mr. James M. Casey," July 18, 1938, in *Collected Writings,* volume one, p. 209.

30. Casey, "Letter to Venerable Br. Leo, O.F.M. CAP.," February 28, 1943, *Collected Writings,* volume two, p. 120.

31. William Tremblay, March 15, 1979, in *Written Reports.*

32. Mrs. Mary Therese McHugh, December 15, 1978, in *Written Reports.*

33. Elizabeth Ann Maher, April 4, 1977, in *Written Reports.*

34. Mrs. Agnes Juergens, October 27, 1978, in *Written Reports.*

35. Casey, "Letter to Mr. James Casey," January 29, 1943, in *Collected Writings,* volume one, p. 217.

36. Casey, "Letter to Margaret LeDoux," January 26, 1937, in *Collected Writings,* volume one, p. 16.

37. Casey, "Letter to Mrs. Margaret LeDoux," January 26, 1937, in *Collected Writings,* volume one, p. 16.

38. Casey, radio speech on station CKLW Detroit, June 11, 1937, in *Collected Writings,* volume one, pp. 94–95.

39. Casey, "Letter to Father Maurice Casey," December 15, 1938, in *Collected Writings,* volume one, pp. 147–148.

40. Leo Wollenweber, O.F.M. CAP., recollections shared with Michael H. Crosby, O.F.M., CAP.

41. Daniel Brady, O.F.M. CAP., "Letter to Michael H. Crosby," February 20, 1983.

42. Casimera Scott, March 2, 1977, in *Written Reports.*

43. Mrs. Hazel Maisano, February 12, 1978, in *Written Reports.* Mrs. Maisano does not say what kind of birth control she was practicing, nor what Solanus said about it—just that he could tell she was practicing birth control.

44. Derum, p. 186.

45. Sister Joyce Pranger, *Rise Early to Meet Your Lord* (adapted) (Denville, N.J.: Dimension), 1977, pp. 41–43.

46. Gerald Walker, O.F.M., CAP., April 14, 1980, in *Written Reports*.

47. *Chronicle*, St. Bonaventure, Detroit, September 13, 1942.

48. Casey, "Letter to Mrs. Margaret LeDoux," November 17, 1942, in *Collected Writings*, volume one, p. 21.

49. Casey, "Letter to Mrs. Margaret LeDoux," November 17, 1942, in *Collected Writings*, volume one, p. 21.

50. *Chronicle*, St. Bonaventure, Detroit, September 13, 1942.

51. Casey, "Letter to Mrs. Margaret LeDoux," November 17, 1942, in *Collected Writings*, volume one, p. 21.

52. Casey, "Letter to Mr. James Casey," January 29, 1943, in *Collected Writings*, volume one, p. 215.

53. At this time in the Province of Saint Joseph there was a custom that the friars knelt in front of their superior to receive a blessing upon their leaving or returning to the friary.

54. Father Michael Cefai, January 10, 1968, in *Written Reports*.

55. Casey, "Letter to Father Edward Casey," December 12, 1938, in *Collected Writings*, volume one, p. 168.

56. Casey, "Letter to Mr. Charles K. Chisholm," May 12, 1937, in *Collected Writings*, volume one, p. 90.

57. Father Marion Roessler, O.F.M. CAP., March 11, 1980, in *Written Reports*.

58. Casey, "Letter to Father Marion, O.F.M. CAP.," July 9, 1945, in *Collected Writings*, volume two, p. 144.

CHAPTER SIX

1. Most Reverend Clement Neubauer, O.F.M. CAP., unsigned, June 14, 1967 in *Written Reports*. The sheet of paper was a formal statement that was to be signed by Father Clement; it was dictated but not signed. Clement Neubauer became the first American to be minister of the entire Capuchin Franciscan Order. He was first appointed by Pope Pius XII at the conclusion of World War II, and then elected in his own right after six years' absence from Rome, which he spent as an associate pastor in Appleton, Wisconsin, and then as local superior at St. Felix Friary, Huntington, Indiana.

2. Brother Ignatius Milne, recollections shared with Michael H. Crosby, O.F.M. CAP., September 1, 1983.

3. Casey, "Letter to Margaret LeDoux," September 9, 1945, in *Collected Writings,* volume one, p. 23.

4. Casey, "Letter to Br. Leo," July 30, 1945. In the next paragraph Solanus urged Leo to burn any photographs of himself except for those of his golden jubilee, especially "the one with all the little grandchildren. Some of them are grandparents now themselves." *Collected Writings,* volume two, p. 121.

5. Casey, "Letter to Muriel Krausmann," August 18, 1945, in *Collected Writings,* volume two, p. 91.

6. Casey, retreat notes, in Notebook 9, August 1945, in *Collected Writings,* volume one, p. 253.

7. Casey, retreat notes, in Notebook 9, August 1945, in *Collected Writings,* volume one, p. 253.

8. Casey, retreat notes, in Notebook 9, August 1945, in *Collected Writings,* volume one, p. 255.

9. Casey, "Postcard to Mrs. Alice Plunkett," 1945, in *Collected Writings,* volume two, p. 2.

10. Casey, "Letter to Ray Garland," October 22, 1945. This letter was found in Solanus's belongings. Whether a copy was sent to Ray Garland is not known. Solanus would often compose many drafts of letters that dealt with difficult issues; thus it is likely that this was one of the drafts. *Collected Writings,* volume two, p. 149.

11. Casey, "Letter to Ray Garland," October 22, 1945. *Collected Writings,* volume two, p. 149.

12. Casey, "Letter to Ray Garland," October 22, 1945. *Collected Writings,* volume two, p. 149.

13. Casey, "Letter to Ray Garland," October 22, 1945. *Collected Writings,* volume two, p. 149.

14. Casey, "Letter to Mrs. Mary Kenny," August 28, 1945, in *Collected Writings,* volume two, p. 146.

15. Father Walter O'Brien, interview with Michael H. Crosby, O.F.M. CAP., January 11, 1983.

16. Father Walter O'Brien, interview with Michael H. Crosby, O.F.M. CAP., January 11, 1983.

17. Casey, "Message to Helena Wilhite," December 14, 1945, in *Collected Writings,* volume one, p. 129. A similar poem was sent to the Wollenwebers.

18. Casey, "Always Christmas Eve—Nay Infinitely More for Daily Communicants," poem in *Collected Writings,* volume two, p. 156.

19. Casey, "Letter to Mrs. Edward Wilhite," February 28, 1946. Solanus must have been very inspired by the purported healing of Mrs. Nagle. He repeated the incident and the return visits in an encouraging letter to Sister Belita in Atlantic City, New Jersey. In a letter of September 15, 1945 (in *Collected Writings,* volume two, p. 147), he said that he was telling her about Mrs. Nagle's recovery because: "I hope this may give you all a little more courage to pray on and with your friends storm heaven. I often advise a proposition to the poor souls. In other words, if an operation is averted I asked that they donate an enrollment for the Poor Souls, a percentage of the costs of the operation, if it is averted, to go to charity or some good cause, besides prayers and Holy Communions." *Collected Writings,* volume one, pp. 130–131.

20. Casey, "Letter to Mrs. Edward Wilhite," February 28, 1946. *Collected Writings,* volume one, pp. 131–132.

21. Casey, "Letter to Mrs. Edward Wilhite," February 28, 1946. *Collected Writings,* volume one, pp. 132–133.

22. Asteria M. Mahoney, August 19, 1977, in *Written Reports.*

23. Casey, "Letter to Mrs. E. L. Eichorn," March 14, 1950, in *Collected Writings,* volume two, p. 297.

24. Casey, "Letter to Mrs. E. L. Eichorn," March 14, 1950, in *Collected Writings,* volume two, p. 297.

25. Casey, "Letter to Mrs. E. L. Eichorn," March 14, 1950, in *Collected Writings,* volume two, p. 298. In the 1940s and early 1950s the term "darky," though offensive to blacks, was commonly used by whites who remained ignorant of the fact.

26. Casey, "Letter to Father Edward Casey," March 28, 1946, in *Collected Writings,* volume one, p. 176.

27. Father Walter O'Brien, interview with Michael H. Crosby, O.F.M. CAP., January 11, 1983.

28. Father Barnabas Keck, O.F.M. CAP., interview with Michael H. Crosby, O.F.M. CAP., January 11, 1983.

29. Father Barnabas Keck, O.F.M. CAP., interview with Michael H. Crosby, O.F.M. CAP., January 11, 1983.

30. Casey, "Letter to Br. Leo Wollenweber," May 23, 1946, in *Collected Writings,* volume two, p. 128.

CHAPTER SEVEN

1. Casey, "Letter to Mrs. Margaret LeDoux," September 22, 1946, in *Collected Writings,* volume one, p. 25.

2. Casey, "Letter to Mrs. Margaret LeDoux," September 22, 1946, in *Collected Writings,* volume one, p. 25.

3. *Chronicle*, St. Felix Friary, Huntington, Indiana, I (1928–1950), May 13, 1946.

4. Father Ambrose deGroot, September 25, 1978, in *Written Reports*.

5. Casey, "Letter to Miss Muriel Krausmann," April 24, 1947, in *Collected Writings*, volume two, p. 99.

6. Dorothy Fletcher, reflections shared with Michael H. Crosby, O.F.M. CAP., January 7, 1983.

7. Dorothy Fletcher, reflections shared with Michael H. Crosby, O.F.M. CAP., January 7, 1983.

8. Casey, "Letter to Mrs. Abraham Trabulsy," unsigned, December 14, 1946, in *Collected Writings*, volume two, pp. 195–196.

9. Casey, "Letter to Mrs. Henry Morgan," December 14, 1946, in *Collected Writings*, volume two, p. 191.

10. Father Ambrose de Groot, Letter to Michael H. Crosby, O.F.M. CAP., June 29, 1984.

11. Casey, "Letter to Mrs. Henry Morgan," December 14, 1946, in *Collected Writings*, volume two, p. 191.

12. Casey, "Letter to Mrs. Geraldine Bieke," September 19, 1946, in *Collected Writings*, volume two, p. 185.

13. Casey, "Letter to Mr. Raymond Taylor," February 8, 1947, in *Collected Writings*, volume two, pp. 214–216.

14. Casey, "Letter to Mr. Raymond Taylor," February 8, 1947, in *Collected Writings*, volume two, p. 216.

15. Casey, "Letter to Rt. Rev. Edward Casey," May 12, 1947, in *Collected Writings*, volume one, p. 182.

16. Casey, "Letter to Father Simon, O.F.M. CAP., c. 1947, in *Collected Writings*, volume two, p. 209.

17. Father Blase Gitzen, O.F.M. CAP., taped interview to Michael H. Crosby, O.F.M. CAP.

18. Father Blase Gitzen, O.F.M. CAP., November 14, 1969, in *Written Reports*.

19. Brother Pius Cotter, O.F.M., CAP., interview with Michael H. Crosby, October 5, 1984.

20. Father Blase Gitzen, O.F.M. CAP., taped interview to Michael H. Crosby, O.F.M. CAP.

21. Casey, "Letter to Mrs. Helena Casey Wilhite," June 1, 1948, in *Collected Writings*, volume one, p. 138.

22. Casey, "Letter to Mrs. Helena Casey Wilhite," June 1, 1948, in *Collected Writings*, volume one, p. 138.

23. Casey, "Letter to Mrs. Geraci," c. 1947, in *Collected Writings*, volume two, p. 179.

24. *Chronicle*, January 12, 1949.

25. Casey, unfinished "Letter to Miss Mae C. Berling," February 7, 1949, in *Collected Writings*, volume two, p. 274.

26. Casey, unfinished "Letter to Miss Mae C. Berling," February 7, 1949, in *Collected Writings*, volume two, p. 274.

27. Casey, "Think Over," typed notes among Solanus's writings, 1948, in *Collected Writings*, volume two, p. 253.

28. Casey, "Think Over," typed notes among Solanus's writings, 1948, in *Collected Writings*, volume two, p. 253.

29. Casey, "Letter to Very Rev. Father Provincial (Edmund Kramer), O.F.M. CAP., July 18, 1949, in *Collected Writings*, volume two, p. 278.

30. Casey, "Letter to Very Rev. Father Provincial (Edmund Kramer), O.F.M. CAP., July 18, 1949, in *Collected Writings*, volume two, p. 278.

31. Father Blase Gitzen, O.F.M. CAP., November 14, 1969, in *Written Reports*.

32. Casey, "Letter to Gramma Kaufman," August 9, 1949, in *Collected Writings*, volume two, p. 281.

33. Casey, "Letter to Gramma Kaufman," August 9, 1949, in *Collected Writings*, volume two, p. 281.

34. Father Michael Cefai, January 10, 1968, in *Written Reports*.

35. James Allen Maher, March 7, 1980, in *Written Reports*.

36. James Allen Maher, March 7, 1980, in *Written Reports*.

37. James Allen Maher, March 7, 1980, in *Written Reports*.

38. James Allen Maher, March 7, 1980, in *Written Reports*.

39. James Allen Maher, March 7, 1980, in *Written Reports*.

40. James Allen Maher, March 7, 1980, in *Written Reports*.

41. Casey, "Letter to Margaret and Frank LeDoux," July 4, 1950, in *Collected Writings*, volume one p. 32

42. Father Elmer Stoffel, O.F.M. CAP., September 1, 1980, in *Written Reports*.

43. Father Blase Gitzen, O.F.M. CAP., November 14, 1969, in *Written Reports*.

44. Father Blase Gitzen, O.F.M. CAP., November 14, 1969, in *Written Reports*.

45. Casey, "Letter to Br. Leo," August 11, 1951, in *Collected Writings*, volume two, p. 132.

46. Brother Booker T. Ashe, O.F.M. CAP., March 21, 1980, in *Written Reports*.

47. Brother Booker T. Ashe, O.F.M. CAP., March 21, 1980, in *Written Reports*.

48. Brother Booker T. Ashe, O.F.M. CAP., March 21, 1980, in *Written Reports*.

49. Casey, "Mystical City of God—Logical Landmarks," c. 1950, in *Collected Writings*, volume one, p. 281.

50. Father Francis Heidenreich, O.F.M. CAP., recollections shared with Michael H. Crosby O.F.M., CAP., January 6, 1983.

51. Casey, "Letter to Sister M. Bernice OP," January 15, 1955, in *Collected Writings*, volume two, p. 352.

52. Sister Kathleen Grimes, February 10, 1978, in *Written Reports*.

53. Casey, "Letter to Margaret Therese LeDoux," May 5, 1953, in *Collected Writings*, volume one, p. 33.

54. Father Benignus of Sant'Ilario M., Min. Gen. O.F.M. CAP., "Letter to Rev. Solanus Casey," Jan. 22, 1953. Documents File, Vice Postulator's Archives, Detroit, Michigan.

55. E.A. Bachelor, Jr., "Detroiters Pay Homage to Priest," *The Detroit Sunday Times*, July 18, 1954.

56. Casey, quoted in E.A. Bachelor, Jr., "Detroiters Pay Homage to Priest," *The Detroit Sunday Times*, July 18, 1954.

57. *Chronicle*, July 28, 1954.

58. Brother Pius Cotter, O.F.M. CAP., reflections shared with Michael H. Crosby O.F.M., CAP., October 5, 1984.

59. Casey, "Letter to Margaret Therese LeDoux," October 19, 1954, in *Collected Writings*, volume one, p. 34.

60. Frank J. Brady, September 23, 1978, in *Written Reports*.

61. Frank J. Brady, September 23, 1978, in *Written Reports*.

62. Frank J. Brady, September 23, 1978, in *Written Reports*.

63. *Chronicle*, July 21, 1955.

CHAPTER EIGHT

1. Father Bernard Burke, O.F.M. CAP., August 9, 1973 in *Written Reports*.

2. Brother Ignatius Milne, O.F.M. CAP., reflections shared with Michael H. Crosby O.F.M., CAP., September 1, 1983.

3. Father Lawrence Merten, O.F.M. CAP., March 21, 1980, in *Written Reports*.

4. Father Elmer Stoffel, O.F.M. CAP., quoted in Father Lawrence Merten, O.F.M. CAP., March 21, 1980, in *Written Reports*.

5. Father Elmer Stoffel, O.F.M. CAP., quoted in Father Lawrence Merten, O.F.M. CAP., March 21, 1980, in *Written Reports*.

6. This is evidenced by an analysis of his handwriting, taken from that period.

7. Father Gerald Walker, O.F.M. CAP., April 14, 1980, in *Written Reports*.

8. Father Daniel Crosby, O.F.M. CAP., June 7, 1984, in *Written Reports*.

9. Casey, Unfinished "Letter to Miss Loretta Mary Gibson," April 1, 1956, in *Collected Writings*, volume two, p. 313.

10. "Prayer for Peace," typewritten copy (by Solanus) in his notes. Since Solanus indicated in his letter to Miss Gibson (above) that he "heard it first, only after coming to Saint Bonaventure's last January" (1956), it would have been typed sometime between then and April 1, 1956. In *Collected Writings*, volume two, p. 343.

11. Father Lawrence Merten, O.F.M. CAP., March 21, 1980, in *Written Reports*.

12. Father Lawrence Merten, O.F.M. CAP., March 21, 1980, in *Written Reports*.

13. Father Lawrence Merten, O.F.M. CAP., March 21, 1980, in *Written Reports*.

14. *Chronicle*, St. Bonaventure, December 2, 1956.

15. Jerry Sullivan, "Life in the Monastery in the Heart of Detroit," *The Detroit Sunday News*, December 2, 1956.

16. *Chronicle*, St. Bonaventure, December 2, 1956.

17. Father Daniel Crosby, O.F.M. CAP., June 7, 1984 in *Written Reports*.

18. Casey, unfinished "Letter to Rev. Edward Casey," March 14, 1957, in *Collected Writings*, volume one, p. 195.

19. Rev. Michael Dalton, November 20, 1977, in *Written Reports*.

20. Mrs. Adeline Striewski, July 15, 1977, in *Written Reports*.

21. Mrs. Edward Klimczak, April 5, 1977, in *Written Reports*.

22. The accounts by Sister Arthur Ann and Sister M. Margaretta are noted in Derum's book on Solanus.

23. Brother Ignatius Milne, O.F.M. CAP., reflections shared with Michael H. Crosby O.F.M., CAP., September 1, 1983.

24. Father Gerald Walker, O.F.M. CAP., April 14, 1980, in *Written Reports*.

25. Father Gerald Walker, O.F.M. CAP., April 14, 1980, in *Written Reports*. Father Gerald Walker's recollections are based on conversations with Monsignor Edward Casey who talked with the nurse who was with Solanus at the time of his death.

26. Father Gerald (Walker) of Detroit, O.F.M. CAP., "Father Solanus Casey, O.F.M. Cap., 1870–1957," *The Messenger*, 21 (February 1958). Detroit: Province of Saint Joseph, pp. 35–36.

27. Bernadette M. Nowak, March 28, 1977, in *Written Reports*.

28. Father Bernard Burke, O.F.M. CAP., August 9, 1973 in *Written Reports*.

29. Father Gerald Walker, O.F.M. CAP., "Funeral Homily," recorded in James Patrick Derum, *The Porter of Saint Bonaventure's: The Life of Father Solanus Casey, Capuchin* (Detroit: Fidelity, 1968), p. 274.

CHAPTER NINE

1. Karl Rahner, "Concern for the Church," *Theological Investigations 20*, Edward Quinn, trans. (New York: Crossroad, 1981), p. 149.

2. Casey, "Letter to Mrs. Helena Casey Wilhite," June 1, 1948, in *Collected Writings*, volume one, p. 138.

3. Casey, "Letter to Walter McClellen," July 1, 1946, in *Collected Writings*, volume two, p. 180.

4. Pope Benedict XVI, Sunday Angelus reflection, June 8, 2008.

5. Casey, "Letter to Mrs. Helena Casey Wilhite," April 16, 1954, in *Collected Writings*, volume one, p. 141.

6. Casey, "On Atheism," c. 1945, in *Collected Writings*, volume two, p. 165.

7. Note written on photo of Solanus Casey by himself, c. 1954, in *Collected Writings*, volume two, p. 342.

8. Casey, "Letter to Mrs. John O'Flaherty," March 23, 1949, in *Collected Writings*, volume two, p. 239.

9. Pope Benedict XVI, All Saints' Day Angelus reflection, November 1, 2007.

10. Casey, "Letter to Br. Leo," February 28, 1943, in *Collected Writings*, volume two, p. 120.

11. Casey, "Letter to Dr. Koch," March 12, 1946, in *Collected Writings*, volume two, p. 168.

12. Casey, "Letter to Miss Medora Louisell," September 10, 1947, in *Collected Writings*, volume two, p. 235.

13. Casey, "Letter to Br. Leo," July 30, 1952, in *Collected Writings*, volume two, p. 134.

14. Casey, "Letter to Father Maurice Joachim Casey," December 15, 1938, in *Collected Writings*, volume one, p. 149.

15. Casey, "Letter to Charles Bracken," January 3, 1943, in *Collected Writings*, volume two, p. 86.

16. Casey, "Letter to Henry S. Morgan," December 14, 1946, in *Collected Writings*, volume two, p. 191.

17. Casey, "Letter to Peter Doyle," September 13, 1951, in *Collected Writings*, volume two, p. 58.

18. Father Daniel Crosby, O.F.M., CAP., June 7, 1984, in *Written Reports*.

19. Father Daniel Crosby, O.F.M., CAP., June 7, 1984, in *Written Reports*.

20. Casey, "Letter to Miss Mildred Maneal," c. 1945, in *Collected Writings*, volume two, p. 162.

21. Benedict J. Groeschel, *Spiritual Passages: The Psychology of Spiritual Development* (New York: Crossroad, 1983), pp. 184–185.

22. Casey, notes written on flyleaf of volume three, *The Mystical City of God*, c. 1939, in *Collected Writings*, volume one, p. 270.

23. Casey, "Letter to Br. Leo," July 30, 1952, in *Collected Writings*, volume two, p. 134.

24. Casey, "Letter to Mrs. Alvera McCarroll," January 27, c. 1948, in *Collected Writings*, volume two, p. 250.

25. Casey, notes written on flyleaf of volume two, *The Mystical City of God*, c., 1939, in *Collected Writings*, volume one, p. 270.

26. Casey, notes written on flyleaf of volume three, *The Mystical City of God,* c., 1939, in *Collected Writings,* volume one, p. 270.

27. Kathleen Pond, *The Spirit of the Spanish Mystics: An Anthology of Spanish Religious Prose from the Fifteenth to the Seventeenth Century* (New York: P.J. Kenedy & Sons, 1958), p. 168.

28. Casey, note written on flyleaf of volume three, *The Mystical City of God,* c. 1939, in *Collected Writings,* volume one, p. 268.

29. Casey, "Letter to Mrs. O'Donnell," August 3, 1949, in *Collected Writings,* volume two, p. 48.

30. Casey, "Letter to Miss Loretta Gibson," September 8, 1951, in *Collected Writings,* volume two, p. 312.

31. Casey, "Letter to Miss Beatrice Lamb," September 17, 1949, in *Collected Writings,* volume two, p. 116.

32. Casey, "Letter to Edwin LeDoux," September 30, 1948, in *Collected Writings,* volume one, p. 29.

33. Casey, "Letter to Mrs. Margaret LeDoux," October 19, 1954, in *Collected Writings,* volume one, p. 34.

34. Casey, "Letter to Mrs. Margaret Lilly," January 16, 1952, in *Collected Writings,* volume one, p. 46.

35. Casey, "Letter to Bridget Ronan," November 24, 1946, in *Collected Writings,* volume two, p. 190.

36. Casey, "Letter to Mr. and Mrs. Joseph O'Donnell," May 16, 1946, in *Collected Writings,* volume two, p. 20.

37. Casey, "Letter to Mrs. Helena Wilhite," February 28, 1946, in *Collected Writings,* volume one, p. 131.

38. Monsignor Edward J. Hickey, December 2, 1969, in *Written Reports.*

39. Monsignor Edward J. Hickey, December 2, 1969, in *Written Reports.*

40. William Tremblay, March 15, 1979, in *Written Reports.*

41. Casey, "Letter to Miss Mae Whelan," September, 1942, in *Collected Writings,* volume two, p. 179.

42. Casey, "Letter to Mrs. Geraci," c. 1947, in *Collected Writings,* volume two, p. 179.

43. Casey, "Letter to Br. Leo," February 28, 1943, in *Collected Writings,* volume two, p. 119.

44. Casey, "Letter to Sister Solania," January 3, 1943, in *Collected Writings,* volume one, p. 85.

45. Casey, "To Recognize the Creator," c. 1948, in *Collected Writings,* volume two, p. 263.

46. Casey, "Letter to Sister M. Joseph," May 21, 1945, in *Collected Writings*, volume two, p. 141.

47. Casey, "Letter to Dorothy Bachor," May 18, 1937, in *Collected Writings*, volume one, p. 96.

48. Casey, "Letter to Monsignor Edward Casey," March 4, 1957, in *Collected Writings*, volume one, p. 195.

49. Casey, "Letter to Muriel Krausman," Sept. 21, 1953, in *Collected Writings*, volume two, p. 111.

50. Casey, "Letter to Mr. and Mrs. Joseph O'Donnell," May 16, 1945, in *Collected Writings*, volume two, p. 20.

51. Casey, "Letter to Miss Mildred Maneal," c. 1945, in *Collected Writings*, volume two, p. 162.

52. Casey, "Letter to Mrs. Margaret LeDoux," April 1, 1915, in *Collected Writings*, volume one, p. 3.

53. Casey, "Letter to John Martin," August 18, 1950, in *Collected Writings*, volume two, p. 299.

54. Casey, "Letter to Mrs. Geraldine Bieke," September 19, 1946, in *Collected Writings*, volume two, p. 185.

55. Casey, "Letter to Mr. and Mrs. Peter Doyle," February 11, 1948, in *Collected Writings*, volume two, p. 57.

56. Casey, "Letter to Miss Loretta Gibson," September 8, 1951, in *Collected Writings*, volume two, p. 312.

57. Casey, "Letter to Peter Doyle," September 13, 1951, in *Collected Writings*, volume two, 58.

58. Casey, "Letter to Miss Winifred Goodwillie," August 5, 1939, in *Collected Writings*, volume two, p. 9.

59. Casey, "Notebook 9," April 12, 1898, in *Collected Writings*, volume one, p. 11.

60. Casey, "Letter to Bernice Schumacher," August 16, 1946, in *Collected Writings*, volume two, p. 183.

61. Casey, "Letter to Tom," April 8, 1955, in *Collected Writings*, volume two, p. 78.

62. Casey, "Letter to Margaret LeDoux," May 17, 1950, in *Collected Writings*, volume one, p. 31.

63. Casey, "Letter to Margaret LeDoux," May 17, 1950, in *Collected Writings*, volume one, p. 31.

64. Casey, "Letter to Father Maurice Casey," April 2, 1946, in *Collected Writings*, volume one, p. 159.

65. Casey, "Letter to Mrs. Charles D'Amico," April 14, 1948, in *Collected Writings*, volume one, p. 248.

66. Casey, "Letter to Mrs. Geraci," c. 1947, in *Collected Writings*, volume two, p. 179.

67. Casey, "Letter to Mr. Joseph O'Donnell," March 28, 1947, in *Collected Writings*, volume two, p. 34.

68. Casey, "Letter to Mrs. Geraci," c. 1947, in *Collected Writings*, volume two, p. 179.

69. E.D. Bachelor, Jr., "Detroiters Pay Homage to Priest," *The Detroit Sunday Times*, July 18, 1954.

70. Pope Benedict XVI, *Spe Salvi*, 14. Available at www.vatican.va.

71. Casey, radio speech on station CKLW Detroit, June 11, 1937, in *Collected Writings*, volume one, p. 94.

72. Reverend Andrew Lawrence, in *Written Reports*.

73. Casey, "Letter to Mrs. Helena Wilhite," June 1, 1948, in *Collected Writings*, volume one, p. 136.

74. Casey, "Letter to Mrs. Helena Wilhite," December 25, 1952, in *Collected Writings*, volume one, p. 251.

75. Casey, "Letter to Margaret LeDoux," January 26, 1937, in *Collected Writings*, volume one, p. 16.

76. Casey, "Letter to James Casey," c. 1948, in *Collected Writings*, volume one, p. 239.

77. Casey, "Letter to Eileen Casey," December 15, 1952, in *Collected Writings*, volume one, p. 252.

78. Casey, "Letter to Dr. J. P. Young," October 4, 1947, in *Collected Writings*, volume two, p. 205.

79. Casey, "Letter to Dr. J. P. Young," October 4, 1947, in *Collected Writings*, volume two, p. 203.

80. Casey, "Letter to Br. Leo," May 23, 1946, in *Collected Writings*, volume two, p. 128.

81. Casey, note written on picture taken at monastery office, c. 1945, in *Collected Writings*, volume two, p. 155.

82. Casey, "Letter to Charles M. Durrell, M.D.," March 1, 1947, in *Collected Writings*, volume two, p. 226.

83. Casey, "Letter to Barbara Bedolfe," August 4, 1949, in *Collected Writings*, volume one, p. 41.

84. Casey, Notes written after the death of Father Maurice Casey, c. 1949, in *Collected Writings*, volume one, p. 162.

85. Casey, "Letter to Wallace Bedolfe," April 18, 1953, in *Collected Writings*, volume one, p. 43.

86. Father Gerald Walker, O.F.M. CAP., in *Written Reports*.

87. Casey, "Think Over," 1948 in *Collected Writings*, volume two, p. 253.

INDEX